Fodor's

SECOND
New
EDITION

Pocket
Atlanta

Fodor's Travel Publications, Inc.
New York • Toronto • London • Sydney • Auckland
www.fodors.com/

Fodor's Pocket Atlanta

EDITOR: Anastasia Redmond Mills

Editorial Contributors: Robert Andrews, Mark Beffart, David Brown, Ren Davis, Jane Garvey, Heidi Sarna, Helayne Schiff, M. T. Schwartzman, Dinah A. Spritzer

Editorial Production: Janet Foley

Maps: David Lindroth, Inc., James Sinclair, Kris Tobiassen, *cartographers*; Steven Amsterdam, *map editor*

Design: Fabrizio La Rocca, *creative director*; Guido Caroti, *associate art director*; Lyndell Brookhouse-Gil, *cover design*; Jolie Novak, *photo editor*

Production/Manufacturing: Mike Costa

Cover Photograph: Copyright © Bill Gornto

Copyright

Special Sales

CONTENTS

5   Nightlife and the Arts   113

6   Outdoor Activities and Sports   127

7   Shopping   135

Index   148

Maps

ON THE ROAD WITH FODOR'S

WE'RE ALWAYS thrilled to get letters from readers, especially one like this:

It took us an hour to decide what book to buy and we now know we picked the best one. Your book was wonderful, easy to follow, very accurate, and good on pointing out eating places, informal as well as formal. When we saw other people using your book, we would look at each other and smile.

Our editors and writers are deeply committed to making every Fodor's guide "the best one"—not only accurate but always charming, brimming with sound recommendations and solid ideas, right on the mark in describing restaurants and hotels, and full of fascinating facts that make you view what you've traveled to see in a rich new light.

About Our Writers

Our success in achieving our goals—and in helping to make your trip the best of all possible vacations—is a credit to the hard work of our extraordinary writers.

Ren Davis is a rare specimen: a third generation Atlantan. He is the coauthor, with his wife, Helen, of *Atlanta Walks, A Guide to Walking, Running, and Bicycling Scenic and Historic Atlanta*. Ren wrote our walking and driving tours and updated the Exploring chapter: After walking hundreds of miles in Atlanta, there's not a corner of the city he doesn't know. Ren and Helen are contributing editors for *Georgia Journal Magazine* and they have led walking tours for groups including delegates to the 1988 Democratic National Convention. Ren, who has degrees in history and public health, is also a freelance magazine writer and a consultant in the fields of health policy and bioethics.

Since 1992, **Jane Garvey,** author of the Dining chapter and updater of every chapter in the book save Chapter 2, has been chasing the ideal food-and-wine match for readers of her *Atlanta Journal-Constitution* column. Jane's a former magazine editor and the coauthor of a residents' guide to Atlanta, where she has nibbled and sipped for more than 25 years.

Mark Beffart, who wrote much of this book, has witnessed the enormous growth of Atlanta firsthand, having moved to the city in 1978 when it was half its present size. Mark is the author of several books and more than 200 magazine articles and is the editorial director of *Travel Books Review* newsletter.

New This Year

We've reformatted this guide to make it easier to use. We've added terrific Great Itineraries that will lead you through the best of the city, taking into consideration how long you have to spend. There are also brand new walking and driving tours and a timing section that tells you how long to allot for each tour.

We're also proud to announce that the American Society of Travel Agents has endorsed Fodor's as its guidebook of choice. ASTA is the world's largest and most influential travel trade association, operating in more than 170 countries, with 27,000 members pledged to adhere to a strict code of ethics reflecting the Society's motto, "Integrity in Travel." ASTA shares Fodor's devotion to providing smart, honest travel information and advice to travelers, and we've long recommended that our readers consult ASTA member agents for the experience and professionalism they bring to the table.

On the Web, check out Fodor's site (www.fodors.com/) for information on major destinations around the world and travel-savvy interactive features. The Web site also lists the 85-plus radio stations nationwide that carry the *Fodor's Travel Show,* a live call-in program that airs every weekend. Tune in to hear guests discuss their wonderful adventures—or call in to get answers for your most pressing travel questions.

How to Use This Book

Organization

Up front is **Essential Information,** an easy-to-use section divided alphabetically by topic. Under each listing you'll find tips and information that will help you accomplish what you need to in Atlanta. You'll also find addresses and telephone numbers of organizations and companies that offer destination-related services and detailed information or publications.

The first chapter in the guide, Destination: Atlanta, helps get you in the mood for your trip. New and Noteworthy cues you in on trends and happenings, What's Where orients you, Pleasures and Pastimes describes the activities and sights that make Atlanta unique, Great Itineraries gives you touring suggestions if you only have a short time in the city, and Festivals and Seasonal Events alerts you to special events you'll want to seek out.

The Exploring chapter is subdivided by neighborhood; each subsection recommends a walking or driving tour and lists neighborhood sights alphabetically, including sights that are off the beaten path. The remaining chapters are arranged in alphabetical order by subject (dining, lodging, nightlife and the arts, outdoor activities and sports, and shopping).

Icons and Symbols

★ Our special recommendations
✕ Restaurant

⊡ Lodging establishment

Ⓒ Good for kids (rubber duckie)

☞ Sends you to another section of the guide for more information

⊠ Address

☎ Telephone number

☺ Opening and closing times

⊡ Admission prices (those we give apply to adults; substantially reduced fees are almost always available for children, students, and senior citizens)

Numbers in white and black circles that appear on the maps, in the margins, and within the tours correspond to one another.

Hotel Meal Plans

Assume that hotels operate on the **European Plan** (EP, with no meals) unless we note they use the **American Plan** (AP, with all meals), the **Modified American Plan** (MAP, with breakfast and dinner), or the **Continental Plan** (CP, with a Continental breakfast).

Credit Cards

The following abbreviations are used: **AE,** American Express; **D,** Discover; **DC,** Diners Club; **MC,** MasterCard; and **V,** Visa.

Don't Forget to Write

You can use this book in the confidence that all prices and opening times are based on information supplied to us at press time;

Fodor's cannot accept responsibility for any errors. Time inevitably brings changes, so always confirm information when it matters—especially if you're making a detour to visit a specific place. In addition, when making reservations be sure to mention if you have a disability or are traveling with children, if you prefer a private bath or a certain type of bed, or if you have specific dietary needs or other concerns.

Were the restaurants we recommended as described? Did our hotel picks exceed your expectations? Did you find a museum we recommended a waste of time? If you have complaints, we'll look into them and revise our entries when the facts warrant it. If you've discovered a special place that we haven't included, we'll pass the information along to our correspondents and have them check it out. So send us your feedback, positive *and* negative: e-mail us at editors@fodors.com (specifying the name of the book on the subject line), or write the Atlanta editor at Fodor's, 201 East 50th Street, New York, New York 10022. Have a wonderful trip!

Karen Cure

Karen Cure
Editorial Director

Georgia

Greater Atlanta

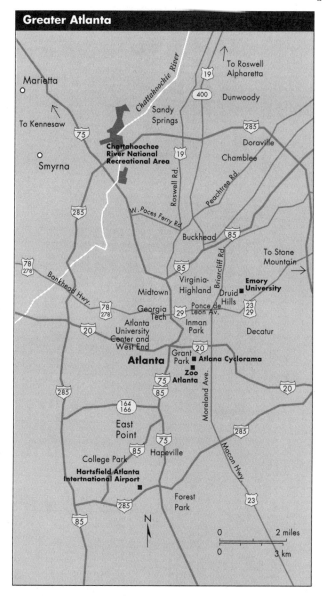

Marietta

To Kennesaw

Smyrna

Chattahoochie River

To Roswell
Alpharetta

19

400

Dunwoody

Sandy
Springs

285

Doraville

Chattahoochee
River National
Recreational Area

19

Chamblee

Peachtree Rd.

75

285

Roswell Rd.

W. Paces Ferry Rd.

Buckhead

85

To Stone
Mountain

78
278

Bankhead Hwy.

85

Briarcliff Rd.

Emory
University

Virginia-
Highland

Druid
Hills

23
29

Midtown

78
278

Ponce de
Leon Av.

29

Georgia
Tech

20

Atlanta
University
Center and
West End

Inman
Park

Decatur

20

Atlanta

Grant
Park

20

■ **Atlana Cyclorama**

■
**Zoo
Atlanta**

Moreland Ave.

20

285

75
85

164
166

285

Macon Hwy.

East
Point

75

College Park

85

Hapeville

Forest
Park

23

**Hartsfield Atlanta
Interntational Airport**
■

285

85

N

0   2 miles

0   3 km

x

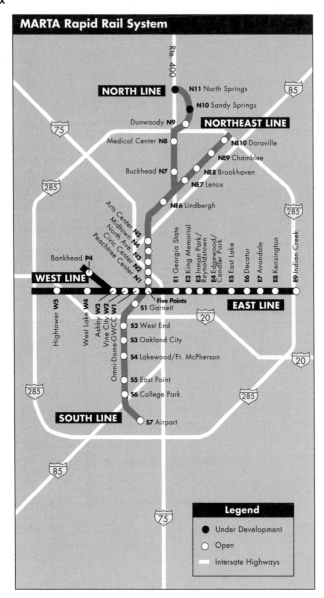

MARTA Rapid Rail System

NORTH LINE

N11 North Springs
N10 Sandy Springs
Dunwoody N9
NORTHEAST LINE
Medical Center N8
NE10 Doraville
NE9 Chamblee
Buckhead N7
NE8 Brookhaven
NE7 Lenox
NE6 Lindbergh
Arts Center N5
Midtown N4
North Ave. N3
Civic Center N2
Peachtree Center N1

E1 Georgia State
E2 King Memorial
E3 Inman Park/Reynoldstown
E4 Edgewood/Candler Park
E5 East Lake
E6 Decatur
E7 Avondale
E8 Kensington
E9 Indian Creek

Bankhead P4

WEST LINE
EAST LINE

Hightower W5
West Lake W4
Ashby W3
Vine City W2
Omni-Dome-GWCC W1

Five Points
S1 Garnett
S2 West End
S3 Oakland City
S4 Lakewood/Ft. McPherson
S5 East Point
S6 College Park

SOUTH LINE
S7 Airport

Legend

● Under Development
○ Open
— Intersate Highways

ESSENTIAL INFORMATION

*Basic Information on Traveling in Atlanta,
Savvy Tips to Make Your Trip a Breeze, and
Companies and Organizations to Contact*

ADDRESSES

Almost all Atlanta addresses are
followed by a NE, NW, SE, or SW
suffix (e.g., 218 Peachtree St. NE).
Most streets north of Five Points
(the official center of Downtown)
have a north designation; those
south of it have a south designation. The east–west dividing line
Downtown is Peachtree Street.
The directional designations are
most useful for postal carriers and
have been left off most addresses
in this book.

AIR TRAVEL

MAJOR AIRLINE OR LOW-COST CARRIER?

Most people choose a flight based
on price. Yet there are other issues
to consider. Major airlines offer
the greatest number of depar-
tures; smaller airlines—including
regional, low-cost, and no-frill
airlines—usually have a more limited number of flights daily.
Major airlines have frequent-flyer
partners, which allow you to
credit mileage earned on one airline to your account with another.
Low-cost airlines offer a definite
price advantage and fewer restrictions, such as advance-purchase
requirements. Safety-wise, low-

cost carriers as a group have a
good history, but **check the safety
record before booking** any low-
cost carrier; call the **Federal Aviation Administration's Consumer
Hotline** (☞ Airline Complaints,
below).

MAJOR AIRLINES➤ Major American
carriers serving Atlanta include
America West (☎ 800/235–9292),
American (☎ 800/433–7300), **Air
South** (☎ 800/247–7688), **Continental** (☎ 800/525–0280), **Delta**
(☎ 800/221–1212), **Northwest**
(☎ 800/225–2525), **TWA** (☎
800/221–2000), **United** (☎ 800/
241–6522), and **US Airways**
(☎ 800/428–4322).

SMALLER AIRLINES➤ For inexpensive, no-frills flights, contact **Kiwi
International** (☎ 800/538–5494),
based in Newark and New York;
Midwest Express (☎ 800/452–
2022), which is based in Milwau-
kee and serves 45 U.S. cities in the
Midwest and on both coasts, including Atlanta; and **ValuJet**
(☎ 770/994–8258 or 800/825–
8538).

FROM THE U.K.➤ **British Airways**
(☎ 0345/222111) and **Delta** (☎
0800/414767) fly daily nonstop
flights from London's Gatwick

Airport to Hartsfield Atlanta International Airport. If service is booked for your dates, several other airlines, including **American Airlines** (☎ 0345/789789), **Continental Airlines** (☎ 01293/776464 or 0800/776464), and **TWA** (☎ 01293/439–0707) fly to New York and other U.S. locations, where you can make a domestic connection to Atlanta.

GET THE LOWEST FARE

The least-expensive airfares to Atlanta are priced for round-trip travel. Major airlines usually require that you **book in advance and buy the ticket within 24 hours,** and you may have to **stay over a Saturday night.** It's smart to **call a number of airlines, and when you are quoted a good price, book it on the spot**—the same fare may not be available on the same flight the next day. Airlines generally allow you to change your return date for a fee of $25–$50. If you don't use your ticket you can apply the cost toward the purchase of a new ticket, again for a small charge. However, most low-fare tickets are nonrefundable. To get the lowest airfare, **check different routings.** If your destination or home city has more than one gateway, compare prices to and from different airports. Also price off-peak flights, which may be significantly less expensive.

To save money on flights from the United Kingdom and back, **look into an APEX or Super-PEX ticket.** APEX tickets must be booked in advance and have certain restrictions. Super-PEX tickets can be purchased at the airport on the day of departure—subject to availability.

DON'T STOP UNLESS YOU MUST

When you book, **look for nonstop flights** and **remember that "direct" flights stop at least once.** Try to **avoid connecting flights,** which require a change of plane. Two airlines may jointly operate a connecting flight, so ask if your airline operates every segment—you may find that your preferred carrier flies you only part of the way.

USE AN AGENT

Travel agents, especially those who specialize in finding the lowest fares (☞ Discounts & Deals, *below*), can be especially helpful when booking a plane ticket. When you're quoted a price, **ask your agent if the price is likely to get any lower.** Good agents know the seasonal fluctuations of airfares and can usually anticipate a sale or fare war. However, waiting can be risky: The fare could go *up* as seats become scarce, and you may wait so long that your preferred flight sells out. A wait-and-see strategy works best if your plans are flexible, but if you must arrive and depart on certain dates, don't delay.

AVOID GETTING BUMPED

Airlines routinely overbook planes, knowing that not everyone with a ticket will show up, but sometimes everyone does. When that happens, airlines ask for volunteers to give up their seats. In return these volunteers usually get a certificate for a free flight and are rebooked on the next flight out. If there are not enough volunteers the airline must choose who will be denied boarding. The first to get bumped are passengers who checked in late and those flying on discounted tickets, so **get to the gate and check in as early as possible,** especially during peak periods.

Always **bring a photo ID to the airport.** You may be asked to show it before you are allowed to check in.

ENJOY THE FLIGHT
For better service, **fly smaller or regional carriers,** which often have higher passenger-satisfaction ratings. Sometimes you'll find leather seats, more legroom, and better food.

For more legroom, **request an emergency-aisle seat**; don't however, sit in the row in front of the emergency aisle or in front of a bulkhead, where seats may not recline.

If you don't like airline food, **ask for special meals when booking.** These can be vegetarian, low-cholesterol, or kosher, for example.

COMPLAIN IF NECESSARY
If your baggage goes astray or your flight goes awry, complain right away. Most carriers require that you file a claim immediately.

AIRLINE COMPLAINTS➤ U.S. Department of Transportation **Aviation Consumer Protection Division** (⊠ C-75, Room 4107, Washington, DC 20590, ☎ 202/366–2220). **Federal Aviation Administration (FAA) Consumer Hotline** (☎ 800/322–7873).

AIRPORTS & TRANSFERS
The major gateway to Atlanta, Hartsfield Atlanta International Airport, 13 mi south of Downtown, can be reached from I–75, I–85, and I–285. These roads are often congested: To and from Downtown locations, **allow at least 30 minutes of travel time.** All ground transportation, including shuttle buses to the rental car company lots, operates from the west exit, a few steps beyond the north terminal baggage claim area; follow the overhead directional signs. The MARTA rapid rail station is here, too.

Distances within the airport can seem never ending: To travel between the airport's five concourses and the main terminal and baggage area, you can **take a minitrain or use the moving sidewalks.**

AIRPORT INFORMATION➤ **Hartsfield Atlanta International Airport** (☎ 404/530–6830).

TRANSFERS
MARTA's rapid-rail service travels between the airport and Down-

town, Buckhead, and several suburbs. At the end and in the middle of some cars, seats have been removed to provide room for luggage. If this open area has a seat belt anchored to the wall, it is reserved for people in wheelchairs. The trip to Downtown's Five Points station, opposite Underground Atlanta, takes 15 minutes (5–10 minutes longer in rush hour); it's 30 minutes to Lenox Square. The fare is $1.50. The trains come directly to the airport, and open-air parking at selected MARTA stations is free. In addition, at Brookhaven and Medical Center stations, patrolled long-term parking costs $3 per day, and $1 per day on the covered decks at Lenox and Lindbergh.

Atlanta Airport Shuttle vans operate from the airport at regular intervals depending upon destination between 7 AM and 11 PM. The Downtown trip ($10 one-way, $17 round-trip) takes about 20 minutes; there are stops at major hotels; to Buckhead ($15 one-way, $24 round-trip). Vans also go to locations around Emory University and Lenox Square Mall.

Other shuttle van companies specialize in routes to northern suburbs; a few companies travel outside the state. For basic information and telephone numbers, **look at the directory at the ground transportation exit.** Most hotels have their own shuttle van or bus, so **check with your hotel.**

Taxi fare between the airport and Downtown hotels is fixed at $18 for one person, $10 each for two people, $24 for three to five persons; the trip takes 15–20 minutes. The fare to hotels in Buckhead and the Lenox Square Mall area is $28 for one person, $30 for two or more people; the ride takes 30–35 minutes. Trip times can vary depending on time of day (☞ Taxis, *below*).

MARTA INFORMATION➤ **MARTA** (☎ 404/848–4711). Information is available in English, Spanish, Japanese, French, and German.

SHUTTLE COMPANIES➤ **Airport Connection** (☎ 770/457–5757). **Atlanta Airport Shuttle** (☎ 404/766–5312 or 404/524–3400). **Atlanta Hotels Connection** (☎ 404/312–2479). **Daytime Transportation** (☎ 770/939–2337). **Interstate Airport Jitney** (☎ 770/932–6757).

BUS TRAVEL

Contact **Greyhound Bus Lines** (✉ 232 Forsyth St., ☎ 800/231–2222 or 404/522–6300).

WITHIN ATLANTA

MARTA operates a fleet of 700 buses on 150 routes covering 1,500 mi. Outside I–285, except for a few important areas of Clayton, DeKalb, and Fulton counties, service is very limited. You can **request a system map that shows every route.**

Bus fare is $1.50; the same tokens used in rail stations are accepted on buses. In most buses, special machines near the driver accept one-dollar bills, or you can use exact change. Request any transfers needed from the driver. Weekend passes and TransCards (☞ Train Travel, *below*) must be shown upon entering the bus.

Selected buses stop at most MARTA rail stations. To identify a bus stop on the street, look for a white cement post with BUS STOP carved into it. Although the routes will take you to most major sights, bus travel can be exasperating. Buses slow down in traffic; **don't plan any meetings around a bus trip.** Avoid them on hot and humid days when the crush of bodies can be overwhelming, especially during rush hour.

SCHEDULES & INFORMATION➤ **MARTA** (☎ 404/848–4711).

CAR RENTAL

Rates in Atlanta begin at $40 a day and $150 a week for an economy car with air-conditioning, an automatic transmission, and unlimited mileage. This does not include tax on car rentals, which is 5%.

MAJOR AGENCIES➤ **Alamo** (☎ 800/327–9633; 0800/272–2000 in the U.K.). **Avis** (☎ 800/331–1212; 800/879–2847 in Canada). **Budget** (☎ 800/527–0700; 0800/181181 in the U.K.). **Dollar** (☎ 800/800–4000; 0990/565656 in the U.K., where it is known as Eu-

rodollar). **Hertz** (☎ 800/654–3131; 800/263–0600 in Canada; 0345/555888 in the U.K.). **National InterRent** (☎ 800/227–7368; 0345/222525 in the U.K., where it is known as Europcar InterRent).

LOCAL AGENCIES➤ **Atlanta Rent-a-Car** (☎ 770/448–6066). **Pay Less** (☎ 800/729–5377). **Rent-a-Wreck** (☎ 404/363–8720). **Thrifty** (☎ 800/367–2277). **Value** (☎ 800/468–2583).

CUT COSTS

To get the best deal, **book through a travel agent who is willing to shop around.** When pricing cars, **ask about the location of the rental lot.** Some off-airport locations offer lower rates, and their lots are only minutes from the terminal via complimentary shuttle. You also may want to **price local car-rental companies,** whose rates may be lower still, although their service and maintenance may not be as good as those of a name-brand agency. Remember to ask about required deposits, cancellation penalties, and drop-off charges if you're planning to pick up the car in one city and leave it in another.

Also **ask your travel agent about a company's customer-service record.** How has it responded to late plane arrivals and vehicle mishaps? Are there often lines at the rental counter, and, if you're traveling during a holiday period, does a confirmed reservation guarantee you a car?

Be sure to **look into wholesalers,** companies that do not own fleets but rent in bulk from those that do and often offer better rates than traditional car-rental operations. Prices are best during off-peak periods.

RENTAL WHOLESALERS➤ The **Kemwel Group** (☎ 914/835–5555 or 800/678–0678, FAX 914/835–5126).

NEED INSURANCE?

When driving a rented car you are generally responsible for any damage to or loss of the vehicle. You also are liable for any property damage or personal injury that you may cause while driving. Before you rent, **see what coverage you already have** under the terms of your personal auto-insurance policy and credit cards.

For about $14 a day, rental companies sell protection, known as a collision- or loss-damage waiver (CDW or LDW) that eliminates your liability for damage to the car; it's always optional and should never be automatically added to your bill.

In most states you don't need CDW if you have personal auto insurance or other liability insurance. However, **make sure you have enough coverage to pay for the car.** If you do not have auto insurance or an umbrella policy that covers damage to third parties, purchasing CDW or LDW is highly recommended.

BEWARE SURCHARGES

Before you pick up a car in one city and leave it in another, **ask about drop-off charges or one-way service fees,** which can be substantial. Note, too, that some rental agencies charge extra if you return the car before the time specified on your contract. To avoid a hefty refueling fee, **fill the tank just before you turn in the car,** but be aware that gas stations near the rental outlet may overcharge.

MEET THE REQUIREMENTS

In Atlanta you must be 21 to rent a car, and rates may be higher if you're under 25. You'll pay extra for child seats (about $3 per day), which are compulsory for children under five, and for additional drivers (about $2 per day). Residents of the United Kingdom will need a reservation voucher, a passport, a U.K. driver's license, and a travel policy that covers each driver, in order to pick up a car.

CHILDREN & TRAVEL

CHILDREN IN ATLANTA

Be sure to plan ahead and **involve your youngsters** as you outline your trip. When packing, include things to keep them busy en route. On sightseeing days try to schedule activities of special interest to your children. If you are renting a car don't forget to **arrange for a car seat** when you reserve.

HOTELS

Most hotels in Atlanta allow children under a certain age to stay in their parents' room at no extra charge, but others charge them as extra adults; be sure to **ask about the cutoff age for children's discounts.**

FLYING

As a general rule, infants under two not occupying a seat fly free. If your children are two or older **ask about children's airfares.**

In general the adult baggage allowance applies to children paying half or more of the adult fare.

According to the Federal Aviation Administration (FAA) it's a good idea to use safety seats aloft for children weighing less than 40 pounds. Airlines, however, can set their own policies: U.S. carriers allow FAA-approved models but usually require that you buy a ticket, even if your child would otherwise ride free, since the seats must be strapped into regular seats. Airline rules vary regarding their use, so it's important to **check your airline's policy about using safety seats during takeoff and landing.** Safety seats cannot obstruct any of the other passengers in the row, so get an appropriate seat assignment as early as possible.

When making your reservation, **request children's meals or a free-standing bassinet** if you need them; the latter are available only to those seated at the bulkhead, where there's enough legroom. Remember, however, that bulk-head seats may not have their own overhead bins, and there's no storage space in front of you—a major inconvenience.

CUSTOMS & DUTIES

ENTERING THE U.S.

Visitors age 21 and over may import the following into the United States: 200 cigarettes or 50 cigars or 2 kilograms of tobacco, 1 liter of alcohol, and gifts worth $100. Prohibited items include meat products, seeds, plants, and fruits.

ENTERING CANADA

If you've been out of Canada for at least seven days you may bring in C$500 worth of goods duty-free. If you've been away for fewer than seven days but more than 48 hours, the duty-free allowance drops to C$200; if your trip lasts 24–48 hours, the allowance is C$50. You may not pool allowances with family members. Goods claimed under the C$500 exemption may follow you by mail; those claimed under the lesser exemptions must accompany you.

Alcohol and tobacco products may be included in the seven-day and 48-hour exemptions but not in the 24-hour exemption. If you meet the age requirements of the province or territory through which you reenter Canada you may bring in, duty-free, 1.14 liters (40 imperial ounces) of wine or liquor *or* 24 12-ounce cans or bottles of beer or ale. If you are 16 or older you may bring in, duty-free, 200 cigarettes and 50 cigars; these items must accompany you.

You may send an unlimited number of gifts worth up to C$60 each duty-free to Canada. Label the package UNSOLICITED GIFT—VALUE UNDER $60. Alcohol and tobacco are excluded.

INFORMATION➤ **Revenue Canada** (✉ 2265 St. Laurent Blvd. S, Ottawa, Ontario K1G 4K3, ☎ 613/993–0534; 800/461–9999 in Canada).

ENTERING THE U.K.

From countries outside the European Union, including the United States, you may import, duty-free, 200 cigarettes or 50 cigars; 1 liter of spirits or 2 liters of fortified or sparkling wine or liqueurs; 2 liters of still table wine; 60 milliliters of perfume; 250 milliliters of toilet water; plus £136 worth of other goods, including gifts and souvenirs.

INFORMATION➤ **HM Customs and Excise** (✉ Dorset House, Stamford St., London SE1 9NG, ☎ 0171/202–4227).

DISABILITIES & ACCESSIBILITY

ACCESS IN ATLANTA

Call MARTA for information about lift vans serving passengers with disabilities and about door-to-door service to and from your destination to rapid rail stations.

TRANSPORTATION➤ **MARTA** (☎ 404/848–5389).

TIPS & HINTS

When discussing accessibility with an operator or reservationist, **ask hard questions.** Are there any stairs, inside *or* out? Are there grab bars next to the toilet *and* in the shower/tub? How wide is the doorway to the room? To the bathroom? For the most extensive facilities meeting the latest legal specifications, **opt for newer accommodations,** which are more likely to have been designed with access in mind. Older buildings or ships may offer more limited facilities. Be sure to **discuss your needs before booking.**

COMPLAINTS➤ **Disability Rights Section** (✉ U.S. Dept. of Justice, Box 66738, Washington, DC 20035-6738, ☎ 202/514–0301 or 800/514–0301, ℻ 202/307–1198, TTY 202/514–0383 or 800/514–0383) for general complaints. **Aviation Consumer Protection Division** (☞ Air Travel, *above*) for airline-related problems. **Civil Rights Office** (✉ U.S. Dept. of Transportation, Departmental Office of Civil Rights, S-30, 400 7th St. SW, Room 10215, Washington, DC 20590, ☎ 202/366–4648) for problems with surface transportation.

TRAVEL AGENCIES & TOUR OPERATORS

The Americans with Disabilities Act requires that travel firms serve the needs of all travelers. That said, you should note that some agencies and operators specialize in making travel arrangements for individuals and groups with disabilities.

TRAVELERS WITH MOBILITY PROBLEMS➤ **Access Adventures** (⊠ 206 Chestnut Ridge Rd., Rochester, NY 14624, ☎ 716/889–9096), run by a former physical-rehabilitation counselor. **Hinsdale Travel Service** (⊠ 201 E. Ogden Ave., Suite 100, Hinsdale, IL 60521, ☎ 630/325–1335), a travel agency that benefits from the advice of wheelchair traveler Janice Perkins. **Wheelchair Journeys** (⊠ 16979 Redmond Way, Redmond, WA 98052, ☎ 206/885–2210 or 800/313–4751), for general travel arrangements.

DISCOUNTS & DEALS

Be a smart shopper and **compare all your options before making a choice.** A plane ticket bought with a promotional coupon may not be cheaper than the least expensive fare from a discount ticket agency. For high-price travel purchases, such as packages or tours, keep in mind that what you get is just as important as what you save. Just because something is cheap doesn't mean it's a bargain.

LOOK IN YOUR WALLET
When you use your credit card to make travel purchases you may get free travel-accident insurance, collision-damage insurance, and medical or legal assistance, depending on the card and the bank that issued it. American Express, MasterCard, and Visa provide one or more of these services, so **get a copy of your credit card's travel-benefits policy.** If you are a member of the American Automobile Association (AAA) or an oil-company-sponsored road-assistance plan, always **ask hotel or car-rental reservationists about auto-club discounts.** Some clubs offer additional discounts on tours, cruises, or admission to attractions. And don't forget that auto-club membership entitles you to free maps and trip-planning services.

DIAL FOR DOLLARS
To save money, **look into "1-800" discount reservations services,** which use their buying power to get a better price on hotels, airline tickets, even car rentals. When booking a room, always **call the hotel's local toll-free number** (if one is available) rather than the central reservations number—you'll often get a better price. Always ask about special packages or corporate rates.

AIRLINE TICKETS➤ ☎ 800/FLY–4–LESS. ☎ 800/FLY–ASAP.

HOTEL ROOMS➤ **Central Reservation Service (CRS)** (☎ 800/548–3311). **Quickbook** (☎ 800/789–9887).

SAVE ON COMBOS

Packages and guided tours can both save you money, but don't confuse the two. When you buy a package your travel remains independent, just as though you had planned and booked the trip yourself. Fly-drive packages, which combine airfare and car rental, are often a good deal. In cities, ask the local visitors bureau about hotel packages. These often include tickets to major museum exhibits and other special events.

JOIN A CLUB?

Many companies sell discounts in the form of travel clubs and coupon books, but these cost money. You must use participating advertisers to get a deal, and only after you recoup the initial membership cost or book price do you begin to save. If you plan to use the club or coupons frequently you may save considerably. Before signing up, find out what discounts you get for free.

DISCOUNT CLUBS➤ **Entertainment Travel Editions** (⊠ 2125 Butterfield Rd., Troy, MI 48084, ☎ 800/445–4137), $23–$48, depending on destination. **Great American Traveler** (⊠ Box 27965, Salt Lake City, UT 84127, ☎ 800/548–2812), $49.95 per year. **Moment's Notice Discount Travel Club** (⊠ 7301 New Utrecht Ave., Brooklyn, NY 11204, ☎ 718/234–6295), $25 per year, single or family. **Privilege Card International** (⊠ 237 E. Front St., Youngstown, OH 44503, ☎ 330/746–5211 or 800/236–9732), $74.95 per year. **Sears's Mature Outlook** (⊠ Box 9390, Des Moines, IA 50306, ☎ 800/336–6330), $14.95 per year. **Travelers Advantage** (⊠ CUC Travel Service, 3033 S. Parker Rd., Suite 1000, Aurora, CO 80014, ☎ 800/548–1116 or 800/648–4037), $49 per year, single or family. **Worldwide Discount Travel Club** (⊠ 1674 Meridian Ave., Miami Beach, FL 33139, ☎ 305/534–2082), $50 per year family, $40 single.

DRIVING

Some residents refer to Atlanta as the Los Angeles of the South, because travel by car is virtually the only way to get to some city sights and the far-reaching parts of the metro area. Although the congestion isn't comparable to L.A.'s yet, Atlantans have grown accustomed to frequent delays, even on the many multilane highways. Always **allow yourself enough time** if you have a meeting; three minutes per mile is a good standard.

Atlantans tend to drive faster than other Southerners. Slower drivers will do best to **stick to the middle lanes** until they need to exit—give plenty of room to speedsters and merging, oncoming traffic.

If you plan to drive into Atlanta, try to **avoid rush hour** (7 AM–9 AM and 4:30 PM–7 PM). The city is crisscrossed by three major interstates: I–85, running northeast–southwest from Virginia to Alabama; I–75, north–south from Michigan to Florida; and I–20, east–west from South Carolina to Texas. Traffic can be intense on these and other major roads anytime, but it should be better before or after these hours.

In addition, Atlanta is bisected by GA 400, a multilane highway that cuts through the east side of Buckhead to connect I–85 to I–285 and continues for nearly 100 mi into north Georgia. I–285, known to residents as the Perimeter, completely encircles the city. On this 63-mi highway, you'll encounter the city's fastest drivers and the most accident- and construction-related slowdowns. The quickest and safest interstate routes are usually straight through the middle of the Perimeter on the Downtown interstates, depending on the time of day you travel. From the airport to Downtown, take I–85 north, which soon joins I–75.

The lack of a grid system in most parts of Atlanta will confuse some drivers. Street names also occasionally change along the same stretch of road: The city's most famous thoroughfare, Peachtree Street, becomes Peachtree Road shortly after it crosses I–85, then Peachtree Industrial Boulevard beyond the Chamblee city limits. To add to the confusion, there are *60* other streets in greater Atlanta with the word Peachtree in them. Before setting out anywhere by car, **get the complete address and precise directions** to your destination.

EMERGENCIES

For **police, fire,** or **ambulance,** ☎ 911.

DOCTORS➤ **Medical Association of Atlanta** (☎ 404/881–1714), open weekdays 9–4, has a referral service listing more than 2,000 physicians in every specialty.

HOSPITALS➤ The following have 24-hour emergency rooms. Downtown: **Grady Memorial Hospital** (✉ 80 Butler St., ☎ 404/616–4307), **Crawford Long Hospital** (✉ 550 Peachtree St., ☎ 404/686–4411), **Emory University** (✉ 1364 Clifton Rd., ☎ 404/712–7021), and **Georgia Baptist Healthcare System** (✉ 303 Parkway Dr., ☎ 404/265–4000). Buckhead: **Piedmont Hospital** (✉ 1968 Peachtree Rd., ☎ 404/605–3297).

DENTISTS➤ The **Georgia Dental Association of Atlanta** (☎ 404/636–7553), open weekdays 8:30–5, will refer you to the dentist closest to your hotel or to one who can accommodate any special needs.

PHARMACIES➤ Some **CVS Drugs** locations offer 24-hour service. **Drug Emporium** has two 24-hour locations (✉ 2625 Piedmont Rd., ☎ 404/233–1048; 4000 LaVista Rd., ☎ 770/939–0370). Many **Kroger** supermarkets (☎ 404/

496–7400), a 24-hour chain, have a full-service pharmacy open daily 9–9. Kroger stores close Saturday at midnight and reopen Sunday at 6 AM.

GAY & LESBIAN TRAVEL

GAY- & LESBIAN-FRIENDLY TRAVEL AGENCIES➤ **Advance Damron** (✉ 1 Greenway Plaza, Suite 800, Houston, TX 77046, ☎ 713/850–1140 or 800/695–0880, ℻ 713/888–1010). **Club Travel** (✉ 8739 Santa Monica Blvd., West Hollywood, CA 90069, ☎ 310/358–2200 or 800/429–8747, ℻ 310/358–2222). **Islanders/Kennedy Travel** (✉ 183 W. 10th St., New York, NY 10014, ☎ 212/242–3222 or 800/988–1181, ℻ 212/929–8530). **Now Voyager** (✉ 4406 18th St., San Francisco, CA 94114, ☎ 415/626–1169 or 800/255–6951, ℻ 415/626–8626). **Yellowbrick Road** (✉ 1500 W. Balmoral Ave., Chicago, IL 60640, ☎ 773/561–1800 or 800/642–2488, ℻ 773/561–4497). **Skylink Women's Travel** (✉ 3577 Moorland Ave., Santa Rosa, CA 95407, ☎ 707/585–8355 or 800/225–5759, ℻ 707/584–5637), serving lesbian travelers.

INSURANCE

Travel insurance is the best way to **protect yourself against financial loss.** The most useful policies are trip-cancellation-and-interruption, default, medical, and comprehensive insurance.

Without insurance you will lose all or most of your money if you cancel your trip, regardless of the reason. It's essential that you **buy trip-cancellation-and-interruption insurance,** particularly if your airline ticket, cruise, or package tour is nonrefundable and cannot be changed. When considering how much coverage you need, look for a policy that will cover the cost of your trip plus the nondiscounted price of a one-way airline ticket, should you need to return home early. Also **look for comprehensive policies that include trip-delay insurance,** which will protect you in the event that weather problems cause you to miss your flight, tour, or cruise. Insurers that sell both trip-delay insurance and waivers for preexisting medical conditions include Access America, Carefree Travel, Travel Insured International, and Travel Guard (☞ *below*). Also **consider default or bankruptcy insurance,** which protects you against a supplier's failure to deliver.

Always **buy travel insurance directly from the insurance company;** if you buy it from a travel agency or tour operator that goes out of business you probably will not be covered for the agency or operator's default, a major risk. Before you make any purchase, **review your existing health and home-owner's policies** to find out whether they cover expenses incurred while traveling.

Citizens of the United Kingdom can buy an annual travel-insurance policy valid for most vacations during the year in which it's purchased. If you are pregnant or have a preexisting medical condition, make sure you're covered. According to the Association of British Insurers, a trade association representing 450 insurance companies, it's wise to buy extra medical coverage when you visit the United States.

TRAVEL INSURERS➤ In the United States, **Access America** (⊠ 6600 W. Broad St., Richmond, VA 23230, ☎ 804/285–3300 or 800/284–8300), **Carefree Travel Insurance** (⊠ Box 9366, 100 Garden City Plaza, Garden City, NY 11530, ☎ 516/294–0220 or 800/323–3149), **Near Travel Services** (⊠ Box 1339, Calumet City, IL 60409, ☎ 708/868–6700 or 800/654–6700), **Travel Guard International** (⊠ 1145 Clark St., Stevens Point, WI 54481, ☎ 715/345–0505 or 800/826–1300), **Travel Insured International** (⊠ Box 280568, East Hartford, CT 06128-0568, ☎ 860/528–7663 or 800/243–3174), **Travelex Insurance Services** (⊠ 11717 Burt St., Suite 202, Omaha, NE 68154-1500, ☎ 402/445–8637 or 800/228–9792, 🕿 800/867–9531), **Wallach & Company** (⊠ 107 W. Federal St., Box 480, Middleburg, VA 20118, ☎ 540/687–3166 or 800/237–6615). In Canada, **Mutual of Omaha** (⊠ Travel Division, 500 University Ave., Toronto, Ontario M5G 1V8, ☎ 416/598–4083; 800/268–8825 in Canada). In the United Kingdom, **Association of British Insurers** (⊠ 51 Gresham St., London EC2V 7HQ, ☎ 0171/600–3333).

MONEY

ATMS

ATM LOCATIONS➤ **Cirrus** (☎ 800/424–7787). **Plus** (☎ 800/843–7587).

PACKING FOR ATLANTA

Casual clothes are acceptable for most sightseeing and dining; more fashionable casual wear or a jacket and tie may be required in the fancier restaurants. From mid-November to March, pack a sweater and an insulated coat or lined raincoat. For summer, dress in natural fabrics. Some buildings are overly air-conditioned, so a light jacket or sweater is useful, too. In fall and spring, a combination of summer clothes and light wools or synthetics will be adequate for moderate daytime temperatures, but add a jacket or sweater for early morning and evening. Since most of the city is hilly, a sturdy, broken-in pair of walking shoes is a necessity for sightseeing.

Bring an extra pair of eyeglasses or contact lenses in your carry-on luggage, and if you take medication, **pack enough medication** to last the entire trip. It's important that you **don't put prescription**

drugs or valuables in luggage to be checked: It might go astray.

LUGGAGE

In general you are entitled to check two bags on flights within the United States. A third piece may be brought on board, but it must fit easily under the seat in front of you or in the overhead compartment.

Airline liability for baggage is limited to $1,250 per person on flights within the United States. On international flights it amounts to $9.07 per pound or $20 per kilogram for checked baggage (roughly $640 per 70-pound bag) and $400 per passenger for unchecked baggage. Insurance for losses exceeding these amounts can be bought from the airline at check-in for about $10 per $1,000 of coverage; note that this coverage excludes a rather extensive list of items, which is shown on your airline ticket.

Before departure, **itemize your bags' contents** and their worth, and label the bags with your name, address, and phone number. (If you use your home address, cover it so that potential thieves can't see it readily.) Inside each bag, **pack a copy of your itinerary.** At check-in, **make sure that each bag is correctly tagged** with the destination airport's three-letter code. If your bags arrive damaged or fail to arrive at all, file a written report with the airline before leaving the airport.

PASSPORTS & VISAS

CANADIANS

A passport is not required to enter the United States.

U.K. CITIZENS

British citizens need a valid passport to enter the United States. If you are staying for fewer than 90 days on vacation, with a return or onward ticket, you probably will not need a visa. However, you will need to fill out the Visa Waiver Form, 1-94W, supplied by the airline.

INFORMATION➤ **London Passport Office** (☎ 0990/21010) for fees and documentation requirements and to request an emergency passport. **U.S. Embassy Visa Information Line** (☎ 01891/200–290) for U.S. visa information; calls cost 49p per minute or 39p per minute cheap rate. **U.S. Embassy Visa Branch** (✉ 5 Upper Grosvenor St., London W1A 2JB) for U.S. visa information; send a self-addressed, stamped envelope. Write the **U.S. Consulate General** (✉ Queen's House, Queen St., Belfast BTI 6EO) if you live in Northern Ireland.

RADIO STATIONS

AM: WPLO 610: Country; WGST 640: News/Talk; WCNN 680: Sports/Talk; **WSB 750**: News/Talk; **WQXI 790**: Music/Talk; **WNIV 970**: Christian Talk/Music; **WGKA 1190**: Classical. FM: **WABE 90.1**: National Public Radio/Classical/

Jazz; **WCLK 91.9:** Blues/Jazz/Soul; **WZGC 92.9:** Classic Rock; **WPCH 94.9:** Light Rock; **WKLS 96.1:** Album Rock; **WFOX 97.1:** Oldies; **WKHX 101.5:** Country; **WVEE 103.3:** Top 40/Soul.

SENIOR-CITIZEN TRAVEL

To qualify for age-related discounts, **mention your senior-citizen status up front** when booking hotel reservations (not when checking out) and before you're seated in restaurants (not when paying the bill). Note that discounts may be limited to certain menus, days, or hours. When renting a car, **ask about promotional car-rental discounts,** which can be cheaper than senior-citizen rates.

EDUCATIONAL TRAVEL PROGRAMS➤ **Elderhostel** (⊠ 75 Federal St., 3rd floor, Boston, MA 02110, ☎ 617/426–8056).

SIGHTSEEING

If this is your first visit to Atlanta, consider a general-interest tour that covers the city highlights. Most tour companies have pickup service at major hotels. Unless noted, tour prices do not include meals or refreshments.

GENERAL TOURS

Gray Line of Atlanta leads four- and eight-hour tours ranging from $40 to $63 per person of Downtown, Midtown, or Buckhead and tours that cover Atlanta's primary sights and attractions, including the King Center and Stone Mountain.

INFORMATION➤ **Gray Line of Atlanta** (☎ 404/767–0594).

SPECIAL-INTEREST TOURS

Capital City Carriage Company runs half-hour horse-and-buggy tours throughout Downtown Atlanta year round ($25 per person, $45 per couple). Inshirah Horse Drawn Carriages gives 20-minute horse-and-buggy tours of historic Downtown sights in summer from 6 PM to midnight ($25 per person, $20 per person for parties of four or more).

Bill Allison of Classic Biplane flies historic tours of Atlanta and Stone Mountain in a Stearman biplane, which seats two passengers plus the pilot. Downtown or Stone Mountain costs $85, and $150 for both sites; the second passenger rides for half price.

Lowder Event Management offers specialized tours including those of Atlanta's historic sites, black heritage, and nightlife (its "Carter, King, and Coke" tour is popular), for all group sizes; transportation is by limousine, van, or passenger bus. A tour outside Atlanta takes in some Civil War battlefields, Callaway Gardens, and antebellum homes. Tours last three to eight hours and cost $18–$64 per person.

INFORMATION➤ **Capital City Carriage Company** (☎ 404/221–1976; 404/690–9701 for pager). **Classic Biplane** (⊠ Administration Bldg., DeKalb Peachtree Airport, Chamblee, ☎ 404/315–9003). **Inshirah Horse Drawn Carriages** (☎ 404/680–3805). **Lowder Event Management** (☎ 404/874–1349).

WALKING TOURS

The Atlanta Preservation Center has 10 walking tours of historic areas and neighborhoods that occur primarily on weekends; the cost is $5 per adult. Especially noteworthy are tours of Sweet Auburn, the neighborhood associated with Martin Luther King Jr. and other leaders in Atlanta's black community; Druid Hills, the verdant, genteel neighborhood where *Driving Miss Daisy* was filmed; the Fox Theatre, Midtown's elaborate 1920s picture palace; and Inman Park, one of the city's celebrated Victorian districts.

INFORMATION➤ **Atlanta Preservation Center** (✉ 156 7th St., Suite 3, 30308, ☎ 404/876–2041; 404/876–2040 for recorded information).

STUDENTS

To save money, **look into deals available through student-oriented travel agencies.** To qualify you'll need a bona fide student ID card. Members of international student groups are also eligible.

STUDENT IDs & SERVICES➤ **Council on International Educational Exchange** (✉ CIEE, 205 E. 42nd St., 14th floor, New York, NY 10017, ☎ 212/822–2600 or 888/268–6245, FAX 212/822–2699), for mail orders only, in the United States. **Travel Cuts** (✉ 187 College St., Toronto, Ontario M5T 1P7, ☎ 416/979–2406 or 800/667–2887) in Canada.

HOSTELING➤ **Hostelling International—American Youth Hostels** (✉ 733 15th St. NW, Suite 840, Washington, DC 20005, ☎ 202/783–6161, FAX 202/783–6171). **Hostelling International—Canada** (✉ 400-205 Catherine St., Ottawa, Ontario K2P 1C3, ☎ 613/237–7884, FAX 613/237–7868). **Youth Hostel Association of England and Wales** (✉ Trevelyan House, 8 St. Stephen's Hill, St. Albans, Hertfordshire AL1 2DY, ☎ 01727/855215 or 01727/845047, FAX 01727/844126). Membership in the United States, $25; in Canada, C$26.75; in the United Kingdom, £9.30.

TAXIS

In Atlanta, you most often have to **call for a taxi or go to a major hotel or MARTA station,** where they congregate. Fares start at $1.50 for the first ½ mi, with 20¢ for each additional ½ mi; waiting time is $15 per hour. Each additional person is charged $1. Within the Downtown Convention Zone, a flat rate of $5 for one person or $1 per person for two or more passengers is charged for any destination.

A large percentage of Atlanta's taxi drivers are from outside the country; you should **beware of cabbies who speak poor English.** Some don't know much more about the city's geography than its visitors do. The problem compounds when big events or conventions are in town, because taxi drivers arrive from out of town. You should **come armed with good directions** if your destination is not off a primary thoroughfare like Peachtree Street or is something other than a major hotel or popular sight. You also should make sure to have small bills and change when taking a taxi, as drivers often do not carry change for even the smallest bills. Many taxi companies now take credit cards.

CAB COMPANIES➤ **Executive Limousine** (☎ 404/223–2000). **Checker Cab** (☎ 404/351–1111). **Buckhead Safety Cab** (☎ 404/233–1152).

TELEPHONES

Atlanta now has a second area code, 770, for most numbers outside the I–285 Perimeter. Numbers inside the Perimeter generally retain the 404 code. But there are exceptions. Chamblee, although it is inside the Perimeter, uses 770. Sandy Springs still uses 404, despite being outside the Perimeter. This guide reflects the division. As we go to press, a third area code is under discussion.

CALLING HOME

AT&T, MCI, and Sprint long-distance services make calling home

relatively convenient and let you avoid hotel surcharges. Typically you dial an 800 number in the United States.

TO OBTAIN ACCESS CODES➤ **AT&T USADirect** (☎ 800/874–4000). **MCI Call USA** (☎ 800/444–4444). **Sprint Express** (☎ 800/793–1153).

TOUR OPERATORS

Buying a prepackaged tour or independent vacation can make your trip to Atlanta less expensive and more hassle-free. Because everything is prearranged you'll spend less time planning.

Operators that handle several hundred thousand travelers per year can use their purchasing power to give you a good price. Their high volume may also indicate financial stability. But some small companies provide more personalized service; because they tend to specialize, they may also be more knowledgeable about a given area.

A GOOD DEAL?

The more your package or tour includes, the better you can predict the ultimate cost of your vacation. Make sure you know exactly what is covered, and **beware of hidden costs.** Are taxes, tips, and service charges included? Transfers and baggage handling? Entertainment and excursions? These can add up.

If the package or tour you are considering is priced lower than in your wildest dreams, **be skeptical.** Also, **make sure your travel agent knows the accommodations** and other services. Ask about the hotel's location, room size, beds, and whether it has a pool, room service, or programs for children, if you care about these. Has your agent been there in person or sent others you can contact?

BUYER BEWARE

Each year consumers are stranded or lose their money when tour operators—even very large ones with excellent reputations—go out of business. So **check out the operator.** Find out how long the company has been in business, and ask several agents about its reputation. And **don't book unless the firm has a consumer-protection program.**

Members of the National Tour Association and United States Tour Operators Association are required to set aside funds to cover your payments and travel arrangements in case the company defaults. Nonmembers may carry insurance instead. Look for the details, and for the name of an underwriter with a solid reputation, in the operator's brochure. Note: When it comes to tour operators, **don't trust escrow accounts.** Although the Department of Transportation watches over charter-flight operators, no regulatory body prevents tour operators from raiding the till. You may want to protect yourself by buying travel insurance that

includes a tour-operator default provision.

It's also a good idea to choose a company that participates in the American Society of Travel Agents' Tour Operator Program (TOP). This gives you a forum if there are any disputes between you and your tour operator; ASTA will act as mediator.

TOUR-OPERATOR RECOMMENDA-TIONS➤ **National Tour Association** (✉ NTA, 546 E. Main St., Lexington, KY 40508, ☎ 606/226–4444 or 800/755–8687). **United States Tour Operators Association** (✉ USTOA, 342 Madison Ave., Suite 1522, New York, NY 10173, ☎ 212/599–6599, FAX 212/599–6744). **American Society of Travel Agents** (☞ *below*).

USING AN AGENT

Travel agents are excellent resources. In fact, large operators accept bookings made only through travel agents. But it's a good idea to **collect brochures from several agencies,** because some agents' suggestions may be influenced by relationships with tour and package firms that reward them for volume sales. If you have a special interest, **find an agent with expertise in that area;** ASTA (☞ Travel Agencies, *below*) has a database of specialists worldwide. Do some homework on your own, too: Local tourism boards can provide information about lesser-known and small-niche operators, some of which may sell only direct.

SINGLE TRAVELERS

Prices for packages and tours are usually quoted per person, based on two sharing a room. If traveling solo, you may be required to pay the full double-occupancy rate. Some operators eliminate this surcharge if you agree to be matched with a roommate of the same sex, even if one is not found by departure time.

TRAIN TRAVEL

Amtrak's *Crescent* provides daily service to New Orleans, Greenville, Charlotte, Washington, D.C., Baltimore, Philadelphia, and New York from Atlanta's Brookwood Station. The *Gulf Breeze* travels from Atlanta to Birmingham and Mobile, Alabama. The small station is between Midtown and Buckhead, convenient to many Atlanta sights. MARTA Bus 23 stops here and continues 1 mi north to the Arts Center rail station, where you can make other connections.

INFORMATION➤ **Brookwood Station** (✉ 1688 Peachtree St., at Deering Rd., ☎ 404/881–3061 or 800/872–7245). **Amtrak** (☎ 800/872–7245). **Amtrak's Great American Vacations** (☎ 800/321–8684).

WITHIN ATLANTA

To get between major sights, **take MARTA,** the rapid rail system that runs beneath Downtown and

Midtown as a subway, and primarily on elevated rail beds throughout the rest of the city. Although its 46-mi system is limited to two lines, MARTA provides links to the airport, Downtown, Midtown, Lenox Square Mall, several major landmarks, and the suburbs. In this guide, MARTA stops are given for major sights as well as for hotels and restaurants when applicable.

The system's east–west line stops at 14 stations from Hightower near the west side of I–285 to Indian Creek just beyond the east side of I–285; the short Proctor Creek extension line branches beyond the Ashby station to one additional stop. The north–south line, with 18 stations, runs from Hartsfield Atlanta International Airport to Doraville, a suburb just west of the I–85 and I–285 intersection. A new north extension branching off from the Lindbergh station provides three new stops (Buckhead, Medical Center Station, and Dunwoody), with two additional stations under construction.

The lines cross at Downtown's Five Points station; you can transfer free here, by pressing the white button on the turnstile (use the same procedure at any MARTA rapid rail station.) At this station, **get ride information for rail lines and buses** from racks of schedules, information booths, and information kiosks with instructions in a multilingual brochure (English, Spanish, and French). At this station, you also can get a shuttle to the Braves games; a shuttle to Six Flags leaves from Hightower.

Depending on the station, trains run from 4:37 AM to 1:17 AM on weekdays and from 5:30 AM to 1:30 AM on weekends; the interval between trains is 8–15 minutes, depending on the line, day, and time. There is free parking in large lots at selected stations (Lindbergh, Chamblee, Doraville, Medical Center, West End, Lakewood/Ft. McPherson, College Park, Indian Creek, Brookhaven, for example). Some stations (mostly Downtown and Midtown stations) have no parking. MARTA has a good safety record, its own police force, and a closed-circuit television system in stations.

The MARTA fare is $1.50. Special shuttle bus routes may charge a small additional fee. To enter the station, you need exact change or a token, purchased from machines outside the station or at the Airport, Lenox Square, Five Points or Lindbergh Ride Store; hours and days of operation vary, but generally these locations are open weekdays 7 AM–6 PM and Airport is open Saturday and Sunday as well. You can buy 20 tokens for $25 ($1.25 a ride). At your departure station, **obtain free bus transfers** by pressing the white button on the turnstile.

For weekend or lengthier stays, **consider a two- or three-day weekend pass** ($6 and $8) that gives unlimited travel on both trains and buses. Weekly Trans-Cards, good for seven days of unlimited travel, are an especially good bargain at $12; monthly TransCards are $45. The passes and cards can be purchased at the Ride Stores (☞ *above*). Tokens and monthly cards may also be purchased at selected A&P and Kroger stores. Be sure to retrieve your card from the turnstile.

SCHEDULES & INFORMATION➤ **MARTA** (☎ 404/848–4711).

TRAVEL AGENCIES

A good travel agent puts your needs first. Look for an agency that has been in business at least five years, emphasizes customer service, and has someone on staff who specializes in your destination. In addition, **make sure the agency belongs to the American Society of Travel Agents** (ASTA). If your travel agency is also acting as your tour operator, *see* Tour Operators, *above*).

LOCAL AGENT REFERRALS➤ **American Society of Travel Agents** (ASTA, ☎ 800/965–2782 24-hr hot line, FAX 703/684–8319). **Alliance of Canadian Travel Associations** (✉ 1729 Bank St., Suite 201, Ottawa, Ontario K1V 7Z5, ☎ 613/521–0474, FAX 613/521–0805). **Association of British Travel Agents** (✉ 55–57 Newman

St., London W1P 4AH, ☎ 0171/
637–2444, FAX 0171/637–0713).

VISITOR INFORMATION

Contact the Atlanta Convention
and Visitors Bureau for a city map
and brochures about all major
sights and upcoming events. Ask
for their EXPLOR-A-CARD,
which can be used for discounts at
selected sights, hotels, restaurants,
and shops. Five small ACVB visitor centers are located at Hartsfield Atlanta International Airport
(north terminal at west crossover);
Downtown at Peachtree Center
Mall (233 Peachtree St.), Underground Atlanta (65 Upper Alabama St.), and World Congress
Center (285 International Blvd.);
and in Buckhead at Lenox Square
Mall (3393 Peachtree Rd.). Helpful employees staff these centers
from 8:30 to 6. For multilingual
information about Atlanta sights,
call 800/542–9112 and one of the
following extensions: 8266
(French), 5266 (German), 6266
(Italian), 9266 (Japanese), and
5266 (Spanish).

For more information, the Atlanta
Chamber of Commerce will send
you a brochure listing 80 of their
publications, ranging from sights
information, newcomer packages,
and economic surveys.

The Georgia Department of Industry, Trade, and Tourism can an-
swer most of your questions about
travel in the state. The free, 176-
page *Georgia on My Mind* magazine offers a wealth of information.

The Welcome South Visitors Center has information and exhibits
about Atlanta and the entire
southern United States and also
has a Thomas Cook office for currency exchange, AAA Club South,
and other services.

In the United Kingdom, also contact the United States Travel and
Tourism Administration.

INFORMATION➤ **Atlanta Convention & Visitors Bureau** (✉ ACVB,
233 Peachtree St., Suite 2000,
30303, ☎ 404/521–6600, 404/
222–6688 for automated information service, or 800/ATLANTA).
Atlanta Chamber of Commerce
(✉ Box 1740, 30301, ☎ 404/
880–9000). **Georgia Department
of Industry, Trade, and Tourism**
(✉ Box 1776, 30301, ☎ 404/
656–3590 or 800/847–4842, FAX
404/656–3567). **Welcome South
Visitors Center** (✉ 200 Spring St.,
☎ 404/224–2000). **United States
Travel and Tourism Administration** (✉ Box 1EN, London W1A
1EN, ☎ 0171/495–4466). For a
free USA pack, write the USTTA at
Box 170, Ashford, Kent TN24
0ZX. Enclose stamps worth £1.50.

WHEN TO GO

Spring and fall, usually with
65°F–80°F temperatures, are the
best seasons to visit Atlanta.
April—when the azaleas and
rhododendrons bloom, and camel-
lias, cherry trees, and dogwoods

flower—invigorates the city with a passionate display of brilliant colors. Various music and crafts fairs take place from spring through the fall; the nine-day Arts Festival of Atlanta, held in September, draws visitors from the entire region.

You may want to check with the Atlanta Convention and Visitors Bureau to see if there will be major conventions in town when you plan to visit; hotels can fill up.

CLIMATE

Because the mountains to the north block the cold air but hold in moisture from the Gulf region, summer is generally hot and humid, with temperatures that may soar to the mid-90s, with 90% humidity. Expect warm temperatures from mid-May to mid-September.

Winter temperatures rarely dip below 40°F during the day, and there is less than two inches of snow per year. The higher humid-

ity, though, can contribute to a damp cold. Atlanta receives up to 50 inches of rain per year, so it's wise always to pack a raincoat and umbrella. October is predictably the driest month.

Average daily maximum and minimum temperatures for Atlanta are in the chart below.

For current conditions and forecasts, plus the local time and helpful travel tips, call the Weather Channel Connection (95¢ per minute) from a Touch-Tone phone. For an Atlanta weather forecast, current temperature, and time, call the hot line that's courtesy of radio station WKLS and the National Weather Service. Or dial 511 and, at the prompt, enter 3660 for a forecast by WSB–TV's meteorologist.

INFORMATION➤ **Weather Channel Connection** (☎ 900/932–8437). **WKLS/NWS weather hot line** (☎ 404/633–3333).

Climate in Atlanta

Jan.	52F	11C	May	79F	26C	Sept.	83F	28C
	36	2		61	16		65	18
Feb.	54F	12C	June	86F	30C	Oct.	72F	22C
	38	3		67	19		54	12
Mar.	63F	17C	July	88F	31C	Nov.	61F	16C
	43	6		70	21		43	6
Apr.	72F	22C	Aug.	86F	30C	Dec.	52F	11C
	52	11		70	21		38	3

1 Destination: Atlanta

CITY ON THE MOVE

ATLANTA SURPRISES and impresses first-time visitors, as well as those who haven't been here recently. People are taken aback by the city's many ultramodern skyscrapers, which are even more compelling at dusk, when the setting sun makes the glassy towers glow in shades of yellow and red, or at night, when they light up the sky for miles. Atlanta's skyline, most of it created since 1980, is its trademark, an assertive symbol of the New South, which refuses to sit still.

Atlanta was founded in 1837 as Terminus (because it was a railroad center), soon became Marthasville, and was named Atlanta in 1845. Its early residents were largely northerners and immigrant Irish, and its reputation, fueled especially by activities on Whitehall Street, where taverns prevailed in that day, was hardly pristine. It did not become the state's capital until after the Civil War, when occupation Federal forces moved it here from Milledgeville.

The romantic images conjured up by the South—lacy moss hanging from massive oak trees, a leisurely pace of life, and sprawling plantations straight out of *Gone With the Wind*—are not found here. Antebellum residential structures do survive in metro Atlanta, although some of these—notably the restaurant Anthonys (☞ Chapter 3) and the plantation structures at Stone Mountain Park—were physically relocated here from other parts of the state. No antebellum commercial buildings remain within the city limits, although some did survive the Battle of Atlanta and the burning of the city November 15, 1864, when General William Tecumseh Sherman and his Army of the Tennessee left the city and headed southeast toward Savannah. Furthermore, those antebellum residences that were built in the Upland South bore little resemblance to the Greek Revival mansions remaining in the southern and eastern parts of the state. The Tullie Smith House (1830s) on the grounds of the Atlanta History Center came from a farm in one of metro Atlanta's counties (DeKalb). Its simple plantation-plain style is far more typical of the kind of house one found here in the early 19th century, especially in rural areas.

Continuing his March to the Sea, Sherman departed Atlanta November 16, 1864, the day after evacuating the city and setting it aflame, leaving most, although not all, of its buildings smoldering. The film *Gone With the Wind* accurately depicts that horrible night, if the words of one of Sherman's officers, likening the scene to a very vision of Hell, are at all credible. Atlanta's strategic importance as a railroad junction and a medical and supply center for the Confederate Army meant any building that could sustain the war effort had to be destroyed. What didn't fall to shot and shell crumbled under the more recent advance of the shopping center. Sherman and his two-column force then cut a wide swath of destruction through the center of the state. The Army of the Tennessee reached the coast and delivered Savannah to President Abraham Lincoln for Christmas. Appomattox only remained to formalize what was already fact: The South had lost the war.

THE CITY suffered another fire in 1917, when many of its Victorian structures burned. Thus, while the city's architecture may lack the venerable history of Savannah's or Charleston's, Atlanta's 20th-century buildings, especially the recent creations by Richard Meier, Michael Graves, Philip Johnson, Marcel Breuer, I. M. Pei, and home-grown architect John Portman, have left their distinctive marks. Former mayor Andrew Young put it this way: "Atlanta is building its history now. This is the golden age of development."

All this explains why visitors quickly discover that Atlanta is not the kind of sleepy-eyed southern town often featured in Hollywood or television portrayals of the South. This myth is exploded as soon as they experience the city's highways, with their bumper-to-bumper high-speed traffic. Atlanta can be a mini–Los Angeles at times, especially when cars grind to a halt because of highway construction, an ongoing project as the city struggles to keep pace with the population growth that has doubled Atlanta's size in the past 20 years.

Atlanta presents a complex demographic profile. As the city gains the world's respect, people are moving here in droves: Of the more than 3.5 million residents in metro Atlanta, it has been estimated that at least 50 percent were born outside the South. While you will still hear true southern drawls, you will also hear the accents of transplants from such places as New York City, Chicago, Vancouver, Los Angeles, Paris, Belfast, Bangkok, Tokyo, and Lagos. There's a large contingent of Latin Americans, a huge African community of Nigerians and Ethiopians, and more than 50,000 Russian Jews, but the best example of the new international presence in Atlanta is the small northeastern suburb of Chamblee, which is home to one of the largest Asian communities in the country. Along a 3-mi strip of Buford Highway lined with commercial businesses and restaurants, nearly all you see are signs atop signs in Chinese, Japanese, Korean, Cambodian, and Vietnamese.

Black and white Georgians interact routinely and amiably every day. Nonetheless, it's not realistic to say there are no racial issues. The state flag reveals one of them: It still incorporates the Confederate Battle Flag's familiar Cross of St. Andrew design, and is a constant source of contention between the black community and good ol' boy politicians. However, the work and enduring legacy of Atlanta native and Nobel Peace Prize winner Dr. Martin Luther King Jr. and many community leaders, both black and white, over the past 30 years have brought a lot of healing to Atlanta and the entire South.

ATLANTA REMAINS a city with economic opportunity for all groups of people, with unemployment consistently less than the national average. Georgia's capital city has become a financial, transportation, communications, and commercial center for the region. It's home to numerous universities and such corporations as Turner Broadcasting, Coca-Cola, Home Depot, Holiday Inn, UPS, and Delta Airlines. More than 730 of the Fortune 1,000 companies have offices here, and with lower taxes than many other big cities, Atlanta provides an excellent atmosphere for starting a business.

Good jobs and the many handsome, tree-filled neighborhoods are only part of the reason people come here. The general high quality of life is addicting; once you get a taste, you've got to have more. It often begins with Atlanta's climate: Although summers can be very humid, it's not impossible for temperatures to be in the 60s in December. The occasional winter ice- or snowstorm that brings the city to a two- or three-day standstill is the worst weather scenario.

As one of Atlanta's nicknames, Hotlanta, indicates, the main draws for visitors are not historical sights and museums—although these exist—but entertainment, shopping, and dining. Atlanta has a symphony and ballet company, a variety of nightspots, more malls and shops than any other U.S. city except Chicago, and restaurants serving any cuisine you can imagine.

Fast-paced and progressive, Atlanta combines northern brashness and efficiency with international sophistication and a touch of time-honored southern hospitality. But there are big-city problems: A reputation for high crime has plagued the city for years, and the urban blights of public housing ghettos and a growing homeless population won't respond to a quick fix. Atlantans, as always, will find solutions. The city swiftly rebuilt from the ashes of the Civil War, absorbed the lessons of the Civil Rights movement, and, over the past three decades, strengthened its economic base. The city's hosting of the 1996 Centennial Olympic Games was a great source of pride—despite the bombing of Centennial Olympic Park and some administrative glitches. Atlanta will continue, like its ever-changing skyline, to make itself look better as it moves forward into the 21st century.

—Mark Beffart
with Jane Garvey

NEW AND NOTEWORTHY

For Atlanta, the Centennial Olympic Games were not only the culmination of years of preparation, but a catalyst for remarkable, ongoing change. Improvements include wider sidewalks, new and beautified public parks, thousands of new trees, eye-catching public art, dramatic restorations within the inner city, and new attractions.

Centennial Olympic Park was especially crafted for the Olympics as a performance and gathering venue. Although it was marred by a bomb explosion early in the games, the park gives Atlanta a new downtown hub for special events. Across the street from the park, a new 20,000-seat sports arena is rising from the site of the OMNI Coliseum and will become the home of the NBA Atlanta Hawks, and possibly an NHL hockey franchise, in 1999.

Turner Field is the new home of the Atlanta Braves. It had been Olympic Stadium and was modified to suit the needs of a baseball field. The dramatic Olympic flame cauldron may or may not remain there; its fate has become something of a controversy, as the Braves want it moved and the artist, Siah Armajani, does not. The old Atlanta-Fulton County Stadium, on the next block, was imploded in summer 1997 to make room for more parking for Turner Field. Fans can tour Turner Field's Ivan Allen Jr. Braves Museum and Hall of Fame and the stadium itself.

New artscapes now dot the city's urban landscape. Most interesting of these is the **John Wesley Dobbs Plaza,** just east of the I–75/I–85 overpass on Auburn Avenue. The work features a life mask of Dobbs, one of former mayor Maynard Jackson's grandfathers and a power behind the development of Auburn Avenue as Atlanta's "Black Wall Street." Visitors may climb inside the mask and view Auburn Avenue from within.

If a walk on the wild side captures your interest, check out **Zoo Atlanta**'s new Conservation Resource Action Center, where you may use the latest satellite technology to track wildlife worldwide.

Georgia's favorite theme park, **Six Flags,** opened its ninth and most exciting attraction, Batman—The Ride, a wild roller coaster that will have riders holding their breath as 4 G's of force push them into their seats high above the ground.

WHAT'S WHERE

Atlanta Neighborhoods

ATLANTA UNIVERSITY CENTER➤ Just west of Downtown are the campuses of the Atlanta University Center, the largest consortium of historically black colleges in the nation: Morris Brown, Morehouse, Clark-Atlanta University, and Spelman. The Alonzo F. Herndon Home, an elegant Georgian Revival house, was built for Herndon, founder of the Atlanta Life Insurance Company and Atlanta's first black millionaire. The Hammonds House Galleries and Resource Center of African-American Art and the Wren's Nest, the former home of Joel Chandler Harris, the author of *Uncle Remus:*

His Songs and Sayings, are also here.

DRUID HILLS AND VIRGINIA-HIGHLAND➤ East of Virginia-Highland between Ponce de Leon Avenue and Emory University, Druid Hills has gracious homes with manicured plantings and dogwood trees that are stunning in the spring. Developed in the early 1900s by Joel Hurt and renowned landscape architect Frederick Law Olmsted, whose firm also designed Central Park in New York City, it is home to the Fernbank Museum of Natural History. The nation caught glimpses of this neighborhood in the film *Driving Miss Daisy,* based on the eponymous Pulitzer Prize–winning play by Atlanta native Alfred Uhry.

Between Midtown and Druid Hills, Virginia-Highland, one of Atlanta's hippest residential areas, takes its name from the intersection of Virginia and North Highland avenues. Longtime residents and young professionals own its small bungalows and two-story traditional homes. The art galleries, shops, bars, restaurants, and music clubs that line North Highland Avenue compete with Buckhead establishments as the in places to shop, dine, and party. Emory University is nearby.

GRANT PARK, INMAN PARK, LITTLE FIVE POINTS➤ Grant Park, a 100-acre park surrounded by Queen Anne mansions and Craftsman bungalows, has two main attractions: Atlanta Cyclorama and Zoo Atlanta. Chief among the charms of the small neighborhood of Inman Park, 3 mi east of Downtown, are its 100 Victorian homes and Callan Castle, a Beaux-Art Classical mansion. The Atlanta History Center is here. In the small business district of Little Five Points, a half mile northeast of Inman Park at the intersection of Euclid and Moreland avenues, funky retail stores sell vintage and offbeat clothes, music, books, and gifts. There are also art galleries, theater companies, bars, and restaurants. Less than a mile northwest of Little Five Points stands the Carter Presidential Center.

Buckhead

A large percentage of Atlanta's wealthy citizens live in Buckhead, on streets near the Governor's mansion and the Atlanta History Center. Buckhead's main drag is Peachtree Road, from I–85 to Lenox Square Mall and Phipps Plaza. The main business district, where Peachtree Road and West and East Paces Ferry roads cross, has the city's most elegant shops, finest restaurants, and its hottest nightlife. SoBuck (South Buckhead, once known as Brookwood) abounds in art galleries, antiques shops, and younger, trend-setting residents.

Downtown

Atlanta's main business and government district, bordered on the south by I–20 and on the east and north by the curves of I–75/I–85, consists primarily of retail and service businesses, office towers, and hotels. Major visitor attractions are the state capitol, the entertainment and shopping complex Underground Atlanta, CNN Center, the Georgia Dome, and Centennial Olympic Park.

Midtown and Ansley Park

Today's Midtown business district has a skyline comparable to that of its neighbor to the south, Downtown. A few blocks east of Peachtree Street are the renovated mansions and bungalows of its residential section. The Fox Theatre, High Museum of Art, and Woodruff Arts Center make this Atlanta's cultural hub. Piedmont Park and the Atlanta Botanical Garden serve as verdant refuges in its northeast corner. SciTrek, the city's science and technology museum, is between Midtown and Downtown. East of the High Museum of Art, between Peachtree Street and Piedmont Avenue, hundreds of large homes on hilly, attractively landscaped lots make up Ansley Park, a respected residential neighborhood.

Sweet Auburn

This historic, predominantly black neighborhood and business district along Auburn Avenue on the eastern edge of Downtown was home to Dr. Martin Luther King Jr., who grew up here and returned in the late 1950s as a leader of the Civil Rights movement. The most dramatic site within the 10-block Martin Luther King Jr. National Historic District is King's raised marble tomb, set in the courtyard of the Martin Luther King Jr. Center for Nonviolent Social Change. The Queen Anne Victorian Martin Luther King Jr. Birth Home is typical of the residential architecture of the neighborhood.

Greater Atlanta

The biggest draw outside the city is Stone Mountain Park, a 3,200-acre family playground built around the largest exposed granite outcropping on earth with the world's largest sculpture, the *Confederate Memorial*—a bas-relief carving of Confederate president Jefferson Davis and generals Stonewall Jackson and Robert E. Lee. There's a steam railroad, plantation homes, a *Gone With the Wind* museum, a zoo, and opportunities for hiking, golf, fishing, tennis, and swimming. There are several other theme parks near the city as well as a winery, a Civil War battlefield, and Roswell, a town that has some of the area's finest antebellum houses.

PLEASURES AND PASTIMES

Civil Rights Legacy

Atlanta's connection with the Civil Rights movement over three decades is felt most powerfully in the Sweet Auburn neighborhood. Here, the Martin Luther King Jr. National Historic District contains Dr. King's birthplace, his pulpit at Ebenezer Baptist Church, and his burial place. The western section of Sweet Auburn was for decades the city's most active and prosperous black community.

Civil War Sites

Although Sherman's army torched much of Atlanta in 1864, some Civil War sites remain, as well as markers that note the movement of troops during the Battle of Atlanta. History buffs should not miss the Kennesaw Mountain National Battlefield Park northwest of the city; Atlanta Cyclorama, a 42-ft circular painting that re-creates the Battle of Atlanta; the Carter Presidential Center, the area from which General Sherman observed the battle; and Oakland Cemetery, at Martin Luther King Jr. Drive. A house that once stood on the cemetery's grounds may have been the location of Confederate General John Bell Hood's observation post; the cemetery is the resting place of 3,723 Civil War soldiers, mostly Confederate, but including 20 Union soldiers who died in local military hospitals and 77 unknowns.

Dining

The city's growing international flavor extends to its restaurants, which have cuisines ranging from French and Italian to Moroccan and Japanese. Many of the best, most stylish eateries are in Buckhead, but Midtown and Virginia-Highland have local favorites, too. The Asian and Mexican restaurants around Buford Highway in suburban Chamblee are appealing alternatives. Both traditional and new-style southern cooking showcase regional foods from crawfish to pork barbecue.

Outdoor Activities and Sports

Atlantans enjoy outdoor pursuits year-round. Tennis courts, golf courses, baseball fields, and other playing surfaces for team sports are widely available throughout the metropolitan area. Atlanta is proud of its numerous green refuges, from tiny neighborhood oases to Midtown's massive Piedmont Park. Atlanta's hilly streets provide an invigorating workout for runners. One of the top events for professional and amateur runners in the United States is the annual July 4th Peachtree Road Race, a 10-km sprint that has 50,000 runners surging down Peachtree Road from Lenox Square Mall to Piedmont Park.

The Chattahoochee River National Recreation Area on the north side of Atlanta has 70 mi of hiking trails ranging from flat riverside strolls to steep climbs up river cliffs. Rafting, canoeing, and kayaking on the river are popular options for cooling down.

Atlanta has four professional sports teams—Braves (baseball), Hawks (basketball), Falcons (football), and Attack (soccer)—besides NCAA college sports from Georgia Tech to satisfy sports fans throughout the year. Annual events include the Coca-Cola 500 professional stock car race; the Bell South Classic, drawing the world's best golfers; and the AT&T Challenge, with top-ranked men's tennis players.

Shopping

Whether it's your favorite collectible, the best bargain on handbags, or the latest designer label, Atlanta's got it. The largest variety of shops and the biggest selection of goods in the Southeast are found here, either in malls, strip shopping centers, or city neighborhoods; the posh boutiques of Buckhead and trendy shops in Virginia-Highland and Little Five Points make great excursions.

ANTIQUES➤ Antiques lovers will discover a wealth of treasures in the SoBuck section of Buckhead, especially the shops on Bennett Street, as well as in stores on Miami Circle and suburban Chamblee's Antique Row.

ARTS AND CRAFTS FESTIVALS➤ Many outdoor festivals, held primarily from May to November in north Georgia towns a short distance from Atlanta, showcase the superb work of Georgia's artisans. A city highlight each September is the nine-day Arts Festival of Atlanta, with an artists' market and professional entertainment in Centennial Olympic Park.

MALLS➤ More than 20 enclosed malls here have at least 100 stores; a few top 200 establishments. To sample the scene, visit Lenox Square Mall, with 268 retailers Atlanta's most popular and largest, on the north edge of Buckhead. Across the street is the glamorous Phipps Plaza, with 200 upscale stores.

GREAT ITINERARIES

A week or more is needed to see the many faces of Atlanta—the gleaming skyscrapers of Downtown, the historical displays of the Atlanta History Center, the living history of Sweet Auburn, the natural beauty of the meandering Chattahoochee River. But if you only are here for a few days, the following suggested itineraries will help you make the best use of your time. See Chapter 2 for more information on the individual sights.

If You Have 1 Day

Start your day **Downtown** with a visit to **Underground Atlanta** and the **World of Coca-Cola.** Walk east on Martin Luther King Jr. Drive for a guided tour of the gold-dome **Georgia State Capitol.** Walk north on Piedmont Avenue (right behind the capitol) and catch the west-bound MARTA train from the Georgia State station and ride

it to the OMNI/Dome/GWCC station. From there it is a short walk to the **CNN Center.** If there is a wait for the CNN Studio Tour, catch a quick lunch in one of the Center's many eateries.

Exit the CNN Center, cross Marietta Street, and stroll along International Boulevard through **Centennial Olympic Park.** Then proceed to Peachtree Street. If you are a shopper, you may want to spend some time in Macy's or in the shops across the street in The Mall. Walk a block south on Peachtree to view the exhibits in the **High Museum of Art's Folk Art and Photography Galleries** in the lobby of the Georgia-Pacific Building.

Continue south past the **Candler Building** and Flatiron Building to **Robert W. Woodruff Memorial Park.** Once you are rested, return to your starting point at Underground Atlanta where you may enjoy dinner and a bit of nightlife in Kenny's Alley.

If You Have 3 Days

Spend your first day exploring **Downtown.** Begin the second day with a visit to the **Martin Luther King Jr. National Historic District** and the surrounding neighborhood of **Sweet Auburn.** Start at the **Martin Luther King Jr. National Historic District Visitor Center** to see the powerful exhibits on the Civil Rights movement, then proceed to the **Martin Luther King Jr. Birth Home,** the **Martin Luther King Jr.**

Center for Nonviolent Social Change, where you may see Dr. King's tomb, and the nearby **Ebenezer Baptist Church.**

After touring Sweet Auburn, head north from Downtown on MARTA to **Midtown.** Exit the train at the Arts Center station and catch a quick lunch at one of the many eateries around Colony Square before visiting the **High Museum of Art.** Follow your museum tour with a stroll through the turn-of-the-century neighborhood of **Ansley Park.** Finish the day with a visit to the landscaped grounds of the **Atlanta Botanical Garden** in **Piedmont Park.**

Your third day starts with a trip to historic **Grant Park** to see the dramatic **Atlanta Cyclorama** painting, followed by a visit to **Zoo Atlanta.** Drive through historic **Inman Park,** with its many beautifully restored Victorian houses, and people-watch over lunch at a **Little Five Points** café. Drive to the **Carter Presidential Center** and tour the museum and grounds. Complete your day with a drive through the parklike neighborhood of **Druid Hills** and a visit to the **Fernbank Museum of Natural History** and its IMAX Theater.

If You Have 5 Days

Follow the 3-day itinerary above and begin your fourth day with a drive to **Buckhead** to visit the **Atlanta History Center,** with its fascinating exhibits, restored houses, and landscaped grounds. Choose a leisurely lunch at the Swan Coach House or a quick bite at an upscale Buckhead café, then walk off your lunch with a stroll through Buckhead's shops, boutiques, and galleries. Climb back in the car for a drive along West Paces Ferry Road and side streets to see Buckhead's lovely mansions. Finish your day with some serious shopping at Lenox Square Mall and Phipps Plaza before returning to the heart of Buckhead for dinner and an evening of entertainment.

You should spend your fifth day at one or two outlying attractions that capture your fancy. Civil War buffs will surely want to visit **Kennesaw Mountain National Battlefield Park,** where Union and Rebel soldiers clashed in June 1864. Wine connoisseurs and golfing enthusiasts may choose to drive north on I–85 to **Chateau Elán** to combine a winery tour and tasting with fine food and a round on championship links. Families will find something to spark everyone's enthusiasm at **Stone Mountain Park,** a 3,200-acre recreation area.

FESTIVALS AND SEASONAL EVENTS

WINTER

DEC.➤ **Egleston Children's Christmas Parade** brings together bands, floats, and giant helium-filled balloons of cartoon characters for a march down Peachtree Street (✉ 3312 Piedmont Rd., Suite 506, 30305, ☎ 404/325–6635).

Peach Bowl, in the Georgia Dome, is one of the key NCAA football bowl games. Sometimes the game occurs in early January (✉ 1 Georgia Dome Dr., ☎ 404/586–8500).

Southeastern Conference Football Championship at the Georgia Dome is one of the nation's premier college sporting events (✉ 1 Georgia Dome Dr., ☎ 800/732–4849).

JAN.➤ **King Week** honors Dr. Martin Luther King Jr. during a weeklong festival, with lectures, interfaith services, films, a parade, and musical entertainment (☎ 404/524–1956).

SPRING

MAR.➤ **St. Patrick's Day** is celebrated in the streets of Buckhead with a parade and partying into the wee hours. The Irish Hibernian Benevolent Society organizes the event (☎ 404/505–1208).

APR.➤ **Steeplechase** is held the first weekend in April on Kingston Downs, a farm near Cartersville, just north of the city. Atlantans come out in droves wearing their finest hats and driving antique cars, and spend the day dining on gourmet fare, drinking fine wines, and watching horses race.

Call well ahead: Admission is by advanced reservation only (✉ Gore Springs Rd., Kingston, ☎ 404/237–7436).

APR.➤ **Dogwood Festival,** a weeklong celebration with concerts, house tours, and crafts shows—timed to match the peak dogwood flowering—is capped by a balloon race that starts in Piedmont Park (✉ Piedmont Ave. at the Prado, ☎ 770/952–9151).

Druid Hills Tour of Homes annually showcases the fine homes of this historic neighborhood, part of Atlanta's Frederick Law Olmsted legacy (✉ Box 363, Decatur, 30031-0363, ☎ 404/524–8687).

Inman Park Festival and Tour of Homes showcases Atlanta's oldest suburb's Victorian mansions and includes an arts and crafts festival, food and drink vendors, and a parade (✉ Euclid Ave., ☎ 770/242–4895).

Salute to American Crafts, sponsored by the American Craft Council, attracts artisans from all over the world to an extraordinary show of fine crafts presented at the Georgia Dome (✉ 1 Georgia Dome Dr., ☎ 404/881–9980).

MAY➢ **Bell South Classic,** held at the Tournament Players Club at Sugarloaf Golf Club, is a four-day PGA golf tournament featuring the nation's best golfers (✉ 2595 Sugarloaf Club Dr., Duluth, ☎ 770/951–8777).

Taste of the South is a sampler of southern art, music, dance, and food at Stone Mountain Park (✉ U.S. 78, Stone Mountain Pkwy., Stone Mountain, ☎ 770/498–5702).

Atlanta Jazz Festival is held on Memorial Day weekend in Piedmont Park (✉ 675 Ponce de Leon Ave., ☎ 404/817–6815).

SUMMER

JUNE–AUG.➢ **Georgia Shakespeare Festival** takes place at Oglethorpe University (✉ 4484 Peachtree Rd., ☎ 404/688–8008).

The Atlanta History Center is an ideal setting for exploring the folk art of Atlanta's ethnic communities at the Center's **International Folk Arts Fair.** Ethnic foods, music, dancing, costuming, and cultural activities attract children and adults (✉ 130 W. Paces Ferry Rd., ☎ 404/814–4000).

JULY 4➢ **Independence Day** celebrations begin with the Peachtree Road Race, followed by a parade and evening fireworks. Check local newspapers or the Atlanta Convention and Visitors Bureau (☎ 404/521–6600) for information.

The Atlanta History Center hosts an annual **Civil War Encampment,**

re-creating both Confederate and Federal encampments. Demonstrations (musket and artillery firings, marching, infantry and cavalry maneuvers), a fife and drum corps, and period handicrafts such as spinning and weaving are part of the event (✉ 130 W. Paces Ferry Rd., ☎ 404/814–4000).

JULY–AUG.➢ The **National Black Arts Festival** is a weeklong celebration of black culture, with art exhibits, films, and music, held in even-numbered years in several venues (✉ 236 Forsyth St., Suite 400, 30303, ☎ 404/730–7315).

AUTUMN

SEPT.➢ **Arts Festival of Atlanta,** a local favorite, draws hundreds of artists and artisans who exhibit and sell their work in Centennial Olympic Park; there's also entertainment day and night (⊠ 285 International Blvd., ☎ 404/885–1125).

Montreux Music Festival brings a week of jazz, soul, and folk music to Chastain and Piedmont parks, beginning Labor Day weekend (⊠ 675 Ponce de Leon Ave., ☎ 404/817–6815).

Powers Crossroads Country Fair and Arts Festival, more than two decades old, is a celebration of country food, music, and crafts. It's held Labor Day weekend 12 mi west of the city in Newnan (⊠ Hwy. 34 West, Newnan, ☎ 770/253–2011).

Yellow Daisy Festival at Stone Mountain Park includes entertainment and exhibits from 400 artists, artisans, and entertainers (⊠ U.S. 78, Stone Mountain Pkwy., Stone Mountain, ☎ 770/498–5600).

Oct.➢ **Scottish Festival and Highland Games** attracts more than 100 clans for a celebration of dance, music, and traditional games at Stone Mountain Park (⊠ U.S. 78, Stone Mountain Pkwy., Stone Mountain, ☎ 770/498–5600).

Nov.➢ The **Lighting of the Great Tree,** the city's Christmas tree at Underground Atlanta, is an annual tradition that is accompanied by choirs and musicians. The spectacle is held Thanksgiving night and draws huge crowds (⊠ Upper Alabama St., ☎ 404/523–7019).

2 Exploring Atlanta

ATLANTA is impossible to stereotype. It is the romance of the Old South and *Gone With the Wind* and the reality of turbulent times. It is downtown towers of stone and steel and gracious mansions under stately shade trees. It is peaceful parks, quiet neighborhoods, and scenic byways amidst the unbridled sprawl created by constant growth.

By Mark Beffart and Ren Davis

Updated by Ren Davis

There are acclaimed museums, Civil War sites, natural wonders, and nearly limitless opportunities to shop. To experience the best of the city, take in the usual tourist attractions, but go beyond them to explore the places just off the beaten path: Sip a cold drink (Coca-Cola, of course) at a sidewalk café in Virginia-Highland or Little Five Points; visit with locals relaxing in Woodruff Park at lunchtime; go for a hike along the banks of the tranquil Chattahoochee River; find a personal treasure in a Buckhead gallery; or simply sit on the porch of the Wren's Nest and listen spellbound while a storyteller spins a tale.

Orientation

From the air, Atlanta's most prominent sight, its Downtown skyline, resembles *The Wizard of Oz*'s Emerald City: Gleaming towers appear to rise right out of the forest. In recent years, mini-enclaves of skyscrapers, rivaling Downtown's for prominence, have sprouted in Midtown, Buckhead, and along the northern perimeter of the city. I–285 encircles much of Atlanta and thus is called the Perimeter. Locations are often referred to in relation to the Perimeter: outside, inside, or near it.

Almost all of these architectural gems are along or near Peachtree Street, a continuous road (though its name changes to Peachtree Road north of I–85) that begins a few blocks south of Downtown's Five Points and snakes its way through the center of the city to the northern suburbs. As the spine of the city and a former east–west dividing line when Atlanta was much smaller, Peachtree Street alone will take you to some of Atlanta's best sights. In fact, you'll often receive street directions within central Atlanta tied to this famous road, because almost all the major byways intersect it somewhere. Just be sure Peachtree Street is meant— a few dozen other roads also use the popular peach tree as part of their name. I–75 and I–85 converge in the city, so don't be confused when given directions that refer to I–75/I–85.

Unlike cities that border an ocean, river, or mountain range, Atlanta has no geographic barriers to impede its sprawling growth. In a mere 20 years, Atlanta has grown rapidly from a minor metropolitan area with just over 1 million people in five counties to a population of 3.5 million residents spread over 20 counties. Despite Atlanta's sprawl, the majority of the best sights and dazzling architecture is in the central part of the city and is best seen on foot. The walking tours that follow guide you through the government and business sections of Downtown, the Sweet Auburn neighborhood and the Martin Luther King Jr. National Historic District, and the cultural diversity of Midtown.

Although Atlanta may impress you with its modernity or its wealth of shopping and entertainment opportunities, you haven't fully explored the "City of Trees" until you visit one of the intimate, exquisitely landscaped residential areas that stretch from the edge of Downtown to the hinterlands. Within the city, the opulent homes of Buckhead, the restored bungalows in chic Virginia-Highland, the Victorian mansions of Inman Park, the quiet streets of West End, and the stately homes in Ansley Park and Druid Hills are local favorites that shouldn't be missed. You will need a car to see these areas properly: Driving tours through these neighborhoods and through Little Five Points and two university areas also follow.

Downtown Atlanta

From its earliest days as a railway construction camp, Atlanta has always been a bustling place, and nowhere is this more evident than in Downtown. Stroll through Woodruff Park at lunchtime, walk up Peachtree through the center of the business district, or stand at Five Points—Atlanta's symbolic heart—at rush hour, and you will see a city on the move. Within these compact city blocks are the stories of Atlanta's birth as raucous village more Wild West than Old South, its destruction during the Civil War, and its meteoric rise to international prominence in the areas of commerce, education, and politics at the close of the 20th century.

Numbers in the text correspond to numbers in the margin and on the Downtown Atlanta and Sweet Auburn map.

A Good Walk

An ideal place to begin a tour of Downtown is at **Underground Atlanta** ①, a six-block entertainment and shopping district. Descend through Peachtree Fountains Plaza onto Lower Alabama Street. Exit through the glass doors at the eastern end of Lower Alabama Street to Depot Plaza. Directly ahead is the Georgia Railroad Freight Depot (✉ Depot Plaza, Central Ave. and Lower Alabama St.), the oldest building in the heart of the city. On your right as you walk south is Kenny's Alley, Underground's nightclub district. Straight ahead is the **World of Coca-Cola** ②.

Cross Martin Luther King Jr. (MLK) Drive to see the Shrine of the Immaculate Conception (✉ 48 MLK Dr., ☏ 404/521–1866), the city's oldest church building. A Roman Catholic church was first built on this site in 1848; the present neo-Gothic structure, with its handsome rose window and unequal towers crowned by elaborate decorations, was built in 1873. Walk up to the corner of MLK Drive and Washington Avenue, past Central Presbyterian Church (✉ 201 Washington Ave.), another of Atlanta's early congregations. Directly across Washington Avenue is the 1889 **Georgia State Capitol** ③, a handsome neoclassical structure modeled after the U.S. Capitol. Several blocks south of the capitol is **Turner Field** ④, where the Atlanta Braves baseball team plays; in the adjacent plaza are a food court, play areas, and Braves' museum.

Return across Washington Avenue and continue west on Mitchell Street, past Georgia Plaza Park. Across from the park is **Atlanta City Hall** ⑤, a handsome neo-Gothic building. Turn right on Pryor Street to see the massive Fulton County Courthouse (✉ 136 Pryor St.), an enormous nine-story 1913 Beaux Arts building, and the Fulton County Government Center (✉ 141 Pryor St.), an airy, futuristic, brick-and-glass structure whose neoclassical lobby has palm trees, a sunken fountain, and a columned archway. Walk left on MLK Drive to the intersection of Forsyth Street. Now you are in the center of the multiblock Federal Government Center. Follow Forsyth north to Alabama Street, turn right on Alabama and continue to Peachtree Street. Walk north on Peachtree, past the sprawling Five Points MARTA station, the hub of the entire rapid-rail system. A block beyond the station is **Five Points** ⑥, the intersection of five streets that is the symbolic heart of the city. Cross to the north side of Marietta Street and turn left. In the Marietta Street median is the statue of journalist Henry Grady. Grady's former newspaper, the *Atlanta Constitution,* is headquartered in the **Atlanta Journal-Constitution Building** ⑦, which you should step into to see the lobby exhibits. Continue west on Marietta to the Atlanta branch of the **Federal Reserve Bank Building** ⑧ and visit its fascinating Monetary Museum.

Follow Marietta across Spring Street and Techwood Drive and enter the massive **CNN Center** ⑨, home of CNN Studios and filled with shops and restaurants. Just south of the building is the construction site of a professional sports arena (⊠ 100 Techwood Dr.), which is scheduled to open in 1999. Beyond the site is the huge **Georgia Dome** ⑩ football stadium, which you can tour. Return along International Boulevard past the sprawling Georgia World Congress Center (⊠ 285 International Blvd.), one of the nation's largest convention and trade-show halls.

Follow International Boulevard north past the Atlanta Chamber of Commerce (⊠ 235 International Blvd.), through the heart of **Centennial Olympic Park** ⑪, the city's lasting legacy of the 1996 Games. Turn right on Techwood Drive, and left on Walton Street. Enter the Fairlie-Poplar Historic District (⊠ North of Marietta St. and south of Carnegie Way; west of Peachtree and east of Spring St.), the turn-of-the-century heart of Downtown that is undergoing a renaissance.

At Forsyth Street, turn left and walk past the fortress-like Atlanta–Fulton County Public Library (⊠ 1 Margaret Mitchell Sq., ☎ 404/730–1700); enter if you're a *Gone With*

20

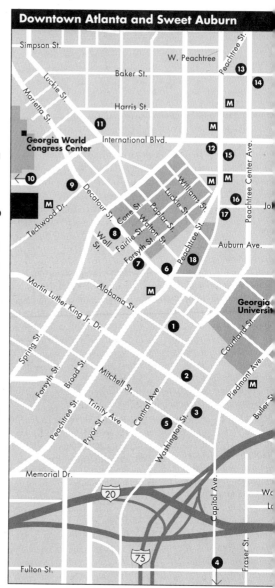

Downtown Atlanta and Sweet Auburn

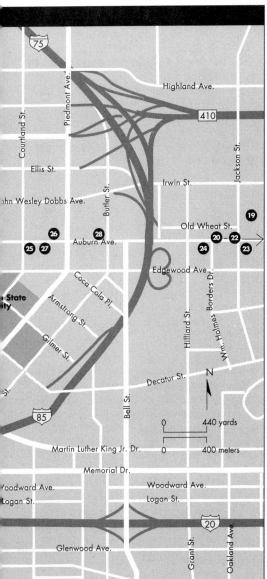

the Wind fan (the library has a permanent collection of *Gone With the Wind* first editions and memorabilia) or are interested in what art exhibits are going on in the basement gallery. Across Forsyth Street is the small, triangular Margaret Mitchell Park (⊠ Peachtree St. at Forsyth St.). Continue north on Peachtree Street, past an entrance to the Peachtree Center MARTA station. On the left, across Ellis Street, is the block-long Macy's department store, a fixture on this site since 1927. Adjacent to the store, the distinctive cylindrical tower of the **Westin Peachtree Plaza Hotel** ⑫ is the highest point in Downtown; you may go up to the Sun Dial, the hotel's revolving bar and restaurant, for a panoramic view.

As you cross International Boulevard, you enter the southern boundary of multiblock Peachtree Center (⊠ Peachtree St. at International Blvd., ☎ 404/654–1296), a trade-show, retail, shopping, and lodging complex. On the east side of Peachtree Street, four office towers, arranged around an open-air plaza and a fountain, anchor the center. Beneath the plaza is The Mall (⊠ 231 Peachtree St.), with 30 specialty retail shops and a variety of restaurants. The **Welcome South Visitors Center** is one floor above the mall. Continue north, crossing Harris Street, past the 1911 Italian Renaissance Capital City Club (⊠ 7 Harris St.), the city's oldest private club.

Two blocks north, at the intersection of Peachtree and West Peachtree streets, is Hardy Ivy Park, the traditional boundary of the Central Business District. Continue on Peachtree to see the First United Methodist Church (⊠ 360 Peachtree St.), whose bell tolled a warning of the Union Army's advance on Atlanta in 1864. This congregation—the city's oldest—was established in 1848 and relocated to this site in 1904. Cross Peachtree and turn right, past the Romanesque Sacred Heart Roman Catholic Church (⊠ 353 Peachtree St.). Soaring above the intersection of Peachtree Street and Peachtree Center Avenue is the gleaming glass tower of **One Peachtree Center** ⑬. Pause to stroll around the building's moat and sculpture garden before walking on.

Continue south on Peachtree Center Avenue, stopping in the Marriott Marquis Hotel and Towers (⊠ 265–285

Peachtree Center Ave.) to marvel at the hotel's 48-story atrium lobby. While in the complex, visit the free **Atlanta International Museum of Art and Design** ⑭, in the Marquis Two Tower. With the impression of the Marriott lobby fresh in your mind, walk up International Boulevard to Peachtree, and turn right to compare the design of the Hyatt Regency Atlanta (✉ 265 Peachtree St.) atrium lobby, completed nearly 20 years before, with the Marriott's. This John Portman–designed hotel was an architectural sensation when it opened in 1967. Many of the features introduced here became Portman trademarks at other hotels worldwide. Take a break in the rooftop Polaris Restaurant if needed.

Return to Peachtree and turn left. Walk past International Boulevard and look up to see the twin steeples of the **One-Ninety-One Peachtree Tower** ⑮. Across Ellis Street is the sharply angular, pink granite Georgia-Pacific Building (✉ 133 Peachtree St.). Inside the lobby, with an entrance on John Wesley Dobbs Avenue, are the **High Museum of Art's Folk Art and Photography Galleries** ⑯. Continue south on Peachtree to see the **Candler Building** ⑰, an opulent turn-of-the-century skyscraper. Do not pass by without admiring the beautiful marble and bronze work in the lobby.

South on Peachtree is the massive blackened-steel-and-glass International Equitable Building (✉ 100 Peachtree St.). Nearby, and dwarfed by comparison, is the sharply triangular 1897 Flatiron Building (✉ 84 Peachtree St.). Anchoring the western boundary of Fairlie-Poplar and facing Peachtree Street, this 11-story building was designed by influential architect Bradford Gilbert, who built the famous New York building of the same name in 1901. Opposite the building is the open green space of **Robert W. Woodruff Memorial Park** ⑱, a popular gathering place. Take time to relax in the park and savor the street life around you. Just west of the park, at the corner of Edgewood Avenue and Hurt Plaza, is the ornate 1913 Hurt Building (✉ 45 Edgewood Ave.) office tower, noted for its intricate grillwork and marble columns, and the elaborate marble staircase in its domed lobby. From Woodruff Park, a two-block walk south on Peachtree Street will return you to Underground Atlanta.

While Downtown is compact, you should plan a full day to explore. This will allow you ample time to enjoy those sights that capture your interest, take a guided tour, linger in a museum or gallery, enjoy a leisurely meal, or shop for that perfect souvenir.

Sights to See

⑤ Atlanta City Hall. Dubbed "The Painted Lady of Mitchell Street" when completed in 1930, this outstanding neo-Gothic building occupies the site of General William T. Sherman's headquarters following the city's September 1864 surrender. Step inside to see the lobby, lavishly decorated with Georgia marble and wood ornamentation. ⊠ *68 Mitchell St. MARTA: Five Points.*

NEED A
BREAK?   **Sylvia's** (⊠ 241 Central Ave., ☎ 404/529-9692), a well-known Harlem-based soul-food eatery, has come south. Especially great are the veggies, cooked the old-fashioned southern way. Expect large crowds at lunchtime, so come early or late.

Atlanta Heritage Row. This multimedia presentation within ☞ **Underground Atlanta** puts the viewer directly into the middle of Atlanta's history. Divided into six historical periods, the touchable, lifelike exhibits—aided by audio- and videotapes and a time line—show the evolution of the city from the days of Cherokee and Creek settlements through its emergence as an international business center. ⊠ *55 Upper Alabama St.,* ☎ *404/584-7879.* ☜ *$3.* ☉ *Tues.–Sat. 10–5, Sun. 1–5. MARTA: Five Points.*

⑭ Atlanta International Museum of Art and Design. This compact museum, on two floors of the Marquis Two Tower, displays arts and crafts from cultures around the world. ⊠ *285 Peachtree Center Ave.,* ☎ *404/688-2467.* ☜ *Free.* ☉ *Tues.–Sat. 11–5. MARTA: Peachtree Center.*

⑦ Atlanta Journal-Constitution Building. This building is the headquarters of the state's two largest newspapers. Founded independently, the *Atlanta Constitution* (morning) in 1868 and the *Atlanta Journal* (afternoon) in 1883, the two rival papers came under common ownership when they were purchased by James Cox in 1950. They are still owned by the Cox family and the papers combine for the Saturday and Sunday editions. The papers' building has a lobby that contains an old typesetting machine, copies of front-page news stories documenting historic events, and photographs of famous individuals, such as Margaret Mitchell and Lewis Grizzard, who have worked for the newspaper. In front of the building, in the median of Marietta Street, is an 1891 statue of *Atlanta Constitution* editor Henry Grady. Call ahead to arrange a guided tour. ⊠ *72 Marietta St.,* ☎ *404/614–2688.* 🖾 *Free. MARTA: Five Points.*

⓱ Candler Building. Coca-Cola Company founder Asa G. Candler spared no expense in constructing this 1906 monument to his success. Sheathed in white Georgia marble, the 17-story building has lavish carvings on the exterior including life-size sculpted lions for cornice brackets and profiles of famous men, from Shakespeare to Buffalo Bill Cody, on medallions in each window bay. The interior is no less spectacular with its monumental marble staircase supported by bronze animals, and a frieze incorporating the busts of local politicians and literati. ⊠ *127 Peachtree St. MARTA: Peachtree Center.*

★ ☾ ⓫ Centennial Olympic Park. This 21-acre park, with its rolling landscaped hills, inscribed bricks, whimsical Rings Fountain, and interesting sculptures, is a permanent legacy of the 1996 Olympic Games. ⊠ *Marietta St. at International Blvd. MARTA: OMNI/Dome/GWCC.*

★ ❾ CNN Center. Best known as home to Ted Turner's Cable News Network, this large complex also includes retail shops, restaurants, movie theaters, and the Omni Hotel. A 45-minute tour of CNN Studios begins with a ride up the world's longest escalator to an eighth-floor exhibit on Turner's global broadcasting empire. You can see a short movie about the history of CNN, learn about TelePrompTers and weather reporting, and see the newsroom in action from a glass-enclosed balcony. The VIP tour allows you to visit the newsroom floor, meet broadcast personalities, have a snack in the CNN commissary, and take home a gift pack. CNN's *Talk Back Live* TV show is broadcast daily at 3 PM from the atrium; tickets are free and required. ⊠ *1 CNN*

Center (International Blvd. at Marietta St.), ☎ *404/827–2300.* ☎ *Tours $7, VIP $24.50.* ☾ *Tours daily 9–5:30, reservations recommended. MARTA: OMNI/Dome/GWCC.*

....

NEED A
BREAK?
Reggie's English Pub (☎ 404/525-1437), a CNN Center landmark, has been serving up meat-pies, sandwiches, and an assortment of English brews for 20 years. CNN news-casters often drop in.

....

❽ Federal Reserve Bank Building. This branch is one of the original 12 established by President Woodrow Wilson in 1914. In spite of the strict security checks at the door, the bank's **Monetary Museum** is well worth a visit. Memorable exhibits—including Native American trading beads, gem-stones, a 27-pound gold bar, and $100,000 bills—explain the history of money. You may even take some home—small packets of shredded bills are complimentary. ☒ *104 Marietta St.,* ☎ *404/521–8764.* ☎ *Free.* ☾ *Weekdays 9–4. MARTA: Five Points.*

❻ Five Points. The symbolic heart of Atlanta, this is the intersection of five streets: Marietta Street from the west, Edgewood Avenue and Decatur Street from the east, and Peachtree Street from the north and south. It has been the commercial nucleus of the city since Atlanta's earliest days as a railroad town. The **William-Oliver Building** (☒ 32 Peachtree St.), a 1932 Art Deco gem, has a frieze near the top with patterns of waves, rosettes, and chevrons. Step inside the lobby to enjoy the colorful ceiling mural and brass ornamentation.

The **Five Points MARTA station** (☒ Peachtree St. between Marietta and Alabama Sts.) is the central hub of the rapid-rail system and is the intersecting point for the north–south and east–west lines. Outside the Peachtree Street entrance, a market atmosphere prevails as hucksters try to peddle everything from counterfeit watches to cheap perfume, licensed vendors sell fruit and vegetables, and street preachers expound on life's moral dilemmas. A tunnel beneath Peachtree connects the station with Underground Atlanta. ☒ *Marietta St. at Peachtree St. MARTA: Five Points.*

❿ Georgia Dome. This modern indoor stadium seats 71,500 for football and is home to the NFL Atlanta Falcons. It also hosts the annual Peach Bowl and Heritage Bowl games and other events. The signature white, plum, and turquoise facade and tentlike top, the world's largest cable-supported oval, enclose over 37 acres of space. ✉ *1 Georgia Dome Dr.,* ☎ *404/223–8687 for tour reservations.* 🎟 *Tours $4.* ☉ *Tues.–Sat. 10–4, Sun. noon–4. MARTA: OMNI/Dome/GWCC.*

★ ☕ ❸ **Georgia State Capitol.** This grand, neoclassical building, modeled after the U.S. Capitol, was completed in 1889. One million dollars was appropriated for its construction, and it was completed $118 under budget! The shiny gold-leaf dome is a landmark visible from several downtown locations. It was gilded in 1958 and refurbished in 1981 from gold mined in Dahlonega, a small northeastern Georgia town that was, in the 1830s, the site of the nation's first gold rush. The capitol houses the Georgia State Museum of Science and Industry, with displays about Georgia wildlife and geology, Native American culture, and agriculture and industry. Also on display are tattered flags and banners from Georgia regiments' participation in various wars. The exhibits, on the capitol's upper floors, are free and are open during regular building hours. At press time the capitol was undergoing a multiyear renovation, so sections of the building may be closed.

Outside, shaded by large oak and magnolia trees, historical markers describe the Civil War battle for Atlanta, and statues honor former Georgia governors, including an equestrian sculpture of Confederate general John B. Gordon and a denim-clad Jimmy Carter. Across Washington Avenue from the capitol is Georgia Plaza Park (✉ Washington Ave. and Mitchell St.), a pleasant, terraced, green space with benches and tables for enjoying a picnic lunch. In warmer months, look for the state seal re-created in some of the park's colorful flowers and shrubs. ✉ *206 Washington Ave.,* ☎ *404/656–2844.* 🎟 *Free.* ☉ *Weekdays 8–5, Sat. 10–4, Sun. noon–4. Guided tours weekdays every ½ hr 9:30–11:30 and 1–2. MARTA: Georgia State.*

⓰ **High Museum of Art's Folk Art and Photography Galleries.** An extension of the High Museum in Midtown, the galleries display a superb permanent collection of folk art and photographs as well as small traveling exhibitions. The galleries are in the **Georgia-Pacific Building,** a sleek, pink granite 52-story skyscraper that is headquarters of the international paper products manufacturer. It was built in 1982 on the site of the Loew's Grand Theater (which burned in 1978), where *Gone With the Wind* made its world premiere in 1939. ✉ *30 John Wesley Dobbs Ave.,* ☎ *404/577–6940.* 🎟 *Free.* ☼ *Mon.–Sat. 10–5. MARTA: Peachtree Center.*

⓭ One Peachtree Center. Anchoring the northern end of Peachtree Center, this 60-story glass and gray granite tower has a two-story lobby that bridges a circular reflecting pool surrounded by a sculpture garden. Observed from a distance, the building's slender, joined towers of varying heights resemble jumbled building blocks, topped by a pyramid of dark reflective glass. ✉ *303 Peachtree St. MARTA: Peachtree Center.*

⓯ One-Ninety-One Peachtree Tower. This 50-story skyscraper, completed in 1990, is the work of noted architects Philip Johnson and John Burgee. The postmodern building catches your eye with its six-story skylit atrium and twin-towered top. Adjacent to the Tower is the elegant Ritz-Carlton Hotel. ✉ *191 Peachtree St. MARTA: Peachtree Center.*

★ ☾ ❹ Turner Field. Introduced to the world in 1996 as Centennial Olympic Stadium, the 46,000-seat ballpark was later named in honor of Ted Turner, the media mogul and Atlanta Braves baseball-team owner. The Braves began to play in the stadium in 1997. The adjacent plaza has a giant photo of the baseball Hank Aaron hit for his 715th home run, a restaurant and fast food court, a microbrewery, and the Braves' Clubhouse Store. Flanking the plaza are the Cartoon Network's Tooner Field, a play area for children; and Scout's Alley, an arcade of interactive games and displays of early scouting reports of Braves' past and present stars. Also in Scout's Alley is the **Ivan Allen Museum of Braves' History,** which chronicles the team's origins in Boston to present day. The restaurant, museum, and plaza are open three hours before home games start. ✉ *755 Henry Aaron Dr.,* ☎ *404/522–7630 Atlanta Braves, 404/614–1328 tours, 404/814–4082 museum.* 🎟 *Stadium tour $7, museum $3 ($2 with game ticket).* ☼ *Stadium tours during baseball season Tues.–Sat. 9–5; in off-season Sun. 1–5. MARTA: Georgia State.*

★ ❶ **Underground Atlanta.** Downtown's most popular tourist sight, this six-block entertainment and shopping district is on three levels. It was created from old brick streets, turn-of-the-century buildings, and alleys that went "underground" when viaducts were built over the railroad tracks to accommodate automobile traffic in the 1920s. Merchants moved their storefronts to the building's second story, and the old main floors became storage—abandoned and forgotten until the late 1960s. After a run as an entertainment complex from 1969 to 1981, Underground was resurrected in 1989. Historical markers throughout Underground explain its unusual history.

More than 40 specialty shops selling art, books, clothes, music, regional foods, and souvenirs line Underground's streets, one of which is actually above ground. Upper Alabama Street, a two-block, pedestrian-only street between Peachtree Street and Central Avenue that is dotted with trees, sculpture, and benches, has about 20 retailers on its south side. Also on this level are the **ACVB Visitor Information Center** and ☞ **Atlanta Heritage Row,** a multimedia exhibit. Underground's upper level overlooks **Peachtree Fountains Plaza,** where you may relax and picnic while watching cascading waterfalls and splashing fountains. From the plaza's distinctive 138-ft light tower, a gigantic peach drops at the stroke of midnight during the annual New Year's Eve celebration held here.

The true underground level, Lower Alabama Street, has a festive atmosphere enhanced by about 50 merchants hawking wares from pushcarts in front of the retail stores. The noise level peaks in the food court, where more than 20 fast-food vendors sell everything from gyros and tacos to ice cream and cookies. Entrances to Lower Alabama Street are through an enclosed glass area directly across from the Five Points MARTA station, by connecting tunnel from the station, by steps down along Peachtree Fountains Plaza, or from Depot Plaza just below Central Avenue.

The third and lowest level is Kenny's Alley, an entertainment strip once occupied by Kenny's Tavern and other saloons so rowdy that, in the 1880s, the police set up a precinct house in the alley to control the crowds. The Alley styles itself as Atlanta's version of New Orleans's Bourbon Street, with bars and nightspots offering comedy acts, a variety of music (rock, country, pop, folk, jazz), and dancing. Late-night revelers can enter at Depot Plaza or through Peachtree Fountains Plaza or Upper Alabama Street. Two parking garages serving Underground are on MLK Drive. Trolley Times (☎ 404/352–1419) operates trolleys that cost $3 for unlimited daily rides and connect Underground Atlanta with many downtown hotels as well as several attractions such as the capitol and SciTrek, running roughly 10:30 AM–9 PM. ⊠ *Alabama and Peachtree Sts.,* ☎ *404/523–2311.* ☉ *Mon.–Sat. 10–9:30, Sun. noon–6. MARTA: Five Points.*

Welcome South Visitors Center. Here you can find information about the Southeast, with exhibits on seven states: Alabama, Georgia, Kentucky, Louisiana, North Carolina, South Carolina, and Tennessee. It also has a currency exchange office, bookstore, a AAA Club South office, and ATM. ⊠ *200 Spring St.,* ☎ *404/224–2000.* ☉ *Mon.–Sat. 9–6, Sun. 11–6. MARTA: Peachtree Center.*

⑫ **Westin Peachtree Plaza Hotel.** The second tallest hotel in North America, a city landmark since its opening in 1976, this glass cylinder climbs more than 70 stories above Peachtree Street. The Sun Dial (☎ 404/589–7506), a revolving rooftop bar and restaurant, allows an unsurpassed panoramic view of the city. The hotel is on the site of the John James House, the residence of Georgia's governors from 1868 to 1921. ⊠ *210 Peachtree St. MARTA: Peachtree Center*

⑱ **Robert W. Woodruff Memorial Park.** Within a stone's throw of Five Points, this green space in the heart of the city was a gift from the late Coca-Cola chairman Robert W. Woodruff. At the southern entrance is *Atlanta from the Ashes,* a blackened-bronze sculpture by Italian artist Gambro Quirino. A female personification of Liberty is shown setting a captive bird free, a reference to the mythological phoenix that arose from the ashes of its own fiery destruction. The symbolism recalls Atlanta's rebirth after General Sherman's Union troops burned it during the Civil War; the phoenix appears on the city's seal. ⊠ *Peachtree St. between Edgewood and Auburn Aves. MARTA: Five Points.*

★ ☞ ❷ **World of Coca-Cola.** Step beneath the neon-lit, revolving
Coca-Cola sign to revel in paeans to the world's most popular soft drink. Sample over 100 Coke products from
around the world and marvel over past and present ad-
vertisements and other memorabilia, but forget about look-
ing for Coke's secret formula—it's locked in the vaults of
the company's world headquarters a few blocks away.
Don't miss the replica 1930s soda fountain and the gift shop,
with an array of items to start your own Coke collection.
⊠ *55 MLK Dr.,* ☎ *404/676–5151.* 🎫 *$6.* ☉ *Mon.–Sat.
10–9:30, Sun. noon–6. MARTA: Five Points.*

Sweet Auburn

The historic Sweet Auburn district was from 1890 to 1930
Atlanta's most active and prosperous center of black business, entertainment, and political life. Prevented from participating in the white business community by cultural
biases and segregation, black Atlantans came here to open
businesses, attend church, meet in fraternal organizations,
and enjoy themselves at clubs and restaurants.

Following the Depression, the area went into an economic
decline that deepened when civil rights laws prohibiting segregation opened more areas of the city to black business
and residential development. The area began a slow recovery
in the 1980s, when the residential area where civil rights
leader Rev. Martin Luther King Jr. was born, raised, and
later lived was declared a National Historic District. Today,
the Martin Luther King Jr. Birth Home, tomb, and Ebenezer
Baptist Church are some of the most frequently visited
sights in the city.

*Numbers in the text correspond to numbers in the margin
and on the Downtown Atlanta and Sweet Auburn map.*

A Good Walk

The best place to begin your tour is the **Martin Luther King
Jr. National Historic District Visitor Center** ⑲, where displays
and interactive exhibits will aid your understanding of the
events in the Civil Rights movement, the life of Dr. King,
and the Sweet Auburn community. You may arrange a
tour here of the Martin Luther King Jr. Birth Home. Exit

through the plaza and admire the impressive *Behold* statue. Cross Auburn Avenue at Boulevard and stop at **Fire Station No. 6** ⑳ to see displays on Atlanta's fire-fighting history. In the block east of the station is the **Martin Luther King Jr. Birth Home** ㉑.

Retrace your steps on Auburn Avenue to the **Martin Luther King Jr. Center for Nonviolent Social Change** ㉒ to see some of King's personal effects and his simple marble tomb. Just west of the center is **Ebenezer Baptist Church** ㉓, the spiritual heart of the Civil Rights movement. Take time to tour the simple interior and see the pulpit where three generations of the King family preached.

In the next block is **Wheat Street Baptist Church** ㉔, the city's oldest black congregation. Ahead, at the intersection of Hilliard Street, is the Prince Hall Masonic Lodge (✉ 334 Auburn Ave.), headquarters of the Southern Christian Leadership Conference (SCLC). Walk under the I–75/I–85 bridge and past the Odd Fellows Building (✉ 250 Auburn Ave.), with its fascinating gargoyles flanking the entrance. Step across Auburn, past the 1926 Herndon Building (✉ 231– 245 Auburn Ave.), a center of business during the area's heyday. Turn left and walk south on Butler Street, passing the Butler Street YMCA (✉ 22 Butler St.), a popular spot for generations of inner-city residents. Across Edgewood Avenue is the Sweet Auburn Curb Market (✉ 209 Edgewood Ave., ☎ 404/659–1665), filled with raucous produce vendors and an aromatic atmosphere. At the intersection of Butler and Coca-Cola Place (so named because the first headquarters of the Coca-Cola Company were located here) is Georgia Hall (✉ 36 Butler St.), an 1892 redbrick Romanesque Revival structure that is the original building of the now-sprawling Grady Memorial Hospital complex.

Turn right on Coca-Cola Place and walk to Edgewood Avenue, where you'll turn left and follow it a block to Courtland Street. The eccentric Victorian building on the corner (✉ 125 Edgewood Ave.) was, in 1900, Coca-Cola's first bottling plant. Turn right on Courtland and walk north to the intersection with Auburn Avenue. On the right is the **Auburn Avenue Research Library** ㉕, which contains an extensive collection of works on African-American culture and history and hosts exhibits. Across Auburn is modern Herndon Plaza, headquarters of the **Atlanta Life Insurance Company** ㉖: Peek inside the lobby to see the art collection before recrossing Auburn and walking east to see the exhibits in the **African-American Panoramic Experience (APEX) Museum** ㉗. Next door to the museum is the office of the *Atlanta Daily World* (✉ 145 Auburn Ave.), the nation's oldest black-owned newspaper, founded by W. A. Scott in 1928.

Cross Piedmont Avenue and walk past the Royal Peacock Club (✉ 1861–1862 Auburn Ave.), a mecca for black entertainers going back to the days of Cab Calloway and Count Basie. The final stop is in front of **Big Bethel African-Methodist-Episcopal Church** ㉘. From this point, you may retrace your steps on Auburn Avenue to the MLK Jr. National Historic District Visitor Center or return to Downtown.

TIMING

The blocks are short and the walking is easy, but there is much to see: Plan to spend at least a half-day in Sweet Auburn. To truly capture the flavor of life in this neighborhood, plan a visit during the annual Sweet Auburn Good Times Festival held each April.

Sights to See

㉗ **African-American Panoramic Experience (APEX) Museum.** Through historical exhibits and artwork, this small museum chronicles the African-American experience in the United States—particularly in Atlanta—from slavery days to the present. ✉ *135 Auburn Ave.,* ☎ *404/521–2739.* ▣ *$3.* ☉ *Tues.–Sat. 10–5. MARTA: Five Points.*

㉖ **Atlanta Life Insurance Company.** The centerpiece of Herndon Plaza, this modern stone-and-glass tower houses one of the largest black-owned and -managed companies in Atlanta. It was the largest in the nation when it was established in 1905 by Alonzo F. Herndon, a barber and former slave, who saw the unmet needs of black Americans for low-cost life and burial insurance. The lobby displays a collection of works by African-American artists. The present building was constructed in 1980 to replace the old headquarters at 148 Auburn Avenue. ✉ *100 Auburn Ave.,* ☎ *404/659–2100. MARTA: Five Points.*

㉕ Auburn Avenue Research Library. This branch of the Atlanta–Fulton County Public Library system houses an extensive collection of works on African-American culture and history. The library hosts lectures and exhibits in the Cary McPheeters Gallery. ⊠ *101 Auburn Ave.,* ☎ *404/730–4001.* ⊘ *Mon.–Thurs. noon–8, weekends 2–6. MARTA: Five Points.*

㉘ Big Bethel African-Methodist-Episcopal Church. Best known to many Atlantans for the illuminated JESUS SAVES sign— which is easily seen from I–75/I–85—on its steeple, this rough-stone Romanesque Revival church, built in 1891, has long been a center of Auburn Avenue social life. ⊠ *220 Auburn Ave.,* ☎ *404/659–0248.* ⊘ *Sun. worship 8 and 11 AM. MARTA: Five Points.*

★ **㉓ Ebenezer Baptist Church.** This simple, redbrick Gothic Revival church, built in 1922, was the spiritual center of the Civil Rights movement and was pastored by members of the King family for more than 80 years. Martin Luther King Jr.'s maternal grandfather, Rev. A. D. Williams, arrived at Ebenezer in 1904; Martin Luther "Daddy" King Sr. took over in 1931. Martin Luther King Jr. co-pastored with his father from 1960 to 1968; his funeral was held here in April 1968. ⊠ *407 Auburn Ave.,* ☎ *404/688–7263.* ▱ *Free.* ⊘ *Mon.–Sat. 9–5, Sun. 2–5., Sun. worship 7:45 and 10:45 AM. MARTA: King Memorial.*

㉒ Fire Station No. 6. Built in 1894 as a single-bay station for a horse-drawn engine, this station remained active for more than a century. As a young boy, Martin Luther King Jr. visited the station often. Today, it is the city's oldest existing station and houses a museum displaying the history of the Atlanta Fire Department and its desegregation in the 1960s. ⊠ *39 Boulevard,* ☎ *404/331–6922.* ▱ *Free.* ⊘ *Daily 9–5. MARTA: King Memorial.*

★ **㉑ Martin Luther King Jr. Birth Home.** Built in 1894, this simple, clapboard, two-story Queen Anne house has been restored to its appearance as it was when Dr. King was born in an upstairs bedroom on January 15, 1929. It was his family's residence until 1941. The house contains furnishings, photographs, and other memorabilia providing insight into the Kings' family life. Admission is by guided tour only. National Park Service interpretive staff conduct tours daily; arrange a tour at the ☞ **Martin Luther King Jr. National Historic District Visitor Center.** ⊠ *501 Auburn Ave.,* ☎ *404/331–5190.* 🎫 *Free.* ☉ *Daily 10–5, tours every ½ hr. MARTA: King Memorial.*

★ ㉒ **Martin Luther King Jr. Center for Nonviolent Social Change.** Established by Dr. King's widow, Coretta Scott King, shortly after his assassination in 1968, the center is dedicated to carrying on King's work in the areas of racial equality and social change. Freedom Hall contains artifacts from Dr. King's life, including his clerical robes and personal Bible, as well as memorial gifts given to his family by well-wishers around the world. In the courtyard, on a circular brick pad in the middle of a rectangular meditation pool, is Dr. King's tomb. An eternal flame burns beneath an inscription that reads "Free at Last!" ⊠ *449 Auburn Ave.,* ☎ *404/526–8900.* 🎫 *Free.* ☉ *Daily 9–5. MARTA: King Memorial.*

★ ⑲ **Martin Luther King Jr. National Historic District Visitor Center.** The center, which opened in 1996 and is run by the National Park Service, has memorabilia and interactive exhibits tracing the progress of the Civil Rights movement and Dr. King's central role in it. Especially moving is the life-size re-creation of a portion of the Edmund Pettus Bridge in Selma, Alabama, with plaster statues of marchers as they crossed it in 1965. Outside the center, on the landscaped grounds of the Peace Pavilion, is the sculpture *Behold,* a statue of a black man lifting a child (symbolizing the future) above his head. It was crafted by Patrick Morelli in honor of Dr. King. Tours of the ☞ **Martin Luther King Jr. Birth Home** are arranged here on a first-come, first-served basis. ⊠ *450 Auburn Ave.,* ☎ *404/331–5190.* 🎫 *Free.* ☉ *Daily 9–5. MARTA: King Memorial.*

㉔ **Wheat Street Baptist Church.** This 1920 Gothic Revival church houses Atlanta's oldest black congregation, established in 1870. The late Rev. Williams Holmes Borders, a contemporary and close friend of Dr. Martin Luther King Sr. as well as the church's leader, was another powerful voice in the Civil Rights movement. ⊠ *359 Auburn Ave.,* ☎ *404/659–4328.* ☉ *Sun. worship 10:45 AM. MARTA: King Memorial.*

Midtown

First developed as a posh residential area in the late 19th century, this thriving area just north of Downtown has undergone many transformations. In the late 1960s Midtown was the South's largest hippie district, filled with coffeehouses and offbeat clubs. By the 1980s the coffeehouses had been replaced by upscale clubs and restaurants while the former flower children, now in three-piece suits, were working in skyscrapers at Colony Square and the Promenade. Despite these changes, the creative and cultural spirit fostered here in the '60s remains alive in the area's many art galleries and theaters.

No other area of Atlanta presents this variety of sights to enjoy, or this diversity of architecture and lifestyles. From the bustling Georgia Tech campus, the pleasant meadows of Piedmont Park, the winding lanes of Ansley Park, the soaring towers around Colony Square, and the quiet galleries of the High Museum, there is something for everyone in this part of the city. While Five Points may be the center of Atlanta commerce, Midtown, with its museums, theaters, and galleries, is its cultural heart.

Numbers in the text correspond to numbers in the margin and on the Atlanta Neighborhoods map.

A Good Walk

The multiple personalities of Midtown may be experienced in one day-long walk, or enjoyed in three shorter loops: Lower Midtown–Georgia Tech, Upper Midtown–Ansley Park, and Piedmont Park–Atlanta Botanical Garden. Three MARTA stations—North Avenue, Midtown, and Arts Center—follow the spine of Peachtree Street and are convenient departure points for exploring Midtown.

Begin your explorations of Lower Midtown–Georgia Tech at Atlanta's popular interactive science museum, **SciTrek** ①, which is in the area between Downtown and Lower Midtown. It's an easy three-block walk east from the Civic Center MARTA station, via Ralph McGill Boulevard to Piedmont Avenue.

Then head north to North Avenue; along the way you may wish to stop at the Baltimore Block (⊠ 5–19 Baltimore Pl.), the site of Atlanta's only existing row houses. Built in 1886, the original buildings have now been incorporated into an award-winning, modern, multiuse complex. To get here from SciTrek, turn right on Piedmont, left on Pine, right on West Peachtree; Baltimore Place will be on your left. From here, continue north on West Peachtree, past One Georgia Center (⊠ 600 W. Peachtree St.). Completed in 1967, this was Midtown's first skyscraper. Across North Avenue is the distinctive red-sandstone All Saints Episcopal Church (⊠ 634 W. Peachtree St.). Look east, past the MARTA station, to see old-fashioned Fire Station No. 11 (⊠ 30 North Ave.); built in 1911, it was designed to blend with the residences that surrounded it.

Continue north on West Peachtree and turn right on Linden Avenue. At Peachtree and Linden Avenue is the sprawling complex of Crawford Long Hospital, where the **Crawford W. Long Medical Museum** ② displays old medical instruments. Glance upward to see the graceful, birdcage steeple of the NationsBank Tower (⊠ 600 Peachtree St.), the South's tallest building at 1,023 ft. Atlanta's Eiffel Tower has a high-ceiling marble lobby that provides space for changing exhibits by local artists. If you're interested in seeing the Georgia Institute of Technology (⊠ 225 North Ave., ☎ 404/894–2000) campus, turn left on North Avenue, and walk across I–75/I–85. In 1996 the campus served as the residential village and a sporting venue for athletes and coaches participating in the Centennial Olympic Games. Sights include the Edge Athletic Center (⊠ 220 Bobby Dodd Way, ☎ 404/894–5400), with Tech athletic memorabilia, and the Robert C. Williams American Museum of Papermaking (⊠ 500 10th St., ☎ 404/894–7840). From nearly anywhere on campus, you can clearly see the tower of the Coca-Cola Corporate Headquarters (⊠ 310 North Ave.), with its familiar script "Coca-Cola," looming in the west. Otherwise, follow West Peachtree north to the Southern Bell building shopping arcade and take the escalator up to the Plaza level to visit the **Telephone Museum** ③.

After touring the exhibits, leave the arcade through the doors to the open courtyard where you can get a close-up perspective of the cantilever design of the Southern Bell building. Climb the steps to Peachtree Street, turn right, and you

38

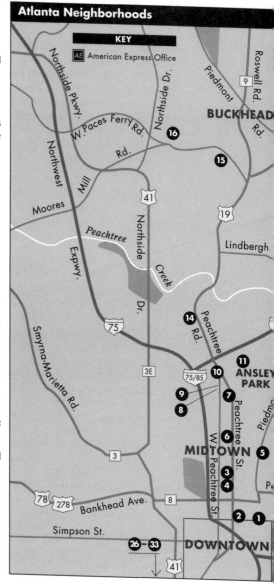

Atlanta Neighborhoods

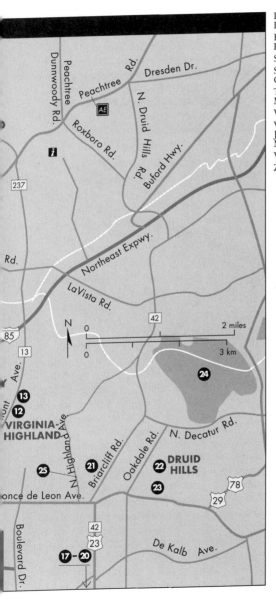

will be in front of the famous **Fox Theatre** ④. The guided
tour is a must if time permits. If you have the energy and
the inclination, you could turn left on Ponce de Leon Avenue and right on Piedmont and walk along the edge of the
Midtown Residential District ⑤; at the end of Piedmont, turn
left on 10th Street and left on Peachtree to reach the **Margaret Mitchell House** ⑥, where the *Gone With the Wind* author once lived. Otherwise, take the North Avenue MARTA
to Midtown, and turn right on 10th Street to Peachtree Street.
On your right is the Margaret Mitchell House.

To begin your tour of Upper Midtown–Ansley Park, walk
north on West Peachtree or take the Midtown MARTA to
the Arts Center station. If you're interested in learning
about the commercial buildings in the area, take the architecture loop (described below) from the Arts Center
MARTA down West Peachtree, 14th Street, and Peachtree.
Otherwise, from the Arts Center MARTA, follow 15th
Street to Peachtree, where you turn left to see the Woodruff
Arts Center. The architecture loop: Walk one block south
on West Peachtree Street to see the soaring, Gothic One Atlantic Center (⊠ 1201 W. Peachtree St.). Completed in
1987 and known to locals as the IBM building, it is Midtown's tallest skyscraper. Turn east and climb 14th Street,
past the stately Four Seasons Hotel Atlanta (⊠ 75 14th St.),
whose styling is reminiscent of the Empire State Building.
At the crest of the hill, on Peachtree Street, is Colony
Square (⊠ 1175–1201 Peachtree St.), the hub of the Midtown commercial district. Completed in 1975, it was the
first high-rise multiuse development in the South. In addition to the two distinctive white business towers, there is
an indoor skylit shopping and dining atrium, athletic club,
condominiums, and the Sheraton Colony Square hotel.
Just south of the intersection is the gleaming green-glass Cam-
panile Building (⊠ 1155 Peachtree St.) and the French
chateau 1898 Wimbish house (⊠ 1150 Peachtree St.). Walk
north on Peachtree, past the mid-rise and high-rise AT&T
Promenade Towers (⊠ 1200–1230 Peachtree St.) and the
eccentric 1910 house with a mix of architectural styles.
Perched atop a fortress-like stone wall, the house is dubbed
the Castle (⊠ 87 15th St.) and is now owned by AT&T.
Grandly dominating the intersection of Peachtree and 15th

streets is the classically styled, copper-domed First Church
of Christ Scientist (✉ 1235 Peachtree St.), which serves as
a transition from the commercial towers of Peachtree to the
residential ambiance of Ansley Park.

Across Peachtree from the church is the imposing, rectangular Woodruff Arts Center, housing the Atlanta Symphony
Orchestra, the Alliance Theatre, and the Atlanta College of
Art. Step inside to see the lobby with its grand marble staircase and to visit the **Atlanta College of Art Gallery.** Sepa-
rated from the center by a small lawn and courtyard is the
dramatically modern, gleaming white **High Museum of
Art** ⑦. On the lawn between the center and the High Museum is the somber statue *The Shade,* sculpted by Auguste
Rodin in 1880. It was a gift to the city from the government
of France, in memory of 122 Atlanta art patrons who were
killed in a 1962 plane crash at Orly Airport in Paris.

Walk north on Peachtree to Pershing Point Park, and then
south on West Peachtree to the crosswalk at 17th Street.
After crossing, walk north to the intersection of 18th Street
and turn left. Directly ahead, across Spring Street, is the **Center for Puppetry Arts** ⑧, a terrific place for kids. And in the
Selig Center, the **William Breman Jewish Heritage Museum** ⑨. If you wish to leave the tour at this point, a good
way to end is with a late afternoon tour and tasting at the
Atlanta Brewing Company, which is in the opposite direction from the rest of the tour but is near the Arts Center
MARTA. To get here from the Center for Puppetry Arts,
walk four blocks south and then west one block on 16th
Street. Turn left on Williams Street and look for the old brick
building that houses the Atlanta Brewing Company.

If you're continuing the tour from the Jewish Heritage Museum, recross Spring Street and walk north to South Rhodes
Center. Turn right and look immediately to your left to see
Rhodes Memorial Hall ⑩, where you may tour the restored
interior and see the stained-glass windows depicting Confederate heroes.

Enter historic **Ansley Park** ⑪ by crossing Peachtree Street
and traveling east on Peachtree Circle. As you walk, no-
tice how these houses, built in the early days of the automobile, differ from the closely spaced residences of Midtown

that were constructed a decade earlier, when commuters still relied on trolleys. Meander east on The Prado and then south on Inman Circle. Enjoy the varied architecture as well as the open green spaces of Winn Park. On the left, just before you return to Peachtree Circle, is the 1917 Robert Crumley house (⊠ 17 Inman Circle). Turn left on Peachtree Circle and look to your left to see the 1912 William Winecoff house (⊠ 37 Peachtree Circle). Just ahead on the left are the Frank Ellis house (⊠ 1 Peachtree Circle), a beautiful 1911 Italianate villa, and the neo-Georgian David Black house (⊠ 186 15th St.). Continue east on 15th Street to see Habersham Memorial Hall (⊠ 270 15th St.), a large Regency building that is the headquarters of the Daughters of the American Revolution. Turn right on Piedmont Avenue, and walk to 14th Street. You may continue the walk here by crossing Piedmont and entering Piedmont Park, or return on 14th Street to Peachtree and the Arts Center MARTA station.

The final loop of your Midtown tour, Piedmont Park–Atlanta Botanical Garden, begins at the 14th Street entrance to **Piedmont Park** ⑫. From the Peace Monument just inside the entrance, follow the loop road to the right, past the whimsical Playscapes and the visitor center, and meander east above the shores of Lake Clara Meer. Continue to your left, past the Park Drive entrance and the tennis courts, as you turn back toward 14th Street. Take the lane on your right, and walk up to the entrance of the **Atlanta Botanical Garden** ⑬, a peaceful way to finish your Midtown tour.

TIMING

It is possible to hit every sight on this tour in one very full day, but most people will want to narrow the selection down for an easier day. If you're an architecture buff, you will probably want to spend two days with this tour, exploring the Midtown Residential District on Piedmont, the Ansley Park neighborhood, and the commercial buildings around Colony Square. You will save a lot of time and energy if you take MARTA at the points indicated instead of walking.

Sights to See

⓫ **Ansley Park.** This picturesque neighborhood was designed by Frederick Law Olmsted's protégé, Solon Ruff, and developed over 20 years, beginning in 1904. The large houses are set back from the street and sheltered by numerous shade trees. Laid out during the advent of the automobile, the curving streets were intended for leisurely motoring, and they wind through the area in an almost haphazard fashion. In fact, the streets are so confusing that many Atlanta motorists compare driving in Ansley Park to navigating the Bermuda Triangle. The more than 600 private homes and numerous small neighborhood parks are best enjoyed on foot. ⊠ *Bounded by Peachtree St. on the west, Piedmont Rd. on the east, 14th St. on the south, and Beverly Rd. on the north. MARTA: Arts Center.*

★ ☺ ⓭ **Atlanta Botanical Garden.** Occupying 30 acres on the north end of Piedmont Park, the property has 15 acres of formal gardens with dazzling displays of perennials, a rose garden, an English herb garden, a fragrance garden for visually impaired visitors, a rock garden, a Japanese garden with a bridge and goldfish pond, and a 15-acre hardwood forest with trails from which you may view many plants native to Georgia. The gardens are especially lovely from April to June. In the Fuqua Conservatory, rare and threatened flora from tropical and desert ecosystems grow within a computer-controlled environment. ⊠ *1345 Piedmont Ave.,* ☎ *404/876–5859.* ☞ *$6; free Thurs. after 1.* ☼ *Nov.–Mar., Tues.–Sun. 9–6; Apr.–Oct., Tues.–Sun. 9–7. MARTA: Arts Center.*

OFF THE BEATEN PATH   **ATLANTA BREWING COMPANY –** Founded in 1994 after changes in Georgia state law allowed the establishment of microbreweries, the Atlanta Brewing Company is the first local brewer established since 1955. Tours of the facility, in a large warehouse, include a discussion of the brewing process followed by a chance to sample the company's Red Brick label ales, lagers, and wheat beers. ⊠ *1219 Williams St.,* ☎ *404/892–4436.* ☞ *Free.* ☼ *Tours Thurs.–Fri. 5:30, Sat. 3. MARTA: Arts Center.*

Atlanta College of Art Gallery. Exciting student exhibits are shown in this space, which is part of the Woodruff Arts Center. ⊠ *1280 Peachtree St.,* ☎ *404/733–5050.* ☞ *Free.* ☼ *Tues., Wed., Sat. 10–5, Thurs.–Fri. 10–9, Sun. noon–5. MARTA: Arts Center.*

🕗 ❽ **Center for Puppetry Arts.** The center's international puppetry museum includes performances, puppet-making workshops, and displays. ✉ *1404 Spring St.,* ☎ *404/873–3391.* ✉ *Museum $5.* ☉ *Mon.–Sat. 9–5. MARTA: Arts Center.*

❷ **Crawford W. Long Medical Museum.** The original white-columned Crawford Long Hospital building houses a medical museum containing Confederate and early 20th-century medical instruments and artifacts belonging to Dr. Crawford Long, the Georgia physician who, in 1842, was the first physician to use ether anesthesia. ✉ *35 Linden Ave.,* ☎ *404/686–4411.* ✉ *Free.* ☉ *Daily 10–5. MARTA: North Avenue.*

NEED A **The Varsity** (✉ 61 North Ave., ☎ 404/881–1706), located
BREAK? between Crawford Long Hospital and Georgia Tech, is an Atlanta institution straight out of *Happy Days.* Atlanta's most famous low-cost eatery, with perhaps its greasiest food, has been serving up hamburgers, chili dogs, onion rings, chocolate malts, and other drive-in fare since the early 1920s. It still has awning-covered curb service for a few cars.

❹ **Fox Theatre.** One of the nation's last surviving movie palaces, this Moorish–Egyptian building was built in 1929. The Shriners designed the building as their Atlanta headquarters, but they were forced to sell it during the Depression to cinema magnate William Fox. For generations, it has hosted films, musicals, rock concerts, dance performances, and operas. Interior features include the grand Egyptian Ballroom and the main auditorium's "sky" ceiling—complete with moving clouds and twinkling stars—above Alhambra-like minarets. ✉ *660 Peachtree St.,* ☎ *404/881–2100 event information, 404/876–2040 tours.* ✉ *Tour $5.* ☉ *Tours Mon., Wed., Thurs. at 10; Sat. at 10 and 11. MARTA: North Avenue.*

❼ **High Museum of Art.** The bold, white-porcelain-paneled museum has a dramatic atrium with a narrow, curving staircase along one wall. In 1991 the American Institute of Architects named this 1983 design by Richard Meier one of the 10 best works of architecture in the 1980s. Best bets among the museum's permanent collections are American decorative arts, sub-Saharan African art, and the Uhry

Print Collection, with works by French impressionists and other European artists. Modern-art lovers will enjoy the large Alexander Calder mobile on the front lawn. The High's gift shop is one of the best in town for art books, prints, and other artful creations. ⊠ *1280 Peachtree St.,* ☎ *404/577–6940.* ▨ *$6.* ☉ *Tues.–Sat. 10–5, Sun. noon–5. MARTA: Arts Center.*

⑥ Margaret Mitchell House. This redbrick building is all that remains of the Windsor House Apartments where Margaret Mitchell lived while writing *Gone With the Wind* from 1926 to 1929. The structure was nearly destroyed by arson in 1994, and was under renovation when it was struck again by a mysterious fire in May 1996. Despite these setbacks, at press time the renovations of the house were nearly complete and the house and adjacent visitor center opened in May 1997. The house contains exhibits about the author and the city. ⊠ *999 Peachtree St.,* ☎ *404/249–7012.* ▨ *$6.* ☉ *Weekends 9–4; call for other possible opening times. MARTA: Midtown.*

⑤ Midtown Residential District. Development began here in the 1890s and continued until the 1920s, so there is a mix of architectural styles, from Victorian mansions to Craftsman bungalows. Much of the area was laid out by real-estate developer Edward Peters, whose 1883 Queen Anne house is now the Mansion Restaurant (⊠ 179 Ponce de Leon Ave.). One of the finer homes along Piedmont Avenue is the W. P. Nicholson house, now the Shellmont Bed & Breakfast Inn (⊠ 821 Piedmont Ave.), an 1892 residence with superb exterior ornamentation. After many years of decline, this area began to rebound in the 1980s with both restoration projects and new construction. In stark contrast to the Victorian houses is the attention-grabbing Rio Shopping Center (⊠ 535 Piedmont Ave.), a U-shape structure with garishly painted red, green, and yellow corrugated walls, and the city's most bizarre plaza. Some 350 large, squatting bronze frogs ride the surface of a reflecting pool lit by submerged fiber-optic strips, and surround a white tubular sphere on the lawn. ⊠ *Piedmont Ave. between North Ave. and 10th St. MARTA: North Avenue or Midtown.*

★ ☺ **⑫ Piedmont Park.** Site of the 1895 Cotton States Exposition, where composer John Philip Sousa introduced his *King*

Cotton March, 185-acre Piedmont Park is Atlanta's oldest and the central city's largest public park. Through the years, the park has hosted many special events, ranging from the state's first football game (an 1892 contest between Georgia and Auburn) to an 1898 reunion of Confederate veterans, as well as hippie love-ins in the 1960s. Today it is best known as the finish line for the Peachtree Road Race, a 10K race that attracts more than 50,000 runners each July 4th. The park is closed to automobile traffic and is popular with joggers, bicyclists, and Rollerbladers. It also has tennis courts, athletic fields, a swimming pool, and a small lake for fishing.

As you stroll through the park, don't miss the dramatic *Peace Monument* at the Piedmont Avenue entrance. A 1911 gift from the citizens of several northern states, the sculpture symbolizes the binding of the nation's wounds after the Civil War. If you have children, plan a visit to the **Playscapes,** on the hill to your right. This recreational area—a series of brightly colored tubes, squares, domes, and other abstract forms with ladders, slides, entry cutouts, or handholds— was created by internationally renowned sculptor Isamu Noguchi. At the 12th Street entrance is the **Piedmont Park Conservancy's Visitor Center,** with displays about the park, its history, and information on guided tours. ⊠ *Piedmont Ave. between 10th St. and Westminster Dr.,* ☎ *404/875– 7275 Visitor Center.* ◰ *Guided tours (seasonal, call for schedule) $5.* ☉ *Park daily 6 AM–midnight; visitor center Tues.–Fri. 10–5, Sat. noon–4, Sun. 1–5. MARTA: Midtown or Arts Center.*

NEED A BREAK?	Across from the park, between 12th and 14th streets, is the **Prince of Wales** (⊠ 1144 Piedmont Ave., ☎ 404/876– 0227), an English pub with cold drinks and thick sandwiches. In warm weather, relax on the patio and watch the Rollerbladers zip by.

⑩ Rhodes Memorial Hall. Built in 1904 for furniture magnate Amos G. Rhodes, this rough-hewn Stone Mountain granite residence resembles a European castle with its four-story square tower and turreted roof. Inside, nine exquisite stained-glass windows, depicting Civil War scenes and 15

Confederate heroes, line a carved mahogany staircase. The Georgia Trust for Historic Preservation, headquartered here, presents exhibits about Georgia architecture of bygone eras. ⊠ *1516 Peachtree St.,* ☏ *404/881–9980.* ⌸ *$3.* ⊙ *Weekdays 11–4. MARTA: Arts Center.*

★ ☝ ❶ **SciTrek.** The Science and Technology Museum of Atlanta, SciTrek occupies 96,000 square ft of space in the Atlanta Civic Center. The museum, one of the top science museums in the nation, contains about 100 interactive exhibits in four halls. Visitors can become human kaleidoscopes and, in Kidspace, two- to seven-year-olds may explore the principles of science through hands-on activities. ⊠ *395 Piedmont Ave.,* ☏ *404/522–5500.* ⌸ *$7.50.* ⊙ *Mon.–Sat. 10–5, Sun. noon–5. MARTA: Civic Center.*

☝ ❸ **Telephone Museum.** The North Avenue MARTA station is adjacent to the Southern Bell building arcade, a mid-rise dining and shopping arcade, where, on the Plaza level, the Telephone Museum has exhibits tracing the evolution of Alexander Graham Bell's invention from its earliest form to the current, high-tech, fiber-optic instruments. Children who have grown up with push-button phones will marvel at the variety of telephones on display. ⊠ *675 W. Peachtree St.,* ☏ *404/223–3661.* ⌸ *Free.* ⊙ *Museum weekdays 11–1. MARTA: North Avenue.*

★ ❾ **William Breman Jewish Heritage Museum.** This museum contains exhibits on Atlanta's Jewish heritage and a pictorial and eyewitness history of the Holocaust. There's also a genealogy center, archives, and the Lillian and A. J. Weinberg Center for Holocaust Education. ⊠ *1440 Spring St.,* ☏ *404/351–8410.* ⌸ *$5.* ⊙ *Mon.–Thurs. 10–5, Fri. 10–3, Sun. 1–5. MARTA: Arts Center.*

Buckhead

To Atlantans, having a Buckhead address is synonymous with being either wealthy or trendy—or, perhaps, both. Often assumed by outsiders to be a suburb, it is instead the city's most prestigious community. The unusual name comes from Henry Irby's 1840s stagecoach-stop tavern that had a buck's head mounted outside its entrance. Because of its desirability, Buckhead has some of the city's most expansive boundaries, ranging from I–85 on the south to Chastain Park and the city limits on the north, and from the Cobb County line on the west to the DeKalb County line on the east—an area of about 28 square mi.

Wherever Buckhead begins and ends, its heart is undeniably at the intersection of Peachtree, East and West Paces Ferry, and Roswell roads, about 6 mi north of Downtown. Concentrated here are about 40 see-and-be-seen restaurants and music clubs, more than 100 chic specialty shops, and numerous art, craft, and antique galleries. Just a short drive away from Peachtree are the impressively landscaped mansions of the rich and famous. A car is required to see all Buckhead sights; MARTA Bus 23 provides transportation to sights along Peachtree Road. For specifics on nightlife and shopping in Buckhead, see Chapters 5 and 7.

Numbers in the text correspond to numbers in the margin and on the Atlanta Neighborhoods map.

A Good Drive

Drive north from Midtown along Peachtree Road. A short distance after crossing over I–85, turn right on Palisades Road into Brookwood Hills, a tree-shaded neighborhood. Turn left on Parkdale and then right on Wakefield. Go left on Brighton Road and return to Peachtree. Continue north on Peachtree and watch for signs pointing left to **Bennett Street** ⑭, where you may search for intriguing antiques and collectibles among scores of shops and studios. Return to Peachtree and continue your neighborhood tour by traveling north. Turn right on Peachtree Hills Avenue and enter Peachtree Hills, a more modest residential area filled with well-kept Craftsman bungalows. Bear right and follow Fairhaven Circle as it meanders back to Peachtree Hills Avenue. Turn left and return to Peachtree Road and continue north. Just ahead on the right is the Peachtree Battle Shopping Center (⊠ 2345 Peachtree Rd.).

Turn left on Peachtree Battle Avenue and enter Peachtree Heights, a neighborhood with large homes on both sides of the landscaped avenue. Turn right on Woodward Way and then right again on Habersham Road. Make an immediate left on West Muscogee Avenue and follow it back to Peachtree Road. Turn right on Peachtree and then left at the traffic light onto Lindbergh Drive. Almost immediately, turn left on Parkside Drive and enter Garden Hills, a blend of pre– and post–World War II houses along both sides of East Wesley Road. Follow Parkside past Peachtree Heights Park, with its pleasant duck pond, to Peachtree Way. Ahead on the left is the Christ the King parochial school. Turn right on Peachtree Way and go several blocks, past a mix of large homes and well-kept bungalows, to Acorn Avenue. Make a left turn and cross East Wesley Road, passing the Garden Hills Community Center and Pool. At the intersection, Acorn becomes Rumson Road and you will follow it back to Peachtree Road.

Turn right and, about a mile ahead, you will come to the fork of Roswell and Peachtree roads. Between the two streets is small, triangular Buckhead Park, marking the heart of Buckhead's shopping and dining district. If time permits, park in one of the nearby lots and explore the galleries, shops, and boutiques along Peachtree and Roswell roads, Buckhead Avenue, North Fulton Drive, East Paces Ferry Road, and around Andrews Drive.

Travel west on West Paces Ferry (no left turn from Peachtree Road), and drive about a half mile to West Andrews Drive. Turn left and enter the **Atlanta History Center** ⑮, which has a museum, two historic homes, and gardens. As you leave the center, return to West Paces Ferry Road and turn left to begin your tour of Buckhead's mansions. While upscale houses seem to be everywhere in Buckhead, there are several magnificent structures located along West Paces Ferry, Tuxedo, Blackland, and Valley roads. Along West Paces Ferry look for the Mount Vernon–like Arden (✉ 456 W. Paces Ferry Rd.), a large 1911 Greek Revival mansion, and directly across the street from it, the massive Greek Revival **Governor's Mansion** ⑯. Turn right on Tuxedo Road and look immediately left to see the Joseph D. Rhodes house (✉ 541 W. Paces Ferry Rd.), a 1926 classical Italian-inspired residence.

Ahead on the right, behind a small rise, is Whitehall (✉ 3425 Tuxedo Rd.), a large, Italian villa once owned by legendary golfer Bobby Jones. At the fork, continue right on

Tuxedo and look left to see the Georgian Windcrofte (⊠ 3640 Tuxedo Rd.), once the home of Coca-Cola chairman Robert W. Woodruff. Turn left on Valley Road and follow it to Northside Drive. Turn right and, at the traffic light, right again on Blackland Road. Climb the hill and look for the gated entrance and rolling lawn of Peninsula House (⊠ 281 Blackland Rd.), a well-proportioned Greek Revival structure. Formerly owned by Prince Faisal of Saudi Arabia, it is one of Atlanta's most photographed buildings.

Turn right on Tuxedo Road and then left on Valley Road. At Habersham Road, turn left, climb the hill, cross Roswell Road to Piedmont Road, and turn right. About a mile ahead on the left, past the Buckhead Loop Road, is the distinctive glass-silhouette of Tower Place (⊠ 3340 Peachtree Rd.), which has stores, restaurants, theaters, and hotels. The center's towering 29-story gleaming glass tower, outlined at night with laser light, has become a Buckhead landmark. Turn left on Peachtree Road and, as you cross GA Route 400, you will pass the imposing pyramidal towers of the Atlanta Financial Center (⊠ 3333 Peachtree Rd.).

When traffic slows to a crawl, you have reached Lenox Square Mall (⊠ 3393 Peachtree Rd.), the South's largest shopping center. Just ahead on the left is the Ritz-Carlton, Buckhead (⊠ 3434 Peachtree Rd.), while across Buckhead Loop Road is the upscale Phipps Plaza (⊠ 3500 Peachtree Rd.), which is loaded with marble, brass, fine woodwork, restaurants, movie theaters, and more than 100 shops. Continue about a mile north on Peachtree to Club Drive, turn left and enter the scenic neighborhood of Brookhaven. Turn right on West Brookhaven Drive, travel past the Capital City Club golf course with its 1928 country-French clubhouse, and return to Peachtree Road, where the tour began.

TIMING

Plan a full day in Buckhead so you will have time to do some serious shopping, take in the Atlanta History Center (plan at least 2–3 hours here), wander in and out of art galleries, and admire the varied neighborhoods with their beautiful homes. If you're interested in touring the Governor's Mansion, be aware that it's only open for tours Tuesday and Thursday mornings. You may wish to stay in Buckhead for the evening, when the restaurant and club scenes get lively.

Sights to See

★ **Atlanta History Center.** On 32 landscaped acres in the heart of Buckhead, the Center is dedicated to preserving, protecting, and displaying the history of Atlanta. The extensive displays are provocative—juxtaposing *Gone With the Wind* romanticism with the grim reality of Ku Klux Klan racism. Also at the center are the elegant **Swan House,** a magnificently furnished 1926 Palladian mansion; the 1836 **Tullie Smith House,** a modest two-story plantation house that depicts life on a frontier farm; **McElreath Hall,** with exhibition space for artifacts, an auditorium for lectures, and the Center's research library and archives; and the Coach House Restaurant (☎ 404/261–0636), which serves southern cuisine lunches until 2:30. The Center's buildings are surrounded by gardens and woodland trails. ⊠ *130 W. Paces Ferry Rd.,* ☎ *404/814–4000.* ⊡ *$7 for museum and gardens, $1 for each house.* ☉ *Mon.–Sat. 10–5:30, Sun. noon–5:30.*

NEED A BREAK?
If touring the galleries makes you feel creative, stop in at **Wired and Fired, A Pottery Playhouse** (⊠ 279 E. Paces Ferry Rd., ☎ 404/842-1919), where you may decorate and fire your own pot while sipping on a glass of wine or munching a sandwich. If a quick bite is the thing, pick up a po-boy from **Henri's Bakery** (⊠ 61 Irby Ave., ☎ 404/237-0202), a local favorite for more than 40 years.

🄯 **Bennett Street.** This side street off Peachtree Road has more than 150 art galleries and antique and decorative furnishings stores in a converted warehouse district. TULA (⊠ 75 Bennett St., ☎ 404/351–3551) is a two-story building that houses the studios and galleries of over 30 artisans. Just north on Peachtree is Brookwood Square (⊠ 2140 Peachtree Rd.), a compact, modern, two-story shopping center. ⊠ *Off 2100 block of Peachtree Rd.*

NEED A BREAK?
If you are hungry for a mid-morning snack or an early lunch, stop at **Huey's** (⊠ 1816 Peachtree Rd., ☎ 404/873-2037) for New Orleans coffee and beignets, or try the popular **Café Intermezzo Coffeehouse** (⊠ 1845 Peachtree Rd., ☎ 404/355-0041) across the street, which has an enticing range of flavored coffees and European pastries.

⑯ Governor's Mansion. Although it is the new kid on the block, this 1967 mansion fits right in with the other large estates that line West Paces Ferry Road. The rambling Greek Revival structure wrapped with white Doric columns is more reminiscent of a Mississippi River plantation than an antebellum Georgia estate. The interior rooms are filled with Federal antiques. You can walk through at your own pace (it takes 20–30 minutes); guides stationed at each roped-off room describe the furnishings and their historical significance. ⊠ *391 W. Paces Ferry Rd.,* ☎ *404/261–1776.* ⎁ *Free.* ☉ *Tues.–Thurs. 10–11:30 AM.*

Grant Park, Inman Park, Little Five Points

The decades after the Civil War were a period of rapid and dramatic change for Atlanta, with little time wasted as the city rebuilt and reclaimed its role as the South's transportation hub. In 1868 Atlanta became the state capital and center for growing business interests. By the advent of the new century, it was the recognized commercial and financial center of the entire South.

As the city's central business district expanded, old homes gave way to commercial development, and new middle- and upper-class suburban neighborhoods developed in Inman Park and Grant Park. Several of these turn-of-the-century residential districts remain relatively intact, and you can tour them to see the fanciful, grand Victorian houses and pleasant parks. Other sights to see along the way include the dramatic cyclorama painting of the 1864 Battle of Atlanta, the highly regarded Zoo Atlanta, and the Carter Presidential Center.

Numbers in the text correspond to numbers in the margin on the Atlanta Neighborhoods map.

A Good Drive

Begin your driving tour by traveling east from Downtown on Memorial Drive to Oakland Avenue. Turn left, then right, through the arched entrance, to **Oakland Cemetery** ⑰. Park and pick up a copy of the cemetery map and continue your explorations of this historic burial ground on foot. Exit the cemetery and go one block west on MLK Drive to Grant

Street. Turn left on Grant and then left on Memorial Drive. Go two blocks and turn right on Cherokee Avenue. Cross over I–20 and proceed south to Grant Park (⊠ Cherokee Ave. and Boulevard, south of Sydney St.), a 100-acre park surrounded by Queen Anne-style mansions and Craftsman bungalows. Plan to visit the park's two main attractions, the **Atlanta Cyclorama** ⑱, and **Zoo Atlanta** ⑲. The parking area for both is on the left at Augusta Avenue. As you leave take a leisurely drive through the rolling, wooded park. Exit on Berne Street and travel east to Boulevard.

Turn left on Boulevard and cross back over I–20, past the eastern boundary of Oakland Cemetery. Looming ahead are the old brick buildings of the Fulton Bag and Cotton Mill (⊠ 170 Boulevard) and the modest houses of Cabbage Town (⊠ Boulevard at Memorial Dr.). Continue on Boulevard and turn right on Edgewood Avenue. In about a half mile you will enter the Victorian-era neighborhood of Inman Park. On July 22, 1864, these rolling, wooded acres were the site of the Battle of Atlanta, and the many historical markers dotting the neighborhood help tell the story of the battle. Bear left on Euclid Avenue and look for the beautifully restored Queen Anne-style red-clapboard Beath-Dickey house (⊠ 866 Euclid Ave.), ahead on the left. Turn right on Elizabeth Street, and look immediately to your left to see Callan Castle (⊠ 145 Elizabeth St.), the grand Greek Revival mansion built by Coca-Cola Company founder Asa Candler in 1903. Just west of the intersection of Edgewood Avenue is the Trolley Barn (⊠ 963 Edgewood Ave.), a reminder of Inman Park's origins as a trolley-commuter neighborhood. Turn left on Edgewood and drive through the small Inman Park commercial district.

Turn right on Hurt Street, past the MARTA Inman Park–Reynoldstown station, and then left on DeKalb Avenue. Turn left on Degress Avenue and, at mid-block, look to your right to see a historical marker in front of a vacant church building. This was the site of the antebellum Troup-Hurt house, a focal point of fighting in the Battle of Atlanta. Follow Degress down the hill to Alta Avenue and turn left, then right on Euclid Avenue. In a few blocks, you will be in the heart of Little Five Points (⊠ Euclid and Moreland Aves.), a small commercial district that is Atlanta's version of Greenwich Village. Aging hippies, artists, grunge rockers, skinheads, and bikers mix with tourists who come to visit the neighborhood's art galleries, music clubs, theaters, health-food stores, restaurants, and off-beat shops. Park and explore then climb back in your car and turn left on Moreland Avenue, then left again on East Freedom Parkway. Cross North Highland Avenue and proceed to the entrance of the **Carter Presidential Center** ⑳. After you have finished your tour, you may follow Freedom Parkway west to I–75/I–85 or north to Ponce de Leon Avenue for Druid Hills.

TIMING

This tour will take almost a full day. Plan at least one hour in both the Oakland Cemetery and the Carter Presidential Center and a half-day at the Cyclorama and Zoo Atlanta.

Sights to See

★ ⑱ **Atlanta Cyclorama.** Gaze spellbound as the sights and sounds of the 1864 Battle of Atlanta surround you in this massive circular painting. Completed by a team of German artists in 1885, it is the largest painting of its type in the world. A three-dimensional foreground gives the image added realism. The building also has an extensive collection of Civil War artifacts. ⊠ *800 Cherokee Ave.,* ☎ *404/624–1071 tickets, 404/658–7625 information.* 🎫 *$5.* ☉ *Sept.–May, daily 9:30–4:30, June–Labor Day, daily 9:30–5:30. MARTA: Transfer to zoo shuttle from Five Points.*

★ ⑳ **Carter Presidential Center.** Established by President Jimmy Carter in 1982, the center includes the Carter Library and Museum, which chronicles the history of the Carter presidency and contains a model of the Oval Office. Across the lobby from the museum is the Copenhill Café, which serves light cafeteria lunches. The low-profile buildings blend with landscaped grounds that include a serene Japanese garden and a patio with a panoramic view of the Downtown skyline. During the Battle of Atlanta, General William T. Sherman had his headquarters on this site. ⊠ *One Copenhill, 441 Freedom Pkwy.,* ☎ *404/331–3942.* 🎫 *$6.* ☉ *Mon.–Sat. 9–4:45, Sun. noon–4:45. MARTA: Inman Park/Reynoldstown.*

NEED A
BREAK?

Two blocks north of the Carter Presidential Center is **Manuel's Tavern** (⊠ 602 N. Highland Ave., ☎ 404/525–3447), where students, social activists, and political types have been enjoying great sandwiches, cold beer, and conversation since 1957.

★ ⑰ **Oakland Cemetery.** In the shadow of Downtown, this cemetery, established in 1850, is Atlanta's oldest public burial ground, and is a treasure of Victorian funerary art. A historical marker is on the site of Confederate General John B. Hood's headquarters during the Battle of Atlanta; many Rebel soldiers who died in the battle are buried in the Confederate section of the cemetery. Look for the dramatic sculpture of the Confederate Lion, carved in 1896 from a single block of marble. Also buried at Oakland are *Gone With the Wind* author Margaret Mitchell and golfer Bobby Jones. ⊠ *MLK Dr. at Oakland Ave.,* ☎ *404/688–2107.* ☞ *Free.* ☉ *Oct.–Apr., daily 8–6, Apr.–Oct., daily 8–7. MARTA: King Memorial.*

★ ☺ ⑲ **Zoo Atlanta.** One of the nation's top zoos, Zoo Atlanta has more than 1,000 animals. The nearly century-old zoo is undergoing a multimillion-dollar renovation that has already produced the Birds of Prey Amphitheater, Ford African Rainforest, Flamingo Lagoon, Masai Mara (re-created plains of Kenya), Sumatran Tiger Exhibit, and a children's OK-to-Touch Corral. ⊠ *800 Cherokee Ave.,* ☎ *404/624–5600.* ☞ *$7.50.* ☉ *Weekdays 9–4:30, weekends 9–5:30. MARTA: Zoo shuttle from Five Points.*

Druid Hills, Emory University, Virginia-Highland

This tour meanders through elegant, Frederick Law Olmsted–designed Druid Hills to the growing campus of Emory University and then to the popular in-town community of Virginia-Highland. Along the way, you will see an exquisite mansion turned fine arts center, the largest natural history museum south of the Smithsonian Institution, a planetarium and observatory in an enchanted forest, fascinating displays of Egyptian and Greek antiquities, and Atlanta's oldest restaurant.

Numbers in the text correspond to numbers in the margin and on the Atlanta Neighborhoods map.

A Good Drive

Travel east on Ponce de Leon Avenue to the intersection with Briarcliff Road (which becomes Moreland Avenue south of the intersection). Turn left on Briarcliff and travel about a half mile to **Callanwolde Fine Arts Center** ㉑. After touring the beautiful estate and galleries, continue north on Briarcliff to The Byway and turn right into the western boundary of **Druid Hills.** Turn right on Springdale Road, past many fine old houses; cross Ponce de Leon Avenue, glancing at the beautiful Olmsted-designed linear parks, and proceed to Fairview Road. Turn left and look immediately to your left to see the French manor-style Walter Rich house (✉ 1348 Fairview Rd.). Turn left on Oakdale Road and re-cross Ponce de Leon. On your right is St. John's Lutheran Church and the Stonehenge house (✉ 1410 Ponce de Leon Ave.). Follow Oakdale, past the Sigmund Montag house (✉ 850 Oakdale Rd.) back to the Byway, and turn right. Turn right again on Lullwater Road. Up a hill on the right, is the Jacob Hirsch house (✉ 822 Lullwater Rd.), which was featured in the movie *Driving Miss Daisy.*

Turn left on Ponce de Leon Avenue and proceed east to Clifton Road. Turn left and then right into the **Fernbank Museum of Natural History** ㉒. After touring the museum, return to Ponce de Leon Avenue and turn left. In about a half mile watch for the intersection of Artwood Drive (it is just before you reach an arched-stone railroad bridge). Turn left, and then right on Heaton Park Drive, to visit **Fernbank Science Center** ㉓.

As you exit the center, turn left on Heaton Park Drive, and then left again on Dyson Road and follow it to East Clifton Road. Go right on East Clifton, and then right again on Clifton Road. Turn left on Oxford Road, cross North Decatur Road and enter the campus of **Emory University** ㉔. A visitor parking lot is ahead on the left and it is a short walk to the quadrangle and the **Michael C. Carlos Museum.**

Leave the campus and turn right on North Decatur Road and travel about a mile to Briarcliff Road. Turn left, and then right on Stillwood Drive. Turn left on North Virginia Avenue, and right on Virginia Avenue to the intersection of North Highland Avenue. You are now in the heart of the **Virginia-Highland** commercial district. Park and browse the interesting shops or meander down a side street to see some of the restored bungalow houses. Travel south on North Highland and explore the early 20th-century neighborhood of **Atkins Park** ㉕ as you conclude your tour.

TIMING

This tour should take you a full day. Count on two hours at the Fernbank Museum of Natural History and its IMAX show, the Fernbank Science Center and its Fernbank Forest, and the Michael C. Carlos Museum and Emory's campus. A visit to Callanwolde should take an hour and the length of your stop in Virginia-Highland will depend on your wallet and your appetite.

Sights to See

㉕ **Atkins Park.** Along North Highland Avenue, in the blocks just north of Ponce de Leon Avenue, Atkins Park was developed in the early 1900s by Edwin Grove, founder of the luxurious Grove Park Inn in Asheville, North Carolina. Large houses and well-preserved old apartment buildings line the side streets, and the commercial district has a mix of shops, taverns, and restaurants. ⊠ *N. Highland Ave. between Ponce de Leon Ave. and St. Louis St.*

NEED A BREAK?   The **Atkins Park Delicatessen** (⊠ 794 N. Highland Ave., ☎ 404/872–2822), Atlanta's oldest restaurant, has been pleasing diners since 1922.

㉑ **Callanwolde Fine Arts Center.** Built in 1917 for Charles H. Candler, eldest son of Coca-Cola Company founder Asa Candler, this exquisite Tudor mansion sits well back from the street on 12 shaded acres. Architect Henry Hornbostel was commissioned for this work after designing the buildings at nearby Emory University. In the early 1970s, the house was acquired by DeKalb County and converted to a fine arts center with studios, classrooms, and galleries. ⊠ *980 Briarcliff Rd.,* ☎ *404/872–5338.* ▣ *Free; guided tours $1.50.* ☉ *Weekdays 9–5:30, Sat. 10–4.*

Druid Hills. In 1892 Inman Park developer Joel Hurt commissioned renowned landscape architect Frederick Law Olmsted to create a new parklike community north of Atlanta. Olmsted drew up the plans, but, due to financial problems the project languished for 8 years until the property was purchased by a consortium headed by Coca-Cola president Asa G. Candler. This group developed the 1500-acre tract into Druid Hills, one of Atlanta's most enduringly popular neighborhoods. The area is noted for its landscaped parks, tree-lined streets, and beautiful homes—many designed by Neel Reid, Walter T. Downing, and other fine architects of the day. Notable Druid Hills structures include: the 1913 Walter Rich house (⊠ 1348 Fairview Rd.), built for the owner of Rich's Department Store; Stonehenge (⊠ 1410 Ponce de Leon Ave.), a rough-hewn stone house (now part of a church complex) built in 1912 by Samuel Venable, who once owned and quarried granite from Stone Mountain; and the Sigmund Montag house (⊠ 850 Oakdale Rd.), built in 1915 by the manufacturer of Montag's Blue Horse writing tablets—a standard for generations of elementary students. A later owner was playwright Alfred Uhrey's grandmother, and his visits to the home became the inspiration for the award-winning play, *Driving Miss Daisy*. The nearby 1922 Jacob Hirsch house (⊠ 822 Lullwater Rd.), was the setting for Miss Daisy's home in the film version of the play.

㉔ Emory University. Founded as a small Methodist college in Oxford, Georgia in 1835, the school moved to this campus in 1917, after Asa G. Candler donated $1 million and land in his Druid Hills development to the college (his brother, Bishop Warren A. Candler, had served as Emory's president). New York architect Henry Hornbostel was commissioned to lay out the new campus and design the buildings. He chose the Italian Renaissance style and constructed the buildings from local marble and red-clay tiles. Today, the university's quadrangle still reflects Hornbostel's original plan. On the quad, is the highly-regarded, Michael Graves-designed, ☞ **Michael C. Carlos Museum.** Today, this once small, rural college, has a bustling campus and outstanding academic programs in medicine, law, and business. ⊠ *North Decatur Rd. at Dowman Dr.*

NEED A
BREAK? **Everybody's Pizza** (⊠ 1593 North Decatur Rd., ☎
404/377-7766), in the heart of Emory Village, has been
serving casual Italian fare since 1973.

★ � ㉒ **Fernbank Museum of Natural History.** This modern museum
maintains the largest natural-history collection south of the
Smithsonian. The permanent exhibits include 15 galleries
that showcase the state's natural beauty and an IMAX theater. ⊠ *767 Clifton Rd.,* ☎ *404/370–0960, 404/370–
0019 (IMAX).* ▦ *Museum $9.50, IMAX $7, museum and
IMAX $14.50.* ⊙ *Mon.–Sat. 10–5 (Fri. IMAX open until
9), Sun. noon–5.*

� ㉓ **Fernbank Science Center.** This 150-acre science and envi-
ronmental education center has a planetarium, an astro-
nomical observatory, and Fernbank Forest, 65 acres of
virgin woods described by naturalists as "a remarkable
treasure." ⊠ *156 Heaton Park Dr.,* ☎ *404/378–4311.* ▦
Center free, planetarium $2. ⊙ *Center Mon. 8:30–5,
Tues.–Fri. 8:30–10, Sat. 10–5, Sun. 1–5.; Observatory
Thurs.–Fri. 8 PM–10:30 PM.*

Michael C. Carlos Museum. This museum on Emory University's campus has a superb collection that includes Egyptian and Greek antiquities, pre-Columbian artifacts, and
contemporary art. ⊠ *571 South Kilgo St.,* ☎ *404/727–4282.*
▦ *$3 (suggested donation)* ⊙ *Mon.–Sat. 10–5, Sun. noon–5.*

Virginia-Highland. Laid out in 1916 as the trolley-commuter
neighborhood of North Boulevard Park (the streetcars used
to travel up North Highland Avenue), Virginia-Highland
became a popular, middle-class community of narrow
streets, lined with comfortable, Craftsman-style bungalows. The area declined after World War II, but rebounded
in popularity in the 1960s and 1970s. Today the gentrified
commercial district attracts a diverse crowd to its mix of
quaint shops and eclectic restaurants. ⊠ *Intersection of N.
Highland and Virginia Aves.*

NEED A
BREAK? The heart of Virginia-Highland has a little something for everyone. Try some hot Buffalo wings at **Taco Mac** (⊠ 1006 N.
Highland Ave., ☎ 404/873-6529), a sandwich and a cold
beer at **Moe's and Joe's Bar and Grill** (⊠ 1033 N. Highland

Ave., ☎ 404/873–6090), or something sweet at **The Dessert Place** (✉ 1000 Virginia Ave., ☎ 404/892–8921).

Atlanta University Center and the West End

Just west of Downtown are the campuses of the Atlanta University Center—the largest consortium of historically black colleges in the nation. Atlanta University was chartered in 1867, and the other schools at the center—Morris Brown, Morehouse, Clark-Atlanta University, and Spelman—were established independently, by churches or missionary associations, all for the purpose of educating freed slaves. Each began modestly, in facilities ranging from church basements to railroad boxcars, and it was a constant struggle to survive. Three of the schools—Morris Brown, Morehouse, and Spelman—pooled their resources and, in 1932, formed the Atlanta University Center. Clark College relocated to the center in 1941, and the Interdenominational Theological Center was created from several small seminaries in 1958. The Morehouse School of Medicine was established in the early 1980s; and in 1988, Clark College consolidated with the Atlanta University graduate schools to form Clark-Atlanta University. A short distance from the campus is the stately home of Alonzo F. Herndon, the former slave who, in the early days of the century, was the richest black man in America.

South of the university campus, along Ralph David Abernathy Drive and the surrounding side streets, is the historic community of West End. Founded as a stagecoach stop in the 1830s, West End became a popular Victorian-era suburb of Atlanta. Many of the turn-of-the-century homes have been restored. Among them are the Wren's Nest cottage, home of author Joel Chandler Harris; and the Hammonds House, an antebellum residence remodeled in the Victorian style in the 1880s.

Numbers in the text correspond to numbers in the margin and on the Atlanta Neighborhoods map.

A Good Drive

Begin your tour by driving west on MLK Drive, past the Georgia Dome to the intersection of Vine Street. Ahead is the campus of **Morris Brown College** ㉖ Atop the hill to the left is Fountain Hall. On the opposite side of MLK Drive is Gaines Hall.

Turn right on Vine Street, and then right again on University Place. As you turn, you will see modern Alonzo F. Herndon Stadium. On your right is the 1910 Professor George Towns house (✉ 594 University Pl.). In 1966 Towns's daughter, Grace Towns Hamilton, became the first black woman to serve in the Georgia legislature. Directly across the street is the **Alonzo F. Herndon Home** ㉗. After touring the house museum, travel south on Walnut Street, across MLK Drive, to the intersection of Beckwith Street. Turn right and follow Beckwith, past the small complex of the Interdenominational Theological Center (✉ 671 Beckwith St., ☎ 404/527–7700), a meeting place that several small seminaries share.

At James P. Brawley Drive turn left past the modern glass and brick Robert Woodruff Library (✉ 111 James P. Brawley Dr.) and travel to the intersection of Fair Street. From this point, Brawley Drive becomes a pedestrian-only pathway between the campuses of **Clark–Atlanta University** ㉘ and **Morehouse College** ㉙. Turn right and follow Fair Street to Ashby Street. Turn left on Ashby and then left on Westview Drive. At the security post, an officer will direct you to convenient parking, either on the street or in a nearby visitor lot.

After parking, continue your tour on foot. Begin with a visit to the Martin Luther King, Jr. International Chapel on Westview Drive. Walk north to the quadrangle and visit the exhibits in the Clark–Atlanta University Art Gallery in Trevor–Arnett Hall. Then walk across the L-shape lawn, past the Research Center for Science and Technology, and on to see the statue of Dr. Benjamin Mays, longtime Morehouse president and mentor to Martin Luther King, Jr. and many other civil rights leaders. Behind the statue is Graves Hall, the symbolic heart of the Morehouse campus.

Retrace your steps, cross Greens Ferry Avenue, and enter the campus of **Spelman College** ㉚. Directly ahead on the right is the modern Cosby Academic Center, containing the Spelman College Museum of Fine Art. After touring the museum, stroll around the small, pastoral campus to see Packard Hall, Sisters' Chapel, and other beautiful buildings.

Return to your car and exit the Atlanta University Center campus. Turn left on Ashby Street, and cross under I–20. Turn right on Ralph David Abernathy Drive and enter the historic community of **West End** ㉛. Ahead on the right is the West End Performing Arts Center (✉ 945 Abernathy Dr.). Continue on Abernathy Drive, past Howell Park, and turn right on Peeples Street. Two blocks ahead, on the left are the **Hammonds House Galleries and Resource Center of African-American Art** ㉜. After a visit to the gallery, retrace your steps to Abernathy Drive and turn right. Just ahead on the left is West Hunter Street Baptist Church (✉ 1040 Abernathy Dr.). Next door to the church is the **Wren's Nest** ㉝, the former home of writer Joel Chandler Harris. To see some Victorian houses before leaving West End, turn left from Abernathy Drive to Lawton Street. At the intersection, turn left on Oglethorpe Avenue: Along Oglethorpe, Peeples Street, and Gordon Place, are a number of renovated structures. Return to Abernathy Drive, turn right, and then turn left on Ashby Street. Follow the signs to I–20 east for the return to downtown Atlanta.

TIMING

If you explore all the campuses, this tour will take a full day; if you are more selective, however, you will be able to cut the tour down to a half day.

Sights to See

★ ㉗ **Alonzo F. Herndon Home.** In 1910 African-American craftspeople designed and built this exquisite Georgian Revival house for Herndon, founder of the Atlanta Life Insurance Company and Atlanta's first black millionaire. The preserved house is now a museum filled with Herndon's furnishings, art collection, and other family memorabilia. Across the street is the **Grace Towns Hamilton house** (✉ 594 University Pl.), the former home of the first African-American woman elected to the Georgia state legislature (1966). ✉ 587 University Pl., ☎ 404/581–9813. 🎟 Free. ☉ Tues.–Sat. 10–4. MARTA: Vine City.

㉘ **Clark-Atlanta University.** Clark College was established in 1865 by the American Missionary Association and it moved to the Atlanta University Center campus in 1941. In 1988 the college consolidated with Atlanta University. A tangible example of the excellent educational and research facilities at Clark-Atlanta is the new Research Center for Science and Technology on the Clark Atlanta–Morehouse quadrangle. Visit the **Clark-Atlanta University Art Gallery** in Trevor-Arnett Hall. ⊠ *James P. Brawley Dr. at Fair St.,* ☎ *404/880–8000; 404/880–6644 gallery.* ⌧ *Gallery free.* ☉ *Gallery Tues.–Fri. 11–4, Sat. noon–4. MARTA: Vine City.*

㉜ Hammonds House Galleries and Resource Center of African-American Art. The galleries occupy a beautiful 1857 house that was remodeled in the Eastlake Victorian style in the 1880s. For many years it was the residence of Dr. O. T. Hammonds, an avid collector of African-American art. His private holdings became the foundation for the current collection. ⊠ *503 Peeples St.,* ☎ *404/752–8730.* ⌧ *$2.* ☉ *Tues.–Fri. 10–6, weekends 1–5. MARTA: West End.*

㉙ Morehouse College. This college may be best known as the alma mater of civil rights leader Dr. Martin Luther King, Jr., Olympian Edwin Moses, former cabinet member Dr. Louis Sullivan, and film director Spike Lee. Morehouse has earned a reputation for preparing leaders in government, business, and medicine, among other disciplines. On the quadrangle, the Romanesque Graves Hall, built in 1889, is a Morehouse landmark while across Westview Avenue, the Martin Luther King, Jr. Interdenominational Chapel, is a gathering place for students from across Atlanta University. ⊠ *830 Westview Dr.,* ☎ *404/681–2800. MARTA: Vine City.*

㉖ Morris Brown College. Founded in the basement of Big Bethel AME Church (☞ *Sweet Auburn, above*) in 1881, Morris Brown moved to the Atlanta University campus in 1932. Landmark campus buildings include the Romanesque-revival Fountain Hall, with its distinctive clock-tower, built in 1882; the Italianate Gaines Hall, the first building on the Atlanta University campus, completed in 1869; and Alonzo F. Herndon Stadium, home of the Morris Brown football team. ⊠ *643 MLK Dr.,* ☎ *404/220–0270. MARTA: Vine City.*

. . . .

NEED A
BREAK?
   Paschal's Restaurant (⊠ 830 MLK Dr., ☎ 404/577–3150) is where many Civil Rights movement leaders met to strategize over plates of chicken, biscuits, and other Southern

dishes. The restaurant and adjacent lodge and conference center are now owned by Clark-Atlanta University.

....

30 **Spelman College.** Established in 1881 as the Atlanta Baptist Female Seminary, this college's first classrooms were in the basement of nearby Friendship Baptist Church. Word of the struggling school reached industrialist John D. Rockefeller, and he made generous financial contributions to support it. In appreciation, the school's name was changed to Spelman Seminary to honor his wife, Laura Spelman. Today, the quiet, cloistered campus is a fine college and is still single sex. Notable campus buildings include the Camille Cosby Academic Center, a gift from actor-comedian Bill Cosby, housing the **Spelman Museum of Fine Art**; Rockefeller Hall, an imposing 1886 Romanesque Revival structure; Sophia Packard Hall, named for one of the school's founders, completed in 1888; and Sister's Chapel, a magnificent Greek Revival auditorium designed by architect Neel Reid, and built in 1923. ⊠ *350 Spelman La.,* ☎ *404/681–3643.* ✆ *Museum $3 suggested donation.* ☉ *Museum Tues.–Fri. 10–5, Sat. noon–5. MARTA: Vine City.*

31 **West End.** Established in 1835 at White Hall Tavern, a stagecoach stop on the Newnan–Decatur Road, this community was Atlanta's first residential suburb. It acquired the name West End in the 1870s, when it was the final stop on the western trolley line from Downtown Atlanta. The convenience to the downtown business district spurred residential growth and by the 1890s, West End had become one of the city's most popular neighborhoods. Notable Atlantans who maintained homes here included *Atlanta Constitution* editor E.P. Howell; author Joel Chandler Harris (☞ Wren's Nest, *below*); and Dean Rusk, who became Secretary of State under President John F. Kennedy.

In the 1950s, West End was bisected by the construction of I–20 and the area went into decline. In the 1960s, black Atlantans, especially staff and professors from nearby Atlanta University, began purchasing and occupying many of the old homes. In the 1980s, some of West End's finest Victorian houses underwent extensive restoration and began attracting both black and white buyers, making West End, today, one of the city's most multicultural communities. ⊠

In case you want to see the world.

At American Express, we're here to make your journey a smooth one. So we have over 1,700 travel service locations in over 120 countries ready to help. What else would you expect from the world's largest travel agency?

do more ®

http://www.americanexpress.com/travel

In case you want to be welcomed there.

We're here to see that you're always welcomed at establishments everywhere. That's why millions of people carry the American Express® Card – for peace of mind, confidence, and security, around the world or just around the corner.

do more ®

Cards

In case you're running low.

We're here to help with more than 118,000 Express Cash locations around the world. In order to enroll, just call American Express before you start your vacation.

do more

Express Cash

And just in case.

We're here with American Express® Travelers Cheques and Cheques *for Two*.® They're the safest way to carry money on your vacation and the surest way to get a refund, practically anywhere, anytime.
Another way we help you...

AMERICAN
EXPRESS

do more ℠

Travelers Cheques

Ralph David Abernathy Blvd. and Ashby St. MARTA: West End.

★ ☪ ㉝ **Wren's Nest.** This home was built in 1867 and remodeled by Joel Chandler Harris, a journalist for the *Atlanta Constitution* and the author of the African American tales known collectively as *Uncle Remus: His Songs and Sayings,* in 1884. The house has been a museum of Chandler memorabilia since 1913; especially popular are the frequent storytelling sessions. ✉ *1050 Ralph David Abernathy Blvd.,* ☎ *404/753–7735.* ≊ *$3.* ☉ *Tues.–Sat. 10–4, Sun. 1–4. MARTA: West End.*

Greater Atlanta

☪ **American Adventures** and **White Water.** These two adjacent theme parks are a kid's dream come true. Highlights of the former include a $1 million tree house, the Foam Factory Funhouse, miniature golf course, and go-kart racetrack. White Water is Atlanta's largest water theme park. ✉ *250 Cobb Pkwy. N,* ☎ *770/424–9283.* ≊ *American Adventures $14.99, White Water $19.99.* ☉ *Memorial Day–Labor Day, Mon.–Thurs. 11–7, Fri.–Sun. 10–9; hrs vary rest of yr, so call ahead.*

Chateau Elán. About 45 minutes from Downtown, the centerpiece of this 3,100-acre winery and resort is the Renaissance French château housing Georgia's premier winery, an art gallery, restaurant, and visitor center. European luxury blends with southern hospitality at this 146-room resort with a spa. Winery tours and tastings are free. The resort has three golf courses, a fishing lake, a tennis facility, and an equestrian center. ✉ *100 Tour de France, I–85 to Exit 48, Braselton,* ☎ *770/932–0900.*

Chattahoochee River National Recreation Area. Spread over 48 mi of the Chattahoochee River, this area provides a wide range of recreational activities: hiking, fly-fishing (a Georgia fishing license is required), or running the river's Class II and III rapids in a raft, canoe, or kayak. ✉ *1978 Island Ford Pkwy.,* ☎ *770/952–4419.* ≊ *Free.*

★ **Kennesaw Mountain National Battlefield Park.** A must for Civil War buffs, this 2,884-acre park with 16 mi of hiking trails was the site of several crucial battles in June 1864. The visitor center contains a small museum with exhibits of Civil War weapons, uniforms, and various items recovered from the battlefield; a 10-minute slide presentation explains the battles. ⊠ *Old U.S. 41 and Stilesboro Rd., Kennesaw (look for signs on I-75N),* ☎ *770/427-4686.* ✆ *Free.* ⊘ *Daily 8:30-5.*

Roswell. Visitors who come to Atlanta in search of *Gone With the Wind*'s legendary plantation, Tara, need only travel about 20 mi north of Downtown to see some of the area's finest surviving antebellum houses. Roswell King established a textile mill (now adapted for use as shops and restaurants) on the Chattahoochee River in 1839, and some of the fine homes that the early settlers built have been preserved. For details on sightseeing, stop in at the **Roswell Visitor Center** (⊠ 617 Atlanta St., ☎ 770/640-3253) on the town square. It is open weekdays 9-5, Saturday 10-4, and Sunday noon-3. ⊠ *Atlanta St. (Roswell Rd.) and GA Rte. 120.*

★ ☾ **Six Flags Over Georgia.** There are more than 100 rides here, many of them heart-stopping roller coasters and water rides. The park also presents well-staged musical revues, diving demonstrations, concerts by top-name artists, and other special events. The newest attraction is Batman—The Ride, a thrilling roller coaster. ⊠ *I-20 at 7561 Six Flags Rd.,* ☎ *770/948-9290.* ✆ *$32.* ⊘ *June-Aug., daily 10 AM-11 PM; Mar.-May and Sept.-Oct., weekends only (closing times vary). From MARTA: Hightower station, take Six Flags shuttle (Bus 201; $2.25).*

☾ **Southeastern Railway Museum.** A delight for rail buffs of all ages, the museum has more than 70 steam and diesel locomotives and passenger and freight cars in addition to more than 7,000 items of railroad memorabilia. Kids may climb on the trains or take short rides on both a full-size and a miniature train (third Saturday of each month). ⊠ *3966 Buford Hwy.,* ☎ *770/476-2013.* ✆ *$5.* ⊘ *Sat. 9-5; also open Sun. noon-5, Apr.-Nov.*

★ ☾ **Stone Mountain Park.** This 3,200-acre family playground, 16 mi east of Downtown, is filled with a variety of recreational opportunities in a beautiful natural setting. Dominating the park is one of the nation's great natural wonders—825-ft Stone Mountain, the largest exposed granite outcropping on earth. On the north face of the mountain is the world's largest sculpture, the *Confederate Memorial*—a bas-relief carving of Confederate president Jefferson Davis and generals Stonewall Jackson and Robert E. Lee. Mount Rushmore sculptor Gutzon Borglum began the carving in 1923; it was completed nearly 50 years later. Visit the park's **Discovering Stone Mountain Museum** to learn more about the natural and human history of the mountain.

You may get a close-up view of the carving from the mountaintop skylift or from the cars of the **Stone Mountain Railroad,** an old steam train that rambles on a 5-mi circle around the mountain's base. The **Antebellum Plantation** was assembled from buildings relocated to the park from throughout Georgia. In the plantation complex is the **Road to Tara Museum,** with displays about Margaret Mitchell and the film version of *Gone With the Wind.* For more Civil War history, visit **Confederate Memorial Hall,** with its diorama. Behind the hall is the historic **Walk-up Trail,** a 1.3-mi footpath that climbs to the summit.

The park has an **Antique Car and Treasure Museum,** a **Wildlife Preserve and Petting Farm,** and excursion rides on Stone Mountain Lake aboard the *Scarlett O'Hara Riverboat.* The park also has two 18-hole golf courses, a tennis center built for the 1996 Olympic Games, and a swimming beach. Summer evenings are capped off with a popular laserlight show beamed across the face of the mountain. Two hotels, a conference center, a campground, and six restaurants are also in the park. Just west of the park is **Stone Mountain Village,** a small 19th-century community filled with quaint shops and cafés. ⊠ *U.S. 78, Stone Mountain Pkwy., Stone Mountain,* ☎ *770/498–5690.* ⊐ *$6 per car; additional fees for individual attractions and special events.* ☉ *Daily 6 AM–midnight. MARTA: Avondale, then take Bus 120 and transfer to Bus 119.*

3 Dining

By Jane
Garvey

ATLANTA HAS COME ALIVE as a restaurant town. You can dine on piroshkis and pecan pie, lap up aromatic Thai soups, or lick barbecue off your fingers. Southern cooking still stews in the many "meat-and-three" establishments that serve several meats with a choice of traditional vegetables, but most of the world is also represented here. Decent French and reasonably authentic Italian restaurants have opened in the past few years. The recent influx of immigrants from Asia has moved Chinese restaurants beyond the egg roll to embrace genuine Asian cooking, and Moroccan, Ethiopian, and Jamaican restaurants add their share of seasoning to the mix.

Prepare to explore two forms of southern food: home-style cooking just like Mother used to make and elegant, refined dishes that use the ingredients of southern cooking in surprising ways. Savor Cajun cuisine at the French Quarter Food Shop, then see what the brash young chefs are doing to redefine this food. Horseradish Grill or South City Kitchen can show you the new, while the Colonnade Restaurant sticks with tradition.

And tradition is everything for the southerner when it comes to food. The term *soul food* notwithstanding, all southerners eat greens and fried chicken. And barbecue, a regional favorite, is more than grilled meat: It's both the process (slow cooking over a low wood fire) and the sauce, which varies widely. At Dusty's, taste North Carolina 'cue, and get a taste of Texas at the Rib Ranch.

Generally, the most chic, adventurous dining spots are in Buckhead. On a weekend night, parking there is at such a premium that taking a taxi is a good idea, even if you have a car. Asian restaurants are scattered throughout the metropolitan area, but some of the best ones line Buford Highway, which leads from Cheshire Bridge and Lenox roads to beyond the Perimeter, I–285. Here, authentic taco parlors sit cheek by jowl with sushi bars. Also look for interesting dining in Virginia-Highland, a renovated neighborhood now brimming with establishments that serve exotic as well as familiar fare. Metro stops are only listed when they are convenient.

Meanwhile, you may savor both simple and sumptuous dining in restaurants in shopping centers and strip malls that house restaurants ranging from ordinary to upscale. When the absolutely opulent Pano's and Paul's opened between a furniture store and a grocery, many forecast its doom. Instead, the owners now operate nine restaurants.

Atlantans enjoy casual and down-at-the-heels establishments, but this is also a town that loves to glitter. When men don jacket and tie, women may be seen in anything from business attire to the classic little black dress. Casual includes everything from designer jeans to silk jumpsuits with rhinestone straps. To some extent, price range should guide patrons: A $$$$ establishment calls for jacket and tie; places listed as $$$ and under may welcome stylish casual attire or jeans. When in doubt, call and ask.

It's wise to make reservations, especially on weekends. Places that generally do not accept reservations may make an exception for a large group. It's worth a call. As for tipping, 15% is a good rule; add 20% to the bill if you're particularly pleased.

If anything frustrates diners in Atlanta, it's the quality of service, which can vary from the most competent to the purely perfunctory. And while many finer restaurants have established good wine lists and hired excellent sommeliers, second-tier restaurants still struggle with wine servers capable of little more than announcing that the house wines are white, blush, and red.

Caveats aside, approach culinary Atlanta with a sense of adventure and a determination to seek out the unfamiliar. Do that, and you'll experience some superb dining.

CATEGORY	COST*
$$$$	over $45
$$$	$35–$45
$$	$25–$35
$	under $25

per person for a three-course meal, excluding drinks, tip, and 6% tax

Downtown

American

$$–$$$ ✕ **The Food Studio.** Stylish and hip, with an adjacent gallery for monumental pieces of art, this fun newcomer packs 'em in. The menu changes frequently, but dishes often have a southern, Italian, or Asian touch. The rabbit enchilada, cheese-tasting plate, turkey (sometimes grilled—sometimes smoked), and cold berry soup for dessert are popular. ⊠ *887 W. Marietta St., Studio K-102, King Plow Arts Center,* ☎ *404/815–6677. Reservations essential on weekends. AE, DC, MC, V.*

$–$$$ ✕ **Pleasant Peasant.** This simple space with brick walls and high, pressed-tin ceilings became a hit for contemporary, casual dining more than two decades ago. The menu, which changes frequently, is listed on chalkboards. Classic French onion soup defines the Peasant's sense of comfort food, as does plum pork—tender pork slices in a plum-sauce glaze, served with mashed sweet potatoes and crisp, tender green beans. Save room for the chocolate mousse cake. ⊠ *555 Peachtree St., at Linden Ave.,* ☎ *404/874–3223. Reservations not accepted. AE, D, DC, MC, V. No lunch weekends. MARTA: North Ave.*

$–$$ ✕ **Sylvia's.** South Carolina–native and Harlem, New York–resident Sylvia Woods has brought her brand of "soul food" to its native turf. Coals to Newcastle? Perhaps. But downtowner office denizens are hungry for her touch with southern classics, including ribs, oxtails, cobbler, and that old southern specialty, red velvet cake. Bring a gang—at least four—and enjoy Sylvia's family style meal for $16.95 per person. ⊠ *241 Central Ave.,* ☎ *404/529–9692. AE, D, MC, V. MARTA: Five Points.*

American/Continental Contemporary

$$$–$$$$ ✕ **The Abbey.** In a desanctified church, The Abbey has
★ been an Atlanta dining institution since 1968. Stained-glass windows in shades of blue remain in place, and a harpist in the former choir loft reinforces the celestial theme. In restaurants like this, gimmickry can overshadow culinary quality, but chef Richard Lindamood produces worthy food. Trust whatever he does with foie gras, snails, breast of duck, sea bass, and salmon. The wine list is weighty. ⊠

72

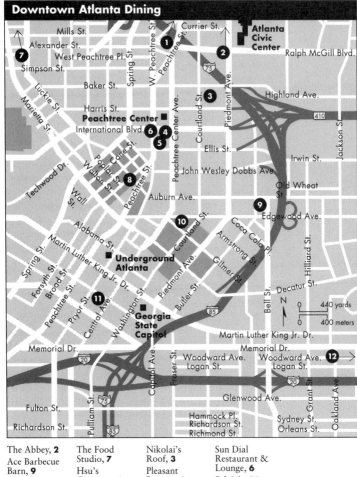

Downtown Atlanta Dining

The Abbey, **2**

Ace Barbecue
Barn, **9**

Café la
Glace, **12**

City Grill, **10**

The Food
Studio, **7**

Hsu's
Gourmet, **4**

Mumbo
Jumbo, **8**

Nikolai's
Roof, **3**

Pleasant
Peasant, **1**

The
Restaurant, **5**

Sun Dial
Restaurant &
Lounge, **6**

Sylvia's, **11**

163 Ponce de Leon Ave., ☎ 404/876–8532. AE, D, DC, MC, V. No lunch. MARTA: North Ave.

$$–$$$$ ✗ **Sun Dial Restaurant & Lounge.** Diners slowly spin around the circular room and enjoy the changing view. While the restaurant is known for its steaks, fish, and chicken, lamb and veal are also good choices. Grilled swordfish with mixed-bean salad and three-pepper stew is superb and healthy. Dinner entrées, priced $29–$49.50, are complete meals, with shrimp cocktail and Caesar salad included. ⌧ *210 Peachtree St., in Westin Peachtree Plaza Hotel, ☎ 404/589–7506. AE, D, DC, MC, V. No lunch Sun. MARTA: Peachtree Center.*

$$–$$$ ✗ **City Grill.** The grand stone staircase in the historic Hurt
★ Building leads to this restaurant's formal yet comfortable clublike interior. The multilevel, high-ceiling spaces are ideal for business discussions. Southern ingredients appear in many dishes, including quail served with traditional cream gravy over raspberry–black pepper biscuits, barbecue shrimp on grits with *maquechoux* (a corn-based relish), and barbecued duck on wilted greens. The extensive wine list is the work of a knowledgeable sommelier. ⌧ *50 Hurt Plaza, ☎ 404/524–2489. Reservations essential on weekends. Jacket and tie. AE, D, DC, MC, V. Closed Sun. No lunch Sat. MARTA: Five Points.*

Barbecue

$ ✗ **Ace Barbecue Barn.** This classic, no-frills hole-in-the-wall fits the bill when you're looking for good barbecue. Besides ribs and the splendid sliced-barbecue sandwich, Ace has superior baked chicken and traditional southern vegetables, such as collard greens. ⌧ *30 Bell St., off Auburn Ave., ☎ 404/659–6630. Reservations not accepted. No credit cards. MARTA: Five Points.*

Chinese

$–$$ ✗ **Hsu's Gourmet.** Winsome Anna and Raymond Hsu work the crowd in their Peachtree Center restaurant, a modern space with Chinese accents that include a fine collection of jade. More Americans than Asians come here, perhaps because the food, in Hong Kong style, reflects some Western influences. The seven shrimp dishes are among the best in town; tops are shrimp with black bean sauce, and asparagus and shrimp with fresh mango. Pay attention to specials, especially if the waiter mentions steamed sea bass with ginger. ⊠ *192 Peachtree Center Ave., at International Blvd.,* ☎ *404/659–2788. AE, D, DC, MC, V. No lunch Sun. MARTA: Peachtree Center.*

Continental Contemporary

$$$$ ✕ **Nikolai's Roof.** At the top of the Atlanta Hilton and Tow-
★ ers, Nikolai's Roof provides a view that makes dining a special experience, for both business and romantic endeavors.
The only remaining Russian touch appears in piroshkis of
beef and chicken, to be dipped into béarnaise sauce. Otherwise, the cooking is classic French Continental, including such
dishes as beef tenderloin with shallot–and–red-wine sauce and
beef marrow, braised lamb shank on truffled risotto, and hot
almond soufflée. The extensive wine list focuses on top vin-
tages and labels from around the world. No à la carte is available; only a fixed-price ($62.50) seven-course dinner is
offered. ⊠ *255 Courtland St., at Harris St.,* ☎ *404/221–
6362. Reservations essential. Set seatings Fri.–Sat. and other
busy evenings at 6:30 and 9:30. Jacket and tie. AE, D, DC,
MC, V. No lunch. MARTA: Peachtree Center.*

$$–$$$$ ✕ **The Restaurant.** Its walls hung with paintings of hunt
scenes, The Restaurant has a plush, masculine formality that
makes an ideal business dining spot. Chef Daniel Schaff-
hauser, a native of Alsace, presents a seasonally changing
menu with Asian and regional American touches. Cornish
hen stuffed with crab meat, buffalo with soft-shell crab, and
cardamom-scented grilled foie gras were among the re-
cently offered treats. Ask about the tasting menu with co-
ordinated wines. An able sommelier administers the
well-selected wine list. ⊠ *Ritz-Carlton, Atlanta, 181
Peachtree St., at Ellis St.,* ☎ *404/659–0400, ext. 6450.
Jacket and tie. AE, D, DC, MC, V. Closed Sun. No lunch
Sat. MARTA: Peachtree Center.*

French

$$–$$$ ✕ **Café la Glace.** This authentic French bistro proves that
★ good food will attract patrons. People come in droves to
this work-in-progress neighborhood for foie gras–stuffed
homemade ravioli, unusual carpaccio (sometimes emu or
buffalo), and homemade desserts. It's a gem! ⊠ *62 Boule-
vard, Grant Park,* ☎ *404/622–3114. AE, D, MC, V. Closed
Sun.–Mon. No dinner Tues.–Wed. No lunch Sat.*

Fusion

$–$$$$ ✕ **Mumbo Jumbo.** This newcomer has quickly become the
★ place to see and be seen. A long bar runs along the left, and
to the right an open kitchen reveals busy chefs. The rear
dining room is centered by a huge fireplace. The menu, with
Asian and Tuscan touches, changes regularly, but you'll find
interesting seafood dishes (any dish with crab or other
shellfish is likely to be stellar), soups, and desserts. Look
for Manila clams in an aromatic broth, sea bass glazed with
cardamom-flavored honey, and chocolate timbale. There's
occasional live music. ✉ *489 Park Pl.,* ☎ *404/523–0330.*
*AE, D, DC, MC, V. No lunch weekends. MARTA: Peachtree
Center.*

Buckhead

American

$$–$$$$ ✕ **Bone's.** Autographed images of celebrities and black-and-
★ white photos depicting Atlanta through the years line the
walls of this masculine steak house. Fish, chicken, and
lamb are also served, but singularly outstanding is the powerfully flavored lobster bisque. The wine list is extensive
and award-winning. ✉ *3130 Piedmont Rd., near Peachtree
Rd.,* ☎ *404/237–2663. AE, DC, MC, V. No lunch weekends. MARTA: Buckhead.*

$$–$$$ ✕ **Canoe.** This location has been a favorite Atlanta enter-
★ tainment site for generations. Prior to that, Union soldiers
crossed the Chattahoochee River here—the river laps at the
banks of the property. Within and on its outdoor dining
spaces, guests come for rock-shrimp cakes, superior beer-
batter fried chicken with sweet potato hash, and, for dessert,
chocolate hazelnut praline cake. The wine list is outstanding. ✉ *4199 Paces Ferry Rd.,* ☎ *770/432–2663. AE, D,
DC, MC, V.*

$–$$$ ✕ **Atlanta Fish Market.** High-energy, contemporary, and,
for some, far too noisy, this large restaurant is nonetheless
very popular. Its upscale modern interior suggests the look
of a train station, with high ceilings and parts seemingly
left unfinished; the more intimate Geechee Porch, adjacent
to the dining room, is quieter. Crab is a specialty: soft-shell
crab, crab cake, crab fries, and stone-crab claws are splen-
did. Fried is the southern way to enjoy fish and seafood,

76

Atlanta Neighborhoods Dining

KEY

AE American Express Office

Northside Pkwy.

W. Paces Ferry Rd.

Northside Dr.

Piedmont

Roswell Rd.

Rd.

Northwest

Mill

Moores

Northside

Peachtree

Creek

Expwy.

Smyrna-Marietta Rd.

Dr.

Lindbergh R

Peachtree

Rd.

**ANSLEY
PARK**

Piedmont Road

Buckhead Loop

Roxboro Rd.

Roswell Rd

237

W. Paces Ferry Rd

Peachtree Road

Maple Dr.

Buckhead Ave.

Pharr Rd.

Lenox Road

Peachtree St.

W. Peachtree St.

MIDTObN

BUCKHEAD

Simpson St.

DOWNTOWN

**SEE DOWNTOWN
ATLANTA
DINING MAP**

Po

57

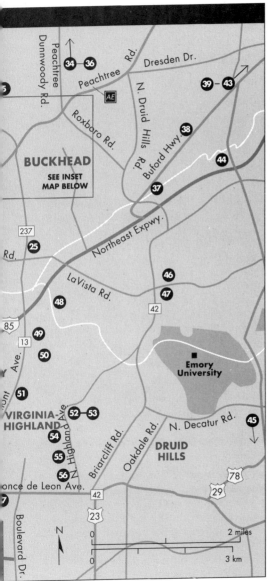

Maggiano's Little Italy, **14**

Mambo Restaurante Cubano, **52**

Mary Mac's Tea Room, **57**

McKendrick's, **34**

McKinnon's Louisiane, **12**

Mi Spia, **36**

NAVA, **10**

Palisades, **32**

Pano's and Paul's, **2**

Phoenix Brew Pub, **33**

Pricci, **13**

Prime, **17**

Rib Ranch, **7**

Riviera, **24**

R.J.'s Uptown Kitchen and Wine Bar, **55**

The Restaurant, **58**

Sa Tsu Ki, **37**

South City Kitchen, **59**

Stringer's Fish Camp and Oyster Bar, **40**

Sundown Cafe, **48**

Terra Cotta, **56**

Thai Chilli, **46**

TomTom, **18**

Toulouse, **29**

Veni Vidi Vici, **60**

Violette, **44**

Zócalo, **61**

but broiled is an option as well. For dessert, consider Key lime pie and white-chocolate-chunk banana crème brûlée. ⊠ *265 Pharr Rd.,* ☎ *404/262–3165. AE, D, DC, MC, V. No lunch Sun.*

$–$$$ ✕ **Blue Ridge Grill.** With its ambiance of sophisticated rustic charm, Blue Ridge Grill takes design notes from the north Georgia mountains. Business and family dining are popular here. Although not every dish is a hit (wood-grilled roasted vegetables come more like charred), signature dishes like smoked trout and crab cake, shrimp and vegetable dumplings with lime sauce, excellent soups (spicy gumbo and Hoppin' John especially), and grilled fish are most worthy. ⊠ *1261 W. Paces Ferry Rd.,* ☎ *404/233–5030. AE, D, DC, MC, V. No lunch Sat.*

$–$$ ✕ **Buckhead Diner.** Outside, this million-dollar faux diner
★ shimmers in chrome, and bands of glowing neon outline it. Inside, inlaid wood, Italian leather, hand-cut marble, and mellow lights establish a languorous ambiance reminiscent of the *Orient Express.* The inventive dishes at this popular restaurant are anything but diner fare: salt-and-pepper squid; fresh goat cheese in a tomato fondue; and a wicked, piled-high banana–and–white-chocolate cream pie. Veal meat loaf, with celeriac-whipped mashed potatoes and shiitake mushrooms, demonstrates substantial, basic good cooking. ⊠ *3073 Piedmont Rd.,* ☎ *404/262–3336. Reservations not accepted. AE, D, DC, MC, V. MARTA: Buckhead.*

$–$$ ✕ **Houston's.** This Atlanta-based chain consistently turns out good food in a neighborhood pub-type atmosphere, with a friendly bar and comfortable seating. Excellent rotisserie chicken with mashed potatoes, grilled fish, and a Thai-inspired grilled chicken salad are popular. ⊠ *3321 Lenox Rd., across from Lenox Sq.,* ☎ *404/237–7534; 4 other locations.*

American/Continental Contemporary

$$$$ ✕ **The Dining Room.** A grand staircase sweeps up to the mez-
★ zanine level of one of the city's finest hotels and leads to its highly rated restaurant, the Dining Room. Tables are well spaced and the warmly lit interior suggests the comfortable formality of a private club. Joel Antunes, a world-class chef, replaced Gunther Seeger in the kitchen in May 1997. The prix-fixe menu ($65 for three courses, $78 for five courses;

add $34 for wine pairings) changes nightly. Dishes have included a creamy vichysoisse-like cold white-bean soup with Parmesan rounds and generous shavings of truffles; meaty black bass with arugula, pecans, gnocchi, and salsify; and white and dark chocolate marble cake with almond cream. Flatware-impaired diners beware. The wine list and the service from a superbly trained sommelier are stunning. ⊠ *Ritz-Carlton, Buckhead, 3434 Peachtree Rd.,* ☎ *404/237–2700. Reservations essential on weekends. Jacket and tie. AE, D, DC, MC, V. No lunch. Closed Sun. MARTA: Lenox Sq.*

$–$$$$ ✕ **Pano's and Paul's.** Pano Karatassos and Paul Albrecht broke the rules when they located their first restaurant in a strip shopping center. Its luxurious, neo-rococo interior that feels like a Venetian palace is a pleasant surprise. The dining room, with walls draped in a soft rose fabric, serves excellent soft-shell crab and foie gras. Look for pheasant and other occasional game dishes, sautéed Gulf red snapper fillet, and cold jumbo lobster tail fried in a light batter and served with Chinese honey mustard. The serious wine list is well administered. ⊠ *1232 W. Paces Ferry Rd.,* ☎ *404/261–3662. Reservations essential. Jacket required. AE, D, DC, MC, V. Closed Sun. No lunch.*

$$$ ✕ **Bacchanalia.** This is one of the city's best restaurants—
★   intimate and romantic, with well-spaced tables. Patrons are upscale, well attired, and interested in good, inventive food. Anne Quatrano and Clifford Harrison, chefs and owners, dazzle diners with cooking they label new American, but which has country-Mediterranean and occasional Asian touches. Dishes change weekly and could include foie gras for a starter and pheasant with wild mushrooms as an entrée. Ice cream made at the restaurant is the star of the dessert list. The fixed price ($40) includes four courses; you can also order à la carte. ⊠ *3125 Piedmont Rd., near Peachtree Rd.,* ☎ *404/365–0410. Reservations essential on weekends. AE, DC, MC, V. No smoking. Closed Sun.–Mon. No lunch. MARTA: Buckhead.*

Barbecue

$ ✕ **Rib Ranch.** The Lone Star flag flies outside this shack-style outpost of Texas barbecue in the heart of Buckhead. Locals plant elbows on red oilcloth table covers while waiting for tender, beautifully executed barbecued beef ribs. Baby-back pork ribs may also be ordered, as well as good turkey and sausage. The thick, tomato-based barbecue sauce, scented generously with cumin, recalls Midwestern-style 'cue. ⊠ *25 Irby Ave.,* ☏ *404/233–7644. Reservations not accepted. AE, MC, V.*

Caribbean

$–$$ ✕ **Arugula.** The flavors of Caribbean cuisine and classical European techniques combine in this bright, youthful environment. Cornmeal-fried calamari comes with a black bean relish; pan-fried mahimahi is accompanied by bananas, roasted almonds, and seasoned rice. ⊠ *3639 Piedmont Rd., near Roswell Rd.,* ☏ *404/814–0959. AE, MC, V. No lunch weekends.*

Continental Contemporary

$–$$$$ ✕ **Palisades.** Occupying the corner of a 1920s commercial strip, Palisades has exposed-brick walls that add texture to the space and provide a casual, neighborhood-bistro ambience. Fried green tomatoes, crumb-crusted lamb with herbs, and crisp duck with sweet-potato pancakes and fresh spinach meld the flavors of the Mediterranean and southern America. In addition to à la carte options, a three-course fixed-price menu is available Sunday through Thursday. ⊠ *1829 Peachtree Rd.,* ☏ *404/350–6755. AE, D, DC, MC, V. No lunch.*

$–$$$$ ✕ **TomTom.** Mall dining of unexpected quality makes a shopping break at TomTom something to plan for. The art-filled, modern space opens onto Lenox Square's plaza level. Afternoon snacking on bistro bites could have one sampling calamari, scallops, and rock shrimp in a spicy sauce or seared tuna with wasabi and ginger. The deep-fried whole catfish with Asian seasonings is a to-share appetizer. Heftier entrées include roast chicken or leg of lamb on mashed potatoes. ⊠ *3393 Peachtree Rd., Lenox Sq.,* ☏ *404/264–1163. Reservations accepted for 8 or more. AE, D, DC, MC, V. MARTA: Lenox Sq.*

$–$$ ✕ **Luna Sí.** This funky, chic restaurant is a hit with gourmets
★ on a budget. The interior, divided by gauze-like fabric drapings, captures the feeling of an artist's loft. The menu changes daily, but dishes are always light on fat and salt—vegetarian dishes stand out. Salmon with a ginger-crumb crust and orange sauce and roast Cornish hen with mashed

potatoes are too popular to leave the menu. Ask about the tasting menu. Desserts, which vary daily, normally include a fabulous crème brûlée. ⊠ *1931 Peachtree Rd.,* ☎ *404/355–5993. Reservations not accepted. AE, D, MC, V. No lunch Sun.*

Cuban

$–$$ ✕ **Coco Loco.** This small, spare establishment, almost lost in a sprawling shopping mall, has earned respect for its cooking among Hispanics and Anglos alike, and it's a favorite hang-out for Spanish-speaking Braves. Cuban-style roast pork (slices of boneless fresh ham marinated in *mojo* sauce—a garlic-cumin-onion-oil mixture—and topped with garlic-and-vinegar-marinated onions), deep-fried ham croquettes, shrimp in garlic sauce, and homemade flan are all favored offerings. ⊠ *2625 Piedmont Rd., Suite G-42, Buckhead Crossing Mall on Sidney Marcus Blvd. side,* ☎ *404/364–0212. AE, D, DC, MC, V. MARTA: Lindbergh.*

French

$$$–$$$$ ✕ **Riviera.** A former private home is now a comfortable, lively dining establishment serving mainly French-Mediterranean fare, such as foie gras, terrines, veal chops, and crème brûlée. ⊠ *519 E. Paces Ferry Rd.,* ☎ *404/262–7112. Reservations essential on weekends. AE, D, DC, MC, V. No lunch. Closed Sun.*

$–$$$ ✕ **Brasserie Le Coze.** The interior of this modern bistro (a relative of New York's Le Bernadin), in one of Atlanta's most important shopping emporiums, has warm tones, well-spaced tables, and comfortable banquettes. The robust, no-nonsense food includes heavenly white-bean soup perfumed with white truffle oil, and a thick pork chop that zings with a whole-grain mustard sauce. Among the desserts is an ice-cream-filled *vacherin* (baked egg-white shell) topped with candied chestnuts. ⊠ *3393 Peachtree Rd., Lenox Sq.,* ☎ *404/266–1440. AE, DC, MC, V. Closed Sun. MARTA: Lenox Sq.*

$–$$$ ✕ **Toulouse.** A quirky location in the rear of an unpretentious low-rise commercial building holds George Tice's comfortable, casual restaurant. A large bar anchors the space, and the open kitchen is in full view of patrons. The culinary tradition of southwestern France is the starting point here. Vegetarians will snap up the roasted vegetable platter with garlic mayonnaise. The well-priced wine list is incredible. ✉ *2293-B Peachtree Rd., Peachtree Walk shopping center,* ☎ *404/351–9533. Reservations not accepted after 7:30. AE, MC, V. No smoking. Closed Sun. No lunch.*

Fusion

$$–$$$ ✕ **Prime.** This sophisticated dining room in Atlanta's busiest shopping mall is the ultimate culinary oxymoron: a sushi bar and a steak house under one roof. Southern touches include grilled salmon on a bed of grits. But there's more: good sandwiches at lunch and wonderful soups (Tuscan white bean is especially popular). ✉ *3393 Peachtree Rd., Lenox Sq.,* ☎ *404/812–0555. AE, D, DC, MC, V. MARTA: Lenox Sq.*

Irish

$–$$ ✕ **Fadó.** Gaelic sayings trim the exterior of this rousing new bar, while within, dark wood, warm lighting, and intimate seating areas attract the denizens of Buckhead. The boxty (potato pancakes with fillings of salmon, vegetables, or corned beef and cabbage) gets raves from homesick Irish, as do the potted salmon, bread pudding, and homemade soda bread. ✉ *3036 Peachtree Rd.,* ☎ *404/841–0066. AE, D, DC, MC, V.*

Italian

$–$$$$ ✕ **Maggiano's Little Italy.** A noisy, frolicking, huge freestanding emporium, this link in a chain has a bakery and outdoor dining. Dishes come straight from the Italian-American repertoire: whole roasted chicken with rosemary and garlic, veal Marsala, shrimp oreganata, eggplant Parmesan. Bring a gang and dine family style. ✉ *3368 Peachtree Rd.,* ☎ *404/816–9650. AE, D, DC, MC, V. MARTA: Buckhead.*

$$–$$$ ✕ **Abruzzi.** The sedate, warmly lit dining room of this enduring restaurant in a bustling shopping center attracts a generally older clientele. The menu is the same at lunch and dinner, although lunch prices are about 20% lower. Gossamer homemade *pappardelle* (broad noodles) with a light game or oxtail sauce, sweetbreads in a mushroom-studded Madeira sauce, and homemade ricotta cheesecake are favorites. ✉ *2355 Peachtree Rd., Peachtree Battle Shopping Center,* ☎ *404/261–8186. Jacket required. AE, DC, MC, V. Closed Sun. No lunch Sat.*

$–$$$ ✕ **La Grotta.** On the lower level of a posh condominium,
★ this elegant, established star is firmly conservative in both
decor and food, and is extremely popular with visiting and
homegrown luminaries. La Grotta specializes in the clas-
sics of Italian cooking: grilled veal chop with garlic, sage,
and lemon; fettuccine with porcini mushrooms and sweet
Italian sausage in a light tomato-basil sauce. ✉ *2637
Peachtree Rd., Peachtree House Condominium,* ☎
*404/231–1368. Reservations essential. Jacket required.
AE, D, DC, MC, V. Closed Sun. No lunch.*

$–$$ ✕ **Pricci.** Pristine white walls with gleaming windows enclose spacious, comfortably arranged tables and banquettes,
but the environment is noisy. High-energy young-at-heart
types make up most of the clientele. The day's risotto is always interesting; a standout is the scallops and spinach
version. Delicious sea bass in parchment paper meets heart-
healthy requirements. The all-Italian wine list is outstanding. ✉ *500 Pharr Rd.,* ☎ *404/237–2941. AE, D, DC, MC,
V. No lunch weekends.*

Japanese

$$–$$$$ ✕ **Kamogawa.** Very formal and correct (patrons must re-
★ move shoes before entering the private tatami rooms),
Kamogawa epitomizes Japanese dining at its most elegant.
Servers slide open the traditional shoji screens and kneel
to take orders and pour sake. Guests will enjoy the perfectly
crisp tempura of soft-shell crabs. ✉ *3300 Peachtree Rd.,
Grand Hyatt Atlanta,* ☎ *404/841–0314. AE, DC, MC, V.
No lunch Sat. Closed Sun. MARTA: Buckhead.*

Moroccan

$$ ✕ **Imperial Fez.** Occupying the street-level space of a con-
dominium high-rise, Imperial Fez seats patrons on luxuri-
ous pillow-backed banquettes after they deposit their shoes
at the door. Traditional veiled dancers entertain during
multicourse dinners, which start with a choice of soup—
light vegetable or thick, flavorful lentil—followed by traditional salads. The fixed-price meal ($35) also includes
pastilla, a flaky puff pastry stuffed with spiced eggs and Cornish hen and perfumed with cinnamon. Lamb and Cornish
hen with couscous are the entrée specialties, but note the
fish *tajine,* an aromatic, traditional Moroccan stew. Vege-
tarians will enjoy the eggplant dishes. ✉ *2285 Peachtree*

Rd., Peachtree Battle Condominiums, ☎ *404/351–0870. Reservations essential. AE, D, DC, MC, V. No lunch.*

Southern

$$–$$$$ ✕ **Anthonys.** A classical revival plantation house brought from southeast Georgia to a spot off Piedmont Road now hums as a restaurant. Out-of-towners looking for the Tara experience as well as locals entertaining guests enjoy the atmosphere of pure romance and nostalgia. Country ham pâté and spicy crab and corn cakes on fried grits are just two that hark back to old Southern ideas. ⊠ *3109 Piedmont Rd., south of Peachtree Rd.,* ☎ *404/262–7379. Jacket and tie. AE, D, DC, MC, V. Closed Sun. No lunch. MARTA: Buckhead.*

$–$$$ ✕ **Horseradish Grill.** Originally a red horse barn, this restau-
★   rant is now painted gray with white trim. Although a bit noisy, this is a must for anyone seeking good southern-style food. The native South Carolina chef translates southern recipes with authority and authenticity. Nestled on a corn cake, his Carolina-style barbecue with cole slaw on top is basically his dad's recipe. The rabbit pot pie appetizer could do main-course duty. The menu changes often, but soups may include such treats as a silky butternut-squash bisque. ⊠ *4320 Powers Ferry Rd.,* ☎ *404/255–7277. Reservations not accepted. AE, D, DC, MC, V.*

$–$$ ✕ **McKinnon's Louisiane.** Billy McKinnon learned to cook classic Creole and Cajun fare in New Orleans and now has a following for his stuffed eggplant—a puree of eggplant and béchamel sauce with shrimp and crab. The restaurant anchors one end of a minuscule strip shopping center. Maquechoux is served on pasta with andouille sausage and shrimp. There's crawfish étouffée, with tomato, onion, and celery, and soft-shell crabs (fried or sautéed). Billy's bread pudding is justifiably famous. ⊠ *3209 Maple Dr.,* ☎ *404/237–1313. AE, D, DC, MC, V. Closed Sun. No lunch.*

Southwestern/Mexican

$–$$$ ✕ **NAVA.** A clever southwestern-motif interior includes handsome kachina dolls as decoration. Two levels fill early and stay that way. Numerous appetizers make good to-share plates, such as the pork carnitas and grilled vegetable quesadillas, the tequila-cured salmon, and the mussels in chipotle broth. For entrées, consider the grilled flank steak fajita style and corn-crusted snapper. Homemade breads are superior, especially the blue corn sticks. The vegetarian platter is extra yummy. ⊠ *3060 Peachtree Rd., near W. Paces Ferry Rd., Buckhead Plaza,* ☎ *404/240–1984. AE, D, DC, MC, V. No lunch weekends.*

$–$$ ✕ **Georgia Grille.** Karen Hilliard and son Billy Kennedy have carved a southwestern niche named not for this state but for artist Georgia O'Keeffe. Young, attractive patrons enjoy inventive fare: the lobster-filled enchiladas are from heaven. If you crave this dish, go early—the restaurant often runs out of it. "Hot shots" are jalapeños stuffed with black beans, deep fried, and accompanied by salsa and sour cream. Potato fritters with sour-cream horseradish sauce are addictive. Have vanilla flan for dessert, with fresh fruit. ⊠ *2290 Peachtree Rd., Peachtree Square Shopping Center,* ☎ *404/352–3517. Reservations not accepted. AE, MC, V. No lunch.*

Thai

$ ✕ **Annie's Thai Castle.** The interior hosts Annie Lai's collection of homeland memorabilia and art. At lunch, quickly prepared dishes, such as chicken in yellow curry and the classic noodle dish *pad Thai* come with a choice of coconut-milk chicken soup or an egg roll. The adventurous dinner menu includes some of the chef's specialties, like roast duck, defatted and deboned, with red curry, *keffer* leaf (a traditional Thai herb), pineapple, and tomato. Shrimp steamed in a clay pot are served with glass noodles made from rice, sliced ginger, and garlic sauce. ⊠ *3195 Roswell Rd.,* ☎ *404/264–9546. Reservations essential on weekends. AE, MC, V.*

Buford Highway–Cheshire Bridge Road and Vicinity

American

$$–$$$ ✕ **The Cabin.** A he-man atmosphere in a log structure with suggestions of hunting accessories on the walls is the headquarters for some of Atlanta's best game cookery. The two nightly game entrees might include venison, elk, or buffalo. Otherwise it's steak, especially aged midwestern beef, and seafood. ⊠ *2678 Buford Hwy.,* ☎ *404/315–7676. AE, D, DC, MC, V. No lunch Sat. Closed Sun.*

Chinese

$–$$$$ ✕ **Little Szechuan.** Enter this restaurant, in a strip shopping
★   center, and join the mostly Asian patrons, including many
families, for authentic Chinese food. Dining inexpensively
never was more delicious. Chicken roll is a dish made by
stuffing the skin of a chicken neck with seasoned minced
pork; it's then deep fried and sliced diagonally. Spicy green
beans, stir-fried spinach, squid, and other treats of Szechuan
cuisine may be enjoyed for precious few dollars. ⊠ *5091-
C Buford Hwy., Northwoods Plaza, Doraville,* ☎ *770/451–
0192. Reservations not accepted. AE, D, DC, MC, V.*

French

$–$$ ✕ **Le Giverny.** This tiny bistro, tucked into a strip mall, has
well-spaced tables and an intimate yet convivial atmo-
sphere. The classics of French bistro cooking make it a hit:
vegetable terrine with goat cheese, rack of lamb, beef bour-
guignonne, snails, sea bass, salmon, and chocolate pâté. ⊠
1355 Clairmont Rd., Decatur, ☎ *404/325–7252. AE, D,
DC, MC, V. Closed Sun. No lunch Sat.*

$–$$ ✕ **Violette.** A native of Alsace, France, operates two loca-
tions that are near each other and share the name; although
they're both good, they couldn't be more different. This flag-
ship location is large, comfortable, bright, and quiet and
is noted for such classic French bistro fare as meltingly ten-
der quiche, steak with Roquefort sauce, monkfish, shrimp
and chicken in lobster sauce, and crème brûlée. ⊠ *2948
Clairmont Rd.,* ☎ *404/633–3363. AE, MC, V. Closed
Sun. No lunch Sat.*

Japanese

$–$$ ✕ **Sa Tsu Ki.** Set back from the road, this great grazing spot
★   occupies its own small building, with nothing but asphalt
leading to the front door. Within lies an Asian aesthetic,
with shoji screens dividing the space. Appetizers range
from well-executed sushi and sashimi to beef *tataki,* a sort
of Japanese carpaccio. Deep-fried shrimp heads are unusual
and compelling. The no-smoking area is not well sepa-
rated from the smokers' corner. ⊠ *3043 Buford Hwy.,* ☎
404/325–5285. AE, DC, MC, V. No lunch.

Southern

$–$$ ✕ **Colonnade Restaurant.** An Atlanta institution since 1927,
★   the Colonnade has a long list of southern specialties. Flo-

ral carpeting, battleship prints in the bar, and hunting scenes in the dining room give the place a down-South feeling. The rib-sticking chicken pot pie overflows with fresh vegetables. Grilled ham steak comes with the round bone smack in the middle. Fried flour-dipped catfish, grilled whole rainbow trout, creamy macaroni and cheese, squash casserole, and favorite regional desserts are all part of the culinary scenario. Everything is homemade, from rolls to corn bread to pastries. ⊠ *1879 Cheshire Bridge Rd.,* ☎ *404/874–5642. Reservations not accepted. No credit cards.*

$–$$ ✕ **Stringer's Fish Camp and Oyster Bar.** With all the local characters here, the people-watching is as good as the food. The deliberately dilapidated freestanding structure evokes a north Georgia fishing camp. Chunky, spicy gumbo, peppery corn relish, and crisp, succulent, nongreasy southern-style fried fish and shellfish are served in huge portions. ⊠ *3384 Shallowford Rd., Chamblee,* ☎ *770/458–7145. Reservations accepted for parties of 6 or more. MC, V. No lunch weekends.*

Southwestern/Mexican

$ ✕ **Sundown Cafe.** Occupying the end of a small strip mall, Sundown Cafe feels like a bit of Taos, with white, adobe-style walls adorned with ceramic plates and textiles. The fundamentals of Mexican and southwestern food dominate this casual neighborhood spot. *Posole,* a stew of pork, hominy, and red chilis, tastes great in cold weather. Eddie's Pork, named for chef Eddie Hernández, combines a thick chop with ancho pepper–accented mashed potatoes and roasted jalapeño gravy. Outstanding turnip greens accompany entrées. A chocolate-stuffed chimichanga, crisp and rich, defies any effort to eat just a few bites. ⊠ *2165 Cheshire Bridge Rd.,* ☎ *404/321–1118. Reservations not accepted. AE, DC, MC, V. Closed Sun. No lunch Sat.*

Thai

$–$$ ✕ **Thai Chilli.** Unpretentious but neat surroundings and a
★   quiet ambience attract neighborhood patrons to one of Atlanta's top Thai restaurants. Nothing here is overgilded or overfussed. *Larb,* ground sirloin with rice powder and mint leaves, is especially fresh tasting. Spicy catfish with basil and Thai eggplant score in the main courses. Vegetarian dishes, mostly tofu-based, are a strength. ⊠ *2169*

Briarcliff Rd., Briarvista Shopping Center, ☎ *404/315–6750. AE, D, MC, V. No lunch weekends.*

Midtown and Virginia-Highland

American

$$ ✕ **R.J.'s Uptown Kitchen & Wine Bar.** Transforming a 1920s corner gas station, Rob Campbell fashioned a casual, bar-centered space with a downstairs wine-tasting room that attracts neighbors from the surrounding residences. A recent turn toward southwestern fare produces spicy accents in dishes. At least 50 different wines are available by the glass; flights (tastes of several wines in a single genre) are also available. Diners should take a taxi, as parking is fierce. ⊠ *870 N. Highland Ave.,* ☎ *404/875–7775. AE, D, DC, MC, V. No lunch.*

Barbecue

$ ✕ **Dusty's.** Customers, both locals and out-of-towners, often pull up to the drive-through window to carry home their treasures from this rustic spot near Emory University; there's seating, too. North Carolina–style barbecue sauce forsakes tomato and instead zings with vinegar and spices. Dusty's version, slathered on tender, slow-cooked pork, is dead-on. ⊠ *1815 Briarcliff Rd.,* ☎ *404/320–6264. Reservations not accepted. AE, D, DC, MC, V.*

Caribbean

$–$$ ✕ **Indigo Coastal Grill.** Trendy coastal cuisine packs in the neighbors at this lively eatery. Conch fritters, lobster corn chowder, and fish with fresh herbs in a twist of parchment are constants on the menu. Don't miss the refreshing Key lime pie. At popular Sunday brunch the jalapeño grits zing, no matter what you have with them, but the Hangtown Scramble, with oysters, eggs, and potatoes, is a top choice. ⊠ *1397 N. Highland Ave.,* ☎ *404/876–0676. Reservations not accepted. AE, MC, V. No sit-down lunch, but take-out service is available at lunch as well as at dinner.*

Continental Contemporary

$$$$ ✕ **The Restaurant.** Sweep up the grand staircase of this exquisite, elegant hotel lobby, and settle into quiet comfort in the fine-dining restaurant. Warm lighting glows from hidden recesses. The food, too, is elegant: start with seared foie gras with turnip pancakes or Beluga caviar and follow with black-pepper–crusted tuna with honey, ginger, and cilantro, or rack of lamb. The berry crème brûlée makes a fine finish. There's also a tasting menu ($40). ⊠ *Four Seasons Hotel, 75 14th St.,* ☎ *404/881–9898. AE, DC, MC, V. Closed Sun. No lunch. MARTA: Arts Center.*

Cuban

$-$$$ ✕ **Mambo Restaurante Cubano.** In a dimly lit, casual storefront, Mambo feeds its mostly local patrons traditional, hearty Cuban fare. Black paella makes judicious use of the squid's ink as well as its meat. *Ropa vieja,* a traditional beef stew, brims with richness. Cuban dishes include black beans and rice, *picadillo* (ground beef, olives, and chilies), and *boliche* (eye of round stuffed with chorizo and braised). Chef Lucy Alvarez specializes in "Chino Latino" dishes, like sea bass poached in lemon-grass ginger sauce. ⊠ *1402 N. Highland Ave.,* ☎ *404/876–2626. AE, DC, MC, V. No lunch.*

French

$$-$$$ ✕ **Ciboulette.** On the south end of a neighborhood commercial center that has everything from a costume shop to ★ an art gallery, this modern French bistro has an open kitchen and a small bar. Patrons enjoy sitting at the tall stools arranged in front of the kitchen area. Try the splendid lump crab cake, Chilean sea bass served either with tomato confit or with a crust of crushed coriander seed, or the house special: bouillabaisse made with lobster as well as fish. Game dishes are frequent specials in season. ⊠ *1529 Piedmont Ave., Clear Creek Shopping Center,* ☎ *404/874–7600. Reservations not accepted Fri.–Sun. AE, DC, MC, V. No lunch. Closed Sun.*

Fusion

$-$$ ✕ **Terra Cotta.** A nondescript, shotgun-style building has been rendered hip and humming by clever design, and its good cooking has made it a mecca for fine casual dining. Accents from myriad cuisines influence southern ideas in such dishes as Thai fish cake with crab, scallions, Japanese bread crumbs, and a chili-soy aioli. Grilled pork tenderloin with garlic roast mashed potatoes and southern greens comes with a sage shiitake jus. ⊠ *1044 Greenwood Ave.,* ☎ *404/853–7888. AE, D, DC, MC, V. No lunch. Closed Mon.*

Italian

$–$$ ✕ **Veni Vidi Vici.** This handsome modern restaurant is a bit
★   noisy because no fabric softens the polished wood walls.
You can dine alfresco on the patio after a game of boccie
ball on an adjacent court. Northern Italian cooking inspires
the menu. Antipasti *piccoli* (small) with savory items such
as calamari with olives, lemon, and olive oil could serve as
a light lunch or late-night snack. Rotisserie-cooked meats
include salmon, pork, and crispy duck. The tiramisu (a lay-
ered cake-and-cream dessert with chocolate) is excellent,
as are all the desserts. ✉ *41 14th St.,* ☎ *404/875–8424.*
*Reservations essential. AE, D, DC, MC, V. No lunch week-
ends. MARTA: Arts Center.*

$ ✕ **Camille's.** Young, urban, and urbane homeowners have
made Camille's their neighborhood dining spot. In nice
weather, the outdoor patio is a treat. This is American-style
Italian food at its best, with slow-simmered, chunky mari-
nara sauces gracing many dishes, including crisp calamari and
plump steamed mussels. There are good pizzas, pastas and
calzones, too. ✉ *1186 N. Highland Ave.,* ☎ *404/872–7203.*
Reservations not accepted. AE, DC, MC, V. No lunch.

Mexican

$–$$ ✕ **Zócalo.** At this casual, fun spot where dining is done only
★   on an outdoor (but protected) patio, Lucero Martínez-
Obregón serves up dishes she learned from her mother in
Mexico City. Among these are superior *mole* (chili-choco-
late sauce) served in fat enchiladas, *arrachera* (the dish
that launched fajitas), and for dessert, crepes filled with
cheeses, drizzled with the family's ranch-made honey, and
topped with toasted pumpkin seeds. ✉ *187 10th St., at Piedmont Ave.,* ☎ *404/249–7576. Reservations not accepted.
AE, D, DC, MC, V. MARTA: Midtown.*

Southern

$–$$ ✕ **Agnes & Muriel's.** Tucked within the walls of an old res-
idence, this restaurant is a bit noisy for some, but the food
is so reminiscent of friendly family fare (but updated) that
no one cares much. Choice morsels include salmon pot pie,
collard greens with sesame seed and lemon, and a French
chocolate pie that makes diners swoon. ✉ *1514 Monroe
Dr., near Piedmont Ave.,* ☎ *404/885–1000. AE, D, DC,
MC, V. No lunch weekends.*

$–$$ ✕ **South City Kitchen.** South Carolina's coastal Low Coun-
★ try guides the cooking at this popular restaurant. The
bright, cleanly designed spaces in a former residence provide good views of the street; the young, trendy patrons also
enjoy the bold modern art that enhances the walls. She-crab
soup, enriched with crab roe, is the city's best. Shrimp and
scallops on creamy stone-ground grits with a garlic-cream
gravy have taken Atlanta by storm. Try catfish here, no matter how the menu offers it. Poached eggs on sublime crab
hash redefines brunch. Chocolate pecan pie and fruit cob-
blers will make you wish they weren't fattening. ⊠ *1144
Crescent Ave., between 14th and 10th Sts.,* ☎ *404/873–
7358. Reservations accepted for dinner only. AE, MC, V.
MARTA: Arts Center.*

$ ✕ **French Quarter Food Shop.** This simple storefront
★ doesn't bother with frills; it's a bit grungy. However, adventurous patrons appreciate the authentic Cajun and Cre-
ole food: étouffées, *muffulettas* (classic New Orleans
sandwiches piled high with deli meats and cheeses and
anointed with olive salad), gumbos made thick, tangy, and
warming, and extraordinary whiskey-sauce bread pudding
all make you grateful for the presence of Cajuns in Atlanta
(or in suburban Dunwoody, where a second location has
opened). ⊠ *923 Peachtree St., at 8th St.,* ☎ *404/875–2489.
Reservations not accepted. AE, D, DC, MC, V. Closed
Sun. MARTA: Midtown.*

$ ✕ **Mary Mac's Tea Room.** A longtime mecca for southern
food, this restaurant has been revived with new ownership,
fresh paint, and bright lighting. Mary Mac's has a loyal following of locals, and out-of-towners seek it out, but other
restaurants serve better versions of this menu. Still, if you're
staying near Midtown, it's handy and does a good job
with country-fried steak, fried chicken, and fresh vegetables. ⊠ *224 Ponce de Leon Ave.,* ☎ *404/876–1800. Reservations accepted for parties of 10 or more. No credit cards.
No dinner Sun. MARTA: North Ave.*

Perimeter Vicinity

American

$$$–$$$$ ✕ **McKendrick's.** Rich, dark wood, warm lighting, a lack
of fuss, and simple presentation characterize this mascu-

line steak house just outside the Perimeter. Nothing is nouvelle here, and portions are substantial. Steak is the main draw, of course, but veal, lamb, buffalo, and grilled fish also grab attention. ⊠ *4505 Ashford-Dunwoody Rd., Park Place Shopping Center, Dunwoody,* ☎ *770/512–8888. AE, D, DC, MC, V. No lunch weekends. MARTA: Dunwoody.*

$–$$ ✕ **Cafe Renaissance.** At the far end of a suburban mall, this unpretentious, comfortable, quiet establishment brings fine dining to barbecue country. Sandwiches and salads at lunch go beyond the usual: the grilled steak salad has strips of meat laced across a bed of romaine and is topped with a blue cheese dressing. Among the appealing sandwiches is grilled tuna with eggplant, onions, oven-dried tomatoes, and caper-laced rémoulade (a spicy mayonnaise) on grilled focaccia. Dinner entrées include steak with glazed shallots and port-wine sauce, and the fresh fish of the day. ⊠ *7050 Jimmy Carter Blvd., Upton's Shopping Center, Norcross,* ☎ *770/441–0291. AE, D, MC, V. Closed Sun. No lunch Sat.*

$–$$ ✕ **Phoenix Brew Pub.** Patrons sit comfortably beneath the pub's operations center, which gleams with shiny copper equipment. Off the entry lies a long, engaging bar. Not content to merely brew great suds, the pub also has a terrific wine list and some of the city's most intriguing food. Venison, light cold dishes in summer, and excellent soups (summer brings the gazpacho du jour), are the high points. ⊠ *5600 Roswell Rd., The Prado Shopping Center, inside the Perimeter,* ☎ *404/843–2739. AE, D, DC, MC, V. No lunch Sat.*

Barbecue

$ ✕ **Holt Bros. Bar-B-Q.** Holt Bros. has quickly gained a reputation for barbecued beef brisket, turkey, chicken, and tender ribs. Crisp fried green tomatoes are a high point. Skip dessert; you won't have room anyway. ⊠ *6539 Jimmy Carter Blvd., at Buford Hwy., Norcross,* ☎ *770/242–3984. Reservations not accepted. AE, D, DC, MC, V.*

Italian

$$–$$$ ✕ **La Grotta at Ravinia.** A handsome restaurant with an exquisite view of surrounding gardens beyond a glass wall, this extension of La Grotta in Buckhead (☞ La Grotta, *above*) provides the adjacent Dunwoody neighborhoods with very good northern Italian food. The sliced veal Mediterranean appetizer with sun-dried tomato vinaigrette is a perfect summer luncheon entrée. Also recommended are the veal chop with Chianti and thyme sauce, the fresh pastas, and *panna cotta* (a flan-like dish literally translated as "cooked cream") for dessert. ✉ *4355 Ashford-Dunwoody Rd., Holiday Inn/Crowne Plaza at Ravinia, Dunwoody,* ☎ *770/395–9925. AE, D, DC, MC, V. Closed Sun. No lunch Sat. MARTA: Dunwoody.*

$–$$ ✗ **Mi Spia.** Lunching outside on the large sidewalk patio is a treat on a fine spring day. Within, the restaurant suggests a trattoria—one surrounded by upscale shops and eateries in an well-landscaped mall. The excellent Italian-inspired menu can also ease the rigors of shopping at nearby Perimeter Mall. Roasted salmon fillet glazed with honey and balsamic vinegar and served with orzo-vegetable salad and crispy leeks is one of the more delectable entrées. Try the white-chocolate napoleon for dessert. ✉ *4505 Ashford-Dunwoody Rd., Park Place, across from Perimeter Mall, Dunwoody,* ☎ *770/393–1333. AE, D, DC, MC, V. No lunch weekends. MARTA: Dunwoody.*

Korean/Japanese

$–$$ ✗ **Hanwoori.** One of Atlanta's best new restaurants, Hanwoori is supremely elegant, yet comfortable. The interior is divided into Korean-food and Japanese-food sections: the Korean side is a better choice—you can get Japanese food there as well. An almost exclusively Asian clientele comes for barbecued eel and spicy squid appetizers, superior tender *boolgogi* (Korean marinated grilled beef), and outstanding sushi. ✉ *4251 N. Peachtree Rd., Chamblee,* ☎ *770/458–9191. AE, D, DC, MC, V.*

4 Lodging

By Mark
Beffart

Updated
by Jane
Garvey

AS ONE OF AMERICA'S three most popular convention destinations, Atlanta has tens of thousands of hotel rooms. The compact Downtown area alone contains more than 12,000 rooms, with the greatest percentage close to Peachtree Center. Other clusters are in Buckhead, Midtown, and in the vicinity of I–285, also known as the Perimeter. Many hotels inside the Perimeter are near Hartsfield Atlanta International Airport; many outside the Perimeter are north of the city. Luxury establishments are centered primarily in Downtown and Buckhead.

Your choice of location depends on whether you're coming for business, entertainment, sightseeing, or shopping. Consider accessibility to your interests and whether you want to drive or use public transportation.

Downtown lodging is convenient to many sights, but don't expect to find a room at the best hotels without a reservation several months in advance. Most downtown hotels are filled with conventioneers and trade-show people rather than tourists. However, these folks are usually gone by the weekend, often leaving the rooms available for weekend getaways at reasonable prices.

Buckhead, with the city's best restaurants, most interesting shops, and Lenox Square and Phipps Plaza malls, is popular with those leisure visitors who can afford it as well as with businesspeople.

With the construction of new office towers in recent years, midtown hotels have become more popular with businesspeople. The area draws visitors attending entertainment events at the Fox Theatre, Woodruff Arts Center, or other venues. Piedmont Park is invitingly near, too.

Of the hotels in other areas of the city, most are near one of the main interstate highways, including a large cluster west of the airport at the junction of I–85 and I–285. Although chain offerings dominate, these lodgings can provide good value and location. We list them under Perimeter Vicinity—Inside. Many Atlanta businesses have offices along or outside I–285, primarily on the north Perimeter between I–75 and I–85; the finest hotels are usually occupied by businesspeople. You'll need a car if you stay outside the Perimeter; public transportation is limited.

To accommodate conventions and conference goers, most Atlanta lodgings have meeting and conference rooms. The larger hotels also have full-service business centers with copiers, fax machines, computers, and other business equipment. Expect hotels in the upper price ranges to have room service, dry cleaning, and other services. Because many conventions and conferences last an entire week, suite-style hotels are the rage. Unless otherwise noted, suites are living room–bedroom–bathroom combinations with stocked minibars, coffeemakers, king-size beds, large-screen televisions, and extra telephones. Regular rooms, unless noted, all have private bath, television, and telephone.

All the hotels listed offer parking. Many downtown, midtown, and Buckhead hotels charge fees that range from $2 to $14, with the average around $8; valet parking is usually a dollar or two higher. Suburban hotels rarely charge anything.

Hotels in prime locations—Downtown, Midtown, Buckhead, and the north Perimeter—are often booked months in advance. If you plan to stay at a particular hotel, make a reservation as soon as possible. Most hotels, especially those connected with a national chain, have weekend rates and special package deals that offer tremendous savings and include tempting extras.

We list hotels by neighborhood, starting with Downtown and proceeding alphabetically to Buckhead, Midtown, Perimeter Vicinity—Inside, and Perimeter Vicinity—Outside. Within neighborhoods, hotels are listed in order of price, starting with the highest. For price explanation, see the price chart below. Metro stops are only given when they are convenient.

Bed-and-Breakfasts

For bed-and-breakfast lodging, check the entries below; you can also contact **Georgia Bed & Breakfast** (☎ 770/493–1930), an agency connecting you with 60 area homes. **Bed & Breakfast Atlanta** (☎ 404/875–0525 or 800/967–3224)

Pick up the phone.
Pick up the miles.

1-800-FLY-FREE

Now when you sign up with MCI you can receive up to 8,000 bonus frequent flyer miles on one of seven major airlines.

Then earn another 5 miles for every dollar you spend on a variety of MCI services, including MCI Card® calls from virtually anywhere in the world.*

You're going to use these services anyway. Why not rack up the miles while you're doing it?

Is this a great time, or what? :-)

Urban planning.

CITYPACKS

The ultimate guide to the city—a complete pocket guide plus a full-size color map.

represents nearly 100 B&Bs. **Great Inns of Georgia** (☎ 800/664–7328) can reserve B&Bs in metro Atlanta as well as in other locations around the state.

CATEGORY	COST*
$$$$	over $160
$$$	$115–$160
$$	$80–$115
$	under $80

The lower end of the price range reflects the lowest rate charged for a standard double room (including weekends and off-peak times); the higher end is the most ever charged for a suite. All prices exclude 14% tax.

Downtown

$$$$ 🏨 **Atlanta Marriott Marquis Hotel and Towers.** Immense and coolly contemporary, the John Portman–designed Marquis seems to go on forever as you stand under the lobby's huge fabric sculpture, which appears to float from the skylighted roof 48 stories above. Each guest room—of average size and redecorated in 1997 with new furniture, light colors, and floral designs—opens onto this atrium. The Southeast's largest-capacity hotel is connected to Peachtree Center and its shops by a skywalk and is a favorite of conventioneers. ⊠ 265 Peachtree Center Ave., 30303, ☎ 404/521–0000 or 800/228–9290, FAX 404/586–6299. 1,671 rooms, 69 suites. 5 restaurants, 4 bars, indoor-outdoor pool, health club, concierge, business services, convention center, meeting rooms. AE, D, DC, MC, V. MARTA: Peachtree Center.

$$$–$$$$ 🏨 **Omni Hotel at CNN Center.** A location adjacent to CNN Center and across the street from the World Congress Center makes this hotel a popular choice with convention visitors. Its lobby combines Old World excellence and modern accents, with marble floors, Oriental rugs, exotic plants and floral arrangements, abstract art, and contemporary furnishings. Large, comfortable rooms were redecorated for the Olympics, and the colors are now intense blue, red, and violet, while walls are painted beige. All guests have access to the Downtown Athletic Club for a $12 fee. ⊠ 100 CNN Center, 30305, ☎ 404/659–0000 or 800/843–6664, FAX 404/525–5050. 458 rooms, 11 suites. 2 restaurants, lobby lounge,

98

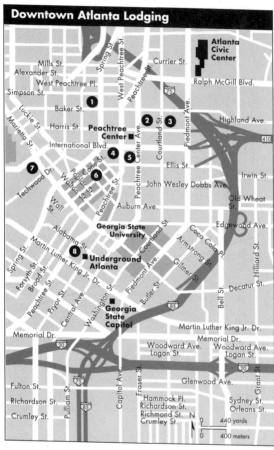

Downtown Atlanta Lodging

Atlanta Hilton and Towers, **3**

Atlanta Marriott Marquis Hotel and Towers, **2**

Hyatt Regency Atlanta, **1**

Omni Hotel at CNN Center, **7**

Quality Hotel, **6**

Ritz–Carlton, Atlanta, **5**

Suite Hotel Underground Atlanta, **8**

Westin Peachtree Plaza Hotel, **4**

concierge, business services, convention center, meeting rooms. AE, D, DC, MC, V. MARTA: OMNI/Dome/GWCC.

$$$-$$$$ ⊞ **Ritz-Carlton, Atlanta.** The mood here is set by the tra-
★ ditional afternoon tea served in the intimate lobby beneath an 18th-century chandelier. Note the 17th-century Flemish tapestry when you enter from Peachtree Street. Spacious guest rooms are luxuriously appointed with marble writing tables and plump sofas, and the suites have four-poster beds. All have white-marble bathrooms. The Café's Sunday brunch spread is spectacular, and in the evenings, live music (☞ Chapter 5) is performed at The Bar upstairs. The Restaurant (☞ Chapter 3) serves Continental cuisine in a clublike setting. Service is efficient, in the style of grand old European hotels. ⊠ 181 Peachtree St., 30303, ☎ 404/659–0400 or 800/241–3333, FAX 404/577–8366. 447 rooms. 2 restaurants, bar, health club, concierge, business center. AE, D, DC, MC, V. MARTA: Peachtree Center.

$$$-$$$$ ⊞ **Suite Hotel Underground Atlanta.** Removed from the flash-and-glitter Downtown hotel district, this understated suites-only hotel, barely noticed by passersby except for its large brass entry doors, can provide a quiet and relaxing stay. Half of its rooms overlook the top level of Underground Atlanta, with the city skyline in the background. The two-tone building, a five-story, 19th-century structure with an addition of several modern floors, has small suites decorated in muted earth tones with solid traditional furniture and modern art prints. Passes to the Peachtree Athletic Center are $15 per visit. ⊠ 54 Peachtree St., 30303, ☎ 404/223–9555 or 800/477–5549, FAX 404/223–0467. 156 suites. Dining room, concierge, business services. AE, D, DC, MC, V. MARTA: Five Points.

$$-$$$$ ⊞ **Atlanta Hilton and Towers.** Occupying an entire square block, this is one of the city's largest hotels, with five dining establishments: The Garden Terrace (casual buffet); Le Café coffee shop; a 24-hour Deli Express; Trader Vic's (Polynesian); and the world-class Nikolai's Roof (Continental Contemporary, ☞ Chapter 3) on the 30th floor. Standard rooms are decorated in restful mauves, greens, and golds, while the separate Towers provides more luxurious accommodations and has a private check-in area. Guests in this section enjoy complimentary evening hors d'oeuvres and Continental breakfast. ⊠ 255 Courtland St., 30303,

☎ 404/659–2000 or 800/445–8667, ℻ 404/221–6368. *1,224 rooms, 41 suites. 3 restaurants, 4 bars, coffee shop, deli, pool, 4 tennis courts, health club, jogging, concierge, business services, convention center, meeting rooms. AE, D, DC, MC, V. MARTA: Peachtree Center.*

$$–$$$$ 🏨 **Hyatt Regency Atlanta.** The Hyatt's 23-story lobby launched the chain's greenery-filled "atrium look" in 1967. Easily identified at night by the brightly lit blue bubble dome over the rooftop Polaris Restaurant, this John Portman–designed creation remains one of Atlanta's more unusual hotels, serving many conventioneers. In addition to rooms overlooking the atrium, there are accommodations in two newer, attached towers. All contain comfortably plush modern furniture. ⊠ *265 Peachtree St., 30303,* ☎ *404/577–1234 or 800/233–1234,* ℻ *404/588–4808 for reservations, 404/588–4137 for guests. 1,278 rooms, 58 suites. 3 restaurants, bar, pool, health club, concierge, business services, convention center, meeting rooms. AE, D, DC, MC, V. MARTA: Peachtree Center.*

$$–$$$$ 🏨 **Westin Peachtree Plaza Hotel.** This cylindrical glass ★ tower, designed by John Portman, is a defining shape in the Atlanta skyline. A five-story atrium surrounds the glass elevator shaft attached to the building's exterior. Caramel-toned marble, upholstered seating, artwork, Oriental rugs, and hanging plants enhance the lobby. Pastel-hued rooms are appointed with dark-toned furniture. For great views of Atlanta, dine in the revolving, dual-level Sun Dial (☞ Chapter 3) restaurant atop the hotel. ⊠ *210 Peachtree St., 30303,* ☎ *404/659–1400 or 800/937–8461,* ℻ *404/589–7424. 1,020 rooms, 48 suites. 3 restaurants, 3 bars, indoor-outdoor pool, sauna, health club, concierge, business services, convention center, meeting rooms. AE, D, DC, MC, V. MARTA: Peachtree Center.*

$–$$ 🏨 **Quality Hotel.** Renovated in 1996, this quiet, small hotel, done in mauve with floral accents, has a lot of charm; some rooms have balconies. The hotel's restaurant, Jimmy D's, serves breakfast and lunch in a delightful retro '50s-diner atmosphere with red leatherette seating. ⊠ *89 Luckie St., 30303,* ☎ *404/524–7991,* ℻ *404/524–0672. 75 rooms. Restaurant. AE, D, DC, MC, V. MARTA: Peachtree Center.*

Buckhead

$$$$ ★ ⊞ **Ritz-Carlton, Buckhead.** Decorated with the Ritz's signature 18th- and 19th-century antiques, this elegant gem bids a discreet welcome. Shoppers from nearby Lenox Square Mall and Phipps Plaza often revive here over afternoon tea or cocktails in the richly paneled Lobby Lounge; at night, The Dining Room (☞ Chapter 3) serves creative contemporary cuisine that has won international acclaim. Ample rooms are furnished with traditional reproductions and have white-marble baths. From the hotel's Club Floors you get a lovely view of Buckhead and an understanding of why Atlanta is known as a city of trees. ⊠ *3434 Peachtree Rd., 30326,* ☎ *404/237–2700 or 800/241–3333,* ㎰ *404/239–0078. 524 rooms, 29 suites. Restaurant, bar, café, lobby lounge, indoor pool, hot tub, health club, concierge, business services, convention center, meeting rooms. AE, D, DC, MC, V. MARTA: Lenox Sq.*

$$$–$$$$ ⊞ **Embassy Suites Hotel.** Just blocks from the Phipps Plaza and Lenox Square malls is this contemporary high-rise with a variety of suites, ranging from deluxe presidential (with wet bars) to more basic suites. ⊠ *3285 Peachtree Rd., 30305,* ☎ *404/261–7733 or 800/362–2779,* ㎰ *404/261–6857. 313 suites. Restaurant, lobby lounge, indoor-outdoor pool, exercise room, concierge. AE, D, DC, MC, V. MARTA: Buckhead.*

$$$–$$$$ ★ ⊞ **Grand Hyatt Atlanta.** A two-tiered lobby facing a courtyard with a 9,000-sq-ft Japanese garden and cascading 35-ft waterfall is the opening statement of this modern, towering hotel. The understated decor is mainly black, gray, and purple; high-quality Japanese art adorns the walls of both public and private areas. Rooms are spacious and luxurious, with a style that's more American than Japanese; there are fax machines in every room. Two excellent restaurants respectively serve Japanese and Mediterranean cuisine. A complimentary shuttle takes guests anywhere within 2 mi of the hotel. ⊠ *3300 Peachtree Rd., 30305,* ☎ *404/365–8100 or 800/233–1234,* ㎰ *404/364–3952 for reservations, 404/233–5686 for guests. 407 rooms, 32 suites. 2 restaurants, bar, lobby lounge, pool, health club, concierge, business services, convention center, meeting rooms. AE, D, DC, MC, V. MARTA: Buckhead.*

102

Atlanta Airport
Hilton, **31**

Atlanta Dream
Hostel, **21**

Buckhead Bed &
Breakfast Inn, **6**

Crowne Plaza
Ravinia, **9**

Days Inn
Peachtree, **28**

Doubletree Guest
Suites Hotel, **30**

Embassy Suites
Hotel, **14**

Emory Inn, **18**

Evergreen
Conference
Center and
Resort, **20**

Four Seasons
Hotel Atlanta, **23**

Grand Hyatt
Atlanta, **10**

Holiday Inn
Atlanta–Decatur
Conference
Center, **22**

JW Marriott, **16**

Lenox Inn, **17**

Marriott
Residence Inn
Atlanta
Midtown, **25**

Renaissance
Atlanta Hotel–
Concourse, **32**

Renaissance
Atlanta Hotel–
Downtown, **29**

Renaissance
Waverly Hotel, **1**

Ritz-Carlton,
Buckhead, **12**

Shellmont Bed &
Breakfast Inn, **27**

Sheraton Colony
Square, **24**

Sierra Suites
Hotel, **4, 8**

Stone Mountain
Inn, **19**

Swissôtel, **13**

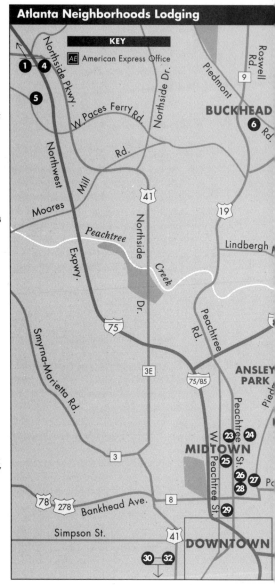

Atlanta Neighborhoods Lodging

KEY

AE   American Express Office

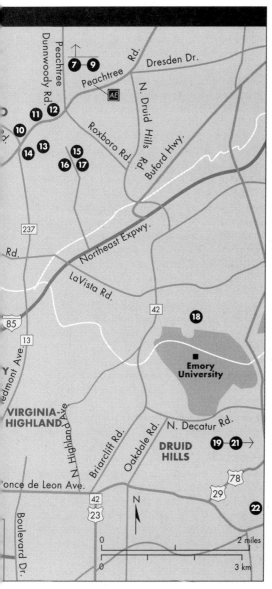

Terrace Garden
Hotel,
Buckhead, **15**

Victorian Inns, **3**

Westin North
Atlanta at
Perimeter, **7**

Whitlock Inn, **2**

Wyndam Garden
Hotel, **11**

Wyndam Garden
Hotel Paces
Ferry, **5**

Wyndam Hotel
Midtown, **26**

$$$–$$$$　🏨 **JW Marriott.** Handsome Chippendale-style furniture graces both the lobby and the guest rooms of this elegant 25-story hotel, which connects with Lenox Square Mall. Off the lobby, which has a marble floor and silver-leaf coffered ceiling, are a series of sitting rooms filled with plush sofas, flowers, and the sound of classical music. Guest rooms, in earth tones with traditional-style furniture, have gilt-framed paintings of Buckhead mansions. All have spacious marble baths with separate shower stalls. ✉ *3300 Lenox Rd., 30326,* ☎ *404/262–3344 or 800/228–9290,* 🆑 *404/262–8689. 361 rooms, 10 suites. Restaurant, bar, lobby lounge, indoor pool, health club, concierge, business services, convention center, meeting rooms. AE, D, DC, MC, V. MARTA: Lenox Sq.*

$$$–$$$$　🏨 **Swissôtel.** Sleek and efficient, this stylish European stunner built in 1991 has a chic glass-and-white-enamel exterior that echoes the facade of the High Museum of Art. Inside the expansive lobby, with its 45-ft windows, are a grand piano and comfortable sofas and chairs; the walls display original 20th-century art by international greats such as Chagall and Schnabel. Rooms, in subtle shades of gray and lavender, are furnished with sophisticated Biedermeier-style furniture, modern accent pieces, and leather-topped desks. Close to Lenox Square Mall, the hotel is a favorite with business travelers. ✉ *3391 Peachtree Rd., 30326,* ☎ *404/365–0065 or 800/253–1397,* 🆑 *404/365–8787. 348 rooms, 17 suites. Restaurant, bar, indoor pool, health club, concierge, business services, convention center, meeting rooms. AE, D, DC, MC, V. MARTA: Buckhead.*

$$–$$$$　🏨 **Terrace Garden Hotel, Buckhead.** This stylish hotel en-
★　　joys a prime location directly across from Lenox Square Mall. Befitting its name, it has one of the prettiest lobbies in town, with ficus trees, flowers, and other greenery. All of its comfortable rooms are furnished with mahogany reproductions of 18th-century French and English furniture and are decorated in green, beige, and mauve color schemes. The Health & Racquet Center will appeal to fitness enthusiasts. ✉ *3405 Lenox Rd., 30326,* ☎ *404/261–9250 or 800/241–8260,* 🆑 *404/848–7391. 355 rooms, 7 suites. Restaurant, bar, indoor pool, sauna, steam room, exercise room, racquetball, concierge, business services, convention center, meeting rooms. AE, D, DC, MC, V. MARTA: Lenox Sq.*

$–$$$$ 🗇 **Wyndham Garden Hotel.** The Wyndham has good-size rooms with traditional mahogany furniture and botanical prints. With reasonable rates and an excellent location between Lenox Square and Phipps Plaza malls in the heart of Buckhead, it's a bargain. Service is adequate, although it doesn't compare with that of luxury establishments in the area. Guests have complimentary access to a neighboring health club. ⊠ *3340 Peachtree Rd., 30326,* ☎ *404/231–1234 or 800/996–3426,* 𝐅𝐀𝐗 *404/231–5236. 217 rooms, 4 suites. Restaurant, bar. AE, D, DC, MC, V. MARTA: Buckhead.*

$–$$$ 🗇 **Lenox Inn.** If the Terrace Garden Hotel (☞ *above*) is full, try this attractive motel next door. It's under the same management, assuring good service at an affordable price. Divided among four two- and three-story buildings, the rooms are more motel-like than the other property's but are nicely decorated in cream, forest green, and mauve with mahogany colonial-style furniture. Only one building has an elevator. The Terrace Garden Inn's Health & Racquet Center is available for guests' use. ⊠ *3387 Lenox Rd., 30326,* ☎ *404/261–5500 or 800/241–0200,* 𝐅𝐀𝐗 *404/261– 6140. 174 rooms, 4 suites. 2 pools. AE, D, DC, MC, V. MARTA: Lenox Sq.*

$$ 🗇 **Buckhead Bed & Breakfast Inn.** Built in 1996 just in time for the Olympic Games, the inn sits on a busy corner but provides the intimacy and coziness that are lacking in the large hotels. Rooms are not especially spacious or intriguingly decorated, but simply utilitarian. The clientele is typically business travelers and sometimes wedding parties, as it's handy to the cluster of cathedrals that forms the hub of Buckhead. A full breakfast, substantial but not gourmet, is included. ⊠ *70 Lenox Pointe, 30324,* ☎ *404/261–8284 or 888/224– 8797,* 𝐅𝐀𝐗 *404/237-9224. 19 rooms. AE, MC, V.*

Midtown

$$$–$$$$ 🗇 **Four Seasons Hotel Atlanta.** Fashioned after Europe's
★ grand hotels, the Four Seasons offers luxury and royal service from the minute you enter its lavish atrium lobby, tiled with Spanish marble. A crystal chandelier hanging from the high ceiling and a sweeping grand staircase set the tone. Occupying the first 19 floors of the GLG Grand Building, the hotel has spacious rooms decorated in mauve

and earth tones, with a combination of traditional and contemporary furnishings that include a desk and sofa; marble bathrooms are well lit. ⊠ *75 14th St., 30309,* ☎ *404/881–9898 or 800/952–0702,* FAX *404/870–4289. 228 rooms, 18 suites. 2 restaurants, bar, indoor pool, health club, concierge, business services. AE, DC, MC, V. MARTA: Arts Center.*

$$–$$$$ 🏨 **Renaissance Atlanta Hotel—Downtown.** Between Downtown and Midtown, this 25-story hotel has a pretty marble-floor lobby and stunning panoramic views of the skyline from upper-story rooms. Rooms are large and have private patios or balconies, hair dryers, three telephones, and voice mail. Club Level suites are deluxe accommodations with a private lounge, and concierge service. ⊠ *590 W. Peachtree St., 30308,* ☎ *404/881–6000 or 800/468–3571,* FAX *404/815–5012. 480 rooms, 24 suites. 2 restaurants, lobby lounge, minibars, pool, health club, concierge floor, business services, convention center, meeting rooms. AE, D, DC, MC, V. MARTA: North Ave.*

$$–$$$$ 🏨 **Sheraton Colony Square.** Theatricality and opulence are epitomized by the dimly lit lobby with overhanging balconies and fresh flowers. Rooms are modern and decorated in muted tones—those on higher floors have nice city views. The best part of this hotel is its location: the 14th Street Playhouse is across the street, and the Woodruff Arts Center and the High Museum of Art are two blocks away. ⊠ *188 14th St., 30361,* ☎ *404/892–6000 or 800/422–7895,* FAX *404/872–9192. 428 rooms, 33 suites. Restaurant, lobby lounge, pool, health club, concierge, business services, convention center, meeting rooms. AE, D, DC, MC, V. MARTA: Arts Center.*

$$–$$$ 🏨 **Days Inn Peachtree.** This hotel is one of Days Inn's best, a striking contrast from standard chain fare. A 12-story former luxury apartment building built in 1920s, it has a sumptuous lobby with four 1920s chandeliers suspended from the lofty mahogany-paneled ceiling, antique furniture, a piano, and Oriental rugs. The rooms further this theme, with mahogany furnishings and mauve, teal, and burgundy decor. This hotel is handy to the Fox Theatre across the street, so guests often include entertainers performing at the Fox. Guests have access to a nearby health club. ⊠ *683 Peachtree St., 30308,* ☎ *404/874–9200 or 800/329–7466,* FAX

404/873–4245. 140 rooms, 2 suites. Coin laundry. AE, D, DC, MC, V. MARTA: North Ave.

$$–$$$ 🏨 **Marriott Residence Inn Atlanta Midtown.** Only a block from the MARTA Midtown station, this seven-story, suites-only hotel evokes a luxury apartment building. Each suite, decorated in soft pastel colors, has a large kitchen and marble-tiled bath, comfortable oak and mahogany 19th-century American and English reproduction furniture, full-length mirrors, ceiling fans, and TVs in every room. A free Continental breakfast is served in a room off the lobby. Grocery shopping service is available. ✉ *1041 W. Peachtree St., 30309,* ☎ *404/872–8885 or 800/331–3131,* FAX *404/872–8885. 66 suites. Restaurant, bar, indoor pool, hot tub, coin laundry, business services, convention center, meeting rooms. CP. AE, D, DC, MC, V. MARTA: Midtown.*

$$–$$$ 🏨 **Shellmont Bed & Breakfast Inn.** In the heart of Midtown's
★ residential district, this delightful, authentically restored 1891 mansion combines Federal, Greek Revival, and Queen Anne architectural styles. Its large, 12-ft-ceiling rooms have ornate plasterwork, claw-foot bathtubs, antique furniture, and Oriental rugs. A cottage (the former carriage house) in back of the house has a living room and kitchen. A full breakfast is served on china with cloth napkins in the downstairs dining room, which has a handsome fireplace. Another fireplace in the living room is inviting on cold winter nights. ✉ *821 Piedmont Ave., 30308,* ☎ *404/872–9290. 4 rooms, 1 cottage. Breakfast room, library. AE, DC, MC, V. MARTA: Midtown.*

$–$$$ 🏨 **Wyndham Hotel Midtown.** The spacious rooms of this 1987 redbrick hotel in the center of Midtown have bay windows and are pale green; each has a large armoire for the television, an armchair with hassock, and a coffeemaker. Executive King rooms are even larger and include a sofa and extra televisions and telephones. ✉ *125 10th St., 30309,* ☎ *404/873–4800 or 800/996–3426,* FAX *404/870–1530. 159 rooms, 32 suites. Restaurant, bar, lobby lounge, indoor pool, hot tub, health club, concierge, business services, convention center, meeting rooms. AE, D, DC, MC, V. MARTA: Midtown.*

Perimeter Vicinity—Inside I-285

$$$-$$$$ ⓣ **Renaissance Waverly Hotel.** Northwest Atlanta's most
     ★ luxurious hotel provides the necessities for conventioneers
and shoppers. The hotel's marble-paneled lobby with its
14-story atrium is a good place in which to relax, and on
the premises are some of the area's best restaurants. De-
spite some uninspiring views of I-285, the ample rooms are
appealingly decorated in rich, autumn hues, with 19th-
century English reproduction mahogany furniture. Rooms
on the east end overlook a small park—a pleasant place for
a walk or a picnic lunch. Club Level rooms share a lounge
and a concierge and come with Continental breakfast. ⊠
2450 Galleria Pkwy., 30339, ☎ *770/953–4500 or 800/468–
3571,* ⒻⒶⓍ *404/953–0740. 504 rooms, 24 suites. 2 restau-
rants, 2 bars, indoor-outdoor pool, health club, racquetball,
concierge, business services, convention center, meeting
rooms. AE, D, DC, MC, V.*

$-$$$$ ⓣ **Atlanta Airport Hilton.** For functions near the airport, this
modern hotel with complete conference facilities offers all
the services you will ever need. Standard rooms, slightly larger
alcove rooms, and suites are decorated in soft earth tones.
In the separate Towers section, a special Concierge Class in-
cludes upgraded amenities such as hair dryers, plusher tow-
els, and 25-inch televisions. All rooms have a data port for
computers and the latest in voice messaging. Sports fans will
end up at the Finish Line Sports Bar, with its 31-inch tele-
visions; just look for the stock car hanging from the ceiling.
⊠ *1031 Virginia Ave., 30354,* ☎ *404/767–9000 or
800/445–8667,* ⒻⒶⓍ *404/768–0185. 441 rooms, 57 alcove
rooms, 5 suites. 2 restaurants, sports bar, indoor-outdoor
pool, beauty salon, tennis court, health club, concierge,
business services, convention center, meeting rooms, airport
shuttle. AE, D, DC, MC, V. MARTA: Airport.*

$-$$$$ ⓣ **Renaissance Atlanta Hotel—Concourse.** Favored by south-
side conference planners and by those on short business trips,
this contemporary atrium hotel with a traditional interior
provides convenience and excellent services. Spacious, com-
fortable rooms, with tan-and-green decor, have private pa-
tios or balconies, hair dryers, and two telephones with
voice mail. Club Level suites offer deluxe accommoda-
tions, a lounge, and other special services. ⊠ *1 Hartsfield
Centre Pkwy., 30354,* ☎ *404/209–9999 or 800/468–*

3571, FAX *404/209–8934. 370 rooms, 17 suites. Restaurant, bar, minibars, indoor-outdoor pool, health club, concierge floor, business services, convention center, meeting rooms. AE, D, DC, MC, V. MARTA: Airport.*

$$-$$$ 🏨 **Emory Inn.** Nearly an institution—anyone who comes to Emory University for business or an event stays here if there's a vacancy—this long-established hotel tucked into a forestlike area provides a peaceful setting away from the bustle of the main business districts. Still, they're a short drive away: 3 mi to Midtown, 5–6 mi to Downtown and Buckhead. At press time, rooms were being renovated; they will have earth-tone color schemes and early American-style pine furniture. The inn is connected to the Emory Conference Center Hotel, a 197-room facility for meetings with a lap pool and health club that guests may use. ⊠ *1641 Clifton Rd., 30329,* ☎ *404/712–6700 or 800/933–6679,* FAX *404/712–6701. 106 rooms, 1 suite. 2 restaurants, pool, hot tub, coin laundry, concierge, business services, convention center, meeting rooms. AE, D, DC, MC, V.*

$$-$$$ 🏨 **Holiday Inn Atlanta–Decatur Conference Center.** A good hotel in the heart of the charming town of Decatur, just 5 mi from Downtown, this striking, postmodern Holiday Inn provides both convenience and value. Within walking distance are the historic Decatur courthouse, now housing the county historical society, and numerous interesting shops and restaurants. Renovated in 1996, the hotel provides ironing boards, hair dryers, faxes, and coffeemakers in the dark green, rust, and burgundy rooms with traditional furnishings. The top floor is the executive level. ⊠ *130 Clairemont Ave., Decatur 30030,* ☎ *404/371–0204 or 800/225–6079,* FAX *404/377–2726. 180 rooms, 4 suites. Restaurant, lobby lounge, indoor pool, hot tub, exercise room, concierge, business services, convention center, meeting rooms. AE, D, DC, MC, V. MARTA: Decatur.*

$-$$$ 🏨 **Wyndham Garden Hotel Paces Ferry.** To get away from busier areas, come to this hotel in the parklike setting of suburban Vinings, a small, exclusive neighborhood near Cumberland Mall, but still convenient to the major business districts (5 mi from Buckhead and a quick trip to Midtown and Downtown on nearby I–75). The Wyndham Garden has efficient service and spacious rooms with plush furniture. It's popular with business travelers visiting the many corporate offices nearby in the I–75/I–285 corridor. Guests have access ($10) to the health club behind the hotel. ⊠ *2857 Paces Ferry Rd., Vinings 30339,* ☎ *770/432– 5555 or 800/822–4200,* FAX *404/436–5558. 141 rooms, 18 suites. Restaurant, lobby lounge, pool, 2 tennis courts, business services. AE, D, DC, MC, V.*

$$ 🏨 **Sierra Suites Hotel.** Studio-style suites with kitchens are decorated in earth tones and forest green. Light wood modern-style furniture with an oak finish is standard. ⊠ *2010 Powers Ferry Rd., 30339,* ☎ *770/933–8010 or 800/474– 3772,* FAX *770/933–8181. 89 suites. Pool, health club, coin laundry. AE, D, DC, MC, V.*

$ 🏨 **Atlanta Dream Hostel.** Basic, clean, and safe dormitory accommodations start at $13 per person at this hostel (students and foreign travelers only; photo ID necessary), while private rooms in the funky St. Agnes Inn next door range from $25 for a single to $36 for a double. Owners John Makar and John McGuinness are especially vigilant about issues of safety and security. Kitchen facilities are shared, and the St. Agnes Tea Garden is an attached restaurant that is open to the public. ⊠ *115 Church St., Decatur, 30030,* ☎ *404/370–0380. Hostel: 40 beds; Inn: 9 beds. Restaurant, kitchen. AE, MC, V. MARTA: Decatur.*

Perimeter Vicinity—Outside I-285

$$$–$$$$ 🏨 **Doubletree Guest Suites Hotel.** Just outside I–285, this primarily suites hotel, with its identifiable mansard roof, is popular with businesspeople in northwest Atlanta. The spacious one-bedroom suites, each with a two-person whirlpool tub and some with connecting single rooms, provide a little more luxury than the average suites hotel. A complimentary Continental breakfast is available in the lobby. ⊠ *2780 Whitley Rd., at U.S. 41, 30339,* ☎ *770/980– 1900 or 800/843–5858,* FAX *770/980–1528. 14 rooms, 141 suites. Restaurant, bar, pool, exercise room. CP. AE, D, DC, MC, V.*

$$$–$$$$ 🏨 **Evergreen Conference Center and Resort.** Only 16 mi from Downtown, near the lakefront among the tall pine trees at Stone Mountain Park, this is a great place for a conference or a family getaway, especially at holiday times (ask about family packages). The lodgelike lobby has a massive

stone fireplace. Rooms are decorated in neutral, woodsy tones and have mahogany 18th-century-style furnishings. In summer and on weekends, the park is fairly crowded, so book far in advance; weekdays are much calmer. ⊠ *1 Lakeview Dr., Stone Mountain 30083,* ☎ *770/879–9900 or 800/722–1000,* FAX *770/469–9013. 220 rooms, 29 suites. Restaurant, indoor-outdoor pool, wading pool, 2 tennis courts, health club, concierge, business services, convention center, meeting rooms. AE, D, DC, MC, V.*

$–$$$$ 🏨 **Crowne Plaza Ravinia.** This pretty hotel offers a taste of luxury. The spacious guest rooms have light pine furniture and neutral color schemes. A waterfall, birds, tropical plants, and a greenhouse dining area enliven the three-story atrium. La Grotta, an extension of the Buckhead restaurant, serves superb Italian cuisine (☞ Chapter 3). On the grounds is a nature area with walking trails and streams. For shopping, Perimeter Mall, Park Place, and myriad other stores line the road. ⊠ *4355 Ashford-Dunwoody Rd., Dunwoody 30346,* ☎ *770/395–7700 or 800/554–0055,* FAX *770/375–9453 for reservations, 770/392–9503 for guests. 459 rooms, 36 suites. 4 restaurants, lobby lounge, indoor pool, outdoor hot tub, basketball, health club, concierge, business services, convention center, meeting rooms. AE, D, DC, MC, V.*

$–$$$$ 🏨 **Westin North Atlanta at Perimeter.** This hotel, with ultramodern glass architecture, is part of the Concourse office park complex. It wins kudos with area businesspeople for its spacious rooms, efficient service, and convenient location near I–285 and GA 400. Guests have access ($10) to the Concourse Athletic Club next door. ⊠ *7 Concourse Pkwy., 30328,* ☎ *770/395–3900 or 800/937–8461,* FAX *770/395–3935. 351 rooms, 19 suites. Restaurant, pool, concierge, business services, convention center, meeting rooms. AE, D, DC, MC, V. MARTA: Medical Center.*

$$–$$$ 🏨 **Whitlock Inn.** In the heart of the Marietta historic district, just one block from Marietta's square, this carefully ★ restored gleaming white Victorian has a wide veranda and exquisite gardens. One room has a canopy bed, another has a sleigh bed, and the bridal suite has a four-poster bed. A ballroom hosts small conferences, weddings, and other events. Snacks and full breakfast are included. ⊠ *57 Whit-*

lock Ave., Marietta 30064, ☎ 770/428–1495, ℻ 770/919–
9620. 5 rooms. AE, D, MC, V.

$–$$$ 🏨 **Victorian Inns.** In suburban Marietta's historic district,
the Stanley House and Marlow House operate together as
Victorian Inns. Stanley House is a beautifully restored,
three-story 1895 Queen Anne B&B inn with a wraparound
porch and 13-ft ceilings. Larger Marlow House, also a
Queen Anne Victorian, was built in 1887. Rooms contain
decorative fireplaces, antiques, and claw-foot bathtubs;
some have showers. Marlow House suites also have kitchens,
sitting rooms with televisions, and private telephone lines.
Both houses have cozy guest parlors, embellished with
plants and working fireplaces. Ample Continental break-
fast for both inns is served at Stanley House in its formal
dining room. The inns are in walking distance to the his-
toric town square, with its park, shops, theater, coffee-
house, and restaurants. ✉ 192 and 236 Church St., Marietta
30060, ☎ 770/426–1881. Stanley House: 4 rooms, 1 suite;
Marlow House: 3 suites. Meeting rooms (one in each inn).
CP. AE, MC, V.

$$ 🏨 **Sierra Suites Hotel.** Studio-style suites with kitchens are
decorated in earth tones and forest green. Light wood mod-
ern-style furniture with an oak finish is standard. ✉ 6330
Peachtree Dunwoody Rd., 30328, ☎ 770/379–0111 or
800/474–3772, ℻ 770/379–9225. 101 suites. Pool, health
club, coin laundry. AE, D, DC, MC, V.

$–$$ 🏨 **Stone Mountain Inn.** This colonnaded two-story hotel
in Stone Mountain Park resembles an antebellum plantation house and has large rooms with reproduction walnut
and mahogany Chippendale furnishings. The food at its buf-
fet-style restaurant, with southern and other American favorites, attracts a local crowd. Recreational opportunities
are abundant in the park. ✉ Stone Mountain Park, U.S.
78, Stone Mountain Pkwy., Stone Mountain 30086, ☎
770/469–3311 or 800/277–0007, ℻ 770/498–5691. 92
rooms. Restaurant, pool, coin laundry, business services.
AE, D, DC, MC, V.

5 Nightlife and the Arts

By Mark
Beffart

Updated
by Jane
Garvey

ATLANTA, the entertainment capital of the south has earned the nickname "Hotlanta." Whether you're seeking black-tie cultural happenings or performances by local musicians in back-alley clubs, you're sure to find something to your liking.

Finding Out What's On

For the most complete schedule of current and upcoming cultural events and entertainment, check the *Atlanta Journal-Constitution*'s Friday Weekend Preview or Saturday Leisure tabloid sections. *Creative Loafing,* a lively and opinionated alternative press distributed weekly for free at restaurants, bars, and bookstores, has the best discussion of the local music and club scenes, besides information about other entertainment. You can also call the 24-hour **Arts Hotline** (☎ 404/853–3278). *The Atlanta Journal-Constitution* displays current arts and entertainment information at its Web site: http://www.accessatlanta.com¢purefun.

Tickets

Attending music concerts by national acts will cost from $20 to $45. Atlanta Symphony Orchestra prices range from $11 to $45; theater prices are from $18 to $35. For convenience, **Ticketmaster** (☎ 404/249–6400) handles tickets for events at some venues; the service charge is $3–$5 per ticket, plus a handling fee per order of $.50–$1.60. Most local theaters and clubs sell tickets directly through their own box offices.

THE ARTS

For many Atlantans, the landmark **Fox Theatre** (✉ 660 Peachtree St., ☎ 404/881–2100) is the number-one place to view entertainment. Despite its 4,518 seats, the Fox feels relatively intimate. The Moorish-Egyptian interior decoration is awesome, and the acoustics are good. Although the **Atlanta Civic Center** (✉ 395 Piedmont Ave., Midtown, ☎ 404/523–6275) seats around 5,000 people, it has clear sight lines and an excellent stage for theater and dance.

Dance

Ballet

Atlanta Ballet Company. Founded in 1929, this company has received international recognition for its productions of classical ballets (*Romeo and Juliet, The Nutcracker*) and contemporary works (*Peter Pan*). Performances are at the Fox Theatre (☞ *above*). ✉ *1400 W. Peachtree St., 30309,* ☎ *404/873–5811.*

Georgia Ballet. Artistic director Iris Hensley formed this company almost 40 years ago to perform classical and contemporary ballets. Performances are at the Cobb Civic Center (✉ 548 S. Marietta Pkwy., Marietta, ☎ 770/528–8450). ✉ *999 Whitlock Ave., Marietta 30064,* ☎ *770/425–0258.*

International Ballet Rotaru. Romanian dancer Pavel Rotaru and his group perform classic, spirited ballet. The company's dancers have been trained in the Kirov method. ✉ *2 Ravinia Dr., Dunwoody 30338,* ☎ *770/395–5322.*

Ruth Mitchell Dance Theatre. Three to four full-length ballets are usually scheduled fall through spring. ✉ *81 Church St., Marietta 30060,* ☎ *770/426–0007.*

Modern Dance

The area's colleges are the best places to find modern dance performances.

Atlanta Jazz Theatre. One of the city's best modern dance troupes, AJT performs twice a year at changing venues. ✉ *5568 Chamblee-Dunwoody Rd., Dunwoody 30338,* ☎ *770/393–9519.*

Lee Harper & Dancers. This company, founded in 1980, performs with the Atlanta Symphony Orchestra in its Symphony Street programs and family concerts. Performances are at a variety of venues. ✉ *721 Miami Circle, Suite 106, 30324,* ☎ *404/261–7416.*

Music and Opera

Chamber and Choral Groups

In Atlanta, numerous choral groups form and disband, performing mainly in churches and academic settings. The area's colleges and universities have many popular musical organizations, the most famous, perhaps, being the **Morehouse**

Chorus and Glee Club (☎ 404/681–2800). What follows is a selection of those that have demonstrated longevity.

Atlanta Boys' Choir. Fletcher Wolfe founded this group in 1955 following the pattern of the Vienna Boys' Choir. The choir tours Europe and Mexico each year and performs often with the Atlanta Symphony Orchestra (ASO). ✉ *1215 S. Ponce de Leon Ave., 30306,* ☎ *404/378–0064.*

Atlanta Chamber Players. This group performs classical and contemporary works by leading composers like Beethoven and Copland at various Atlanta locations during its fall–spring season. ✉ *953 Rosedale Rd.,* ☎ *770/242–2227.*

Atlanta Virtuosi. Founded in 1977, this chamber gives concerts at the Oglethorpe University Museum of Art. ✉ *4484 Peachtree Rd.,* ☎ *770/938–8611.*

Thamyris. For more than a decade, this established group has devoted itself to 20th-century chamber music. Performances are at Emory University's Performing Arts Studio (✉ N. Decatur Rd. at Clifton Rd.). ✉ *2285 Peachtree Rd., Suite 221, 30309,* ☎ *404/352–8144.*

Concerts

Chastain Park Amphitheatre. Performances in this facility, a few miles north of the heart of Buckhead, might be from musicians as diverse as ASO, Bonnie Raitt, and the Pointer Sisters. Several levels of seating are available; you can dine at a table before and during the concert, sit on stone seats (bring a cushion), or sprawl on the lawn. ✉ *4469 Stella Dr.,* ☎ *404/733–4900 ASO, 404/888–9961 Concerts Southern.*

Coca-Cola Lakewood. At this 18,000-seat facility, concerts by such stars as the Allman Brothers, Jimmy Buffet, and Reba McIntyre are held from April to the end of October. ✉ *2002 Lakewood Way, between Downtown and airport,* ☎ *404/627–6739.*

The Coca-Cola Roxy Theater. Buckhead's only concert hall hums with music by popular rock performers like The Wallflowers and Sheryl Crow. Seating is in the balcony and sometimes on folding chairs on the floor. Acoustics are good. ✉ *3110 Roswell Rd.,* ☎ *404/233–7699.*

Georgia State University Recital Hall. Small community choral, chamber, symphonic, and jazz performances are often free and open to the public. ✉ *10 Peachtree Center Ave., at Gilmer St.,* ☎ *404/651–4636.*

Rialto Center for the Performing Arts. A model of urban rehabilitation, this 950-seat venue is the setting for comedy, dance, drama, and music performances. ⊠ *80 Forsyth St., at Luckie St.,* ☎ *404/651–4727.*

Robert Ferst Center for the Arts. This facility hosts the finest in theater, music, comedy, dance, opera, and the visual arts by visiting luminaries. ⊠ *350 Ferst Dr.,* ☎ *404/894–9600.*

Spivey Hall. Scenic Spivey Hall has superb acoustics; it hosts celebrated classical, jazz, and organ concerts. ⊠ *5900 N. Lee St., Clayton College and State University, Morrow,* ☎ *770/961–3683.*

Variety Playhouse. A hip lineup of alternative rock bands, progressive country, and blues are performed here. Light snacks, beer, and wine are available. ⊠ *1099 Euclid Ave., Little Five Points,* ☎ *404/521–1786.*

Opera

Atlanta Opera. Local singers and musicians and internationally known guest artists join forces to stage four full-length operas per year in the Fox Theatre (☞ *above*). Productions include classic and modern operas. ⊠ *1800 Peachtree St., Suite 20, 30309,* ☎ *404/355–3311.*

Savoyards Musical Theatre. Known for performances of Gilbert and Sullivan, this company, with a 26-piece orchestra, has expanded its repertoire to include other kinds of musical productions. Performances are at the Robert Ferst Center for the Arts (☞ *above*). ⊠ *3101 Roswell Rd., N–149, Marietta 30062,* ☎ *770/565–9651.*

Orchestra

Atlanta Symphony Orchestra. Under the musical direction of Yoel Levi, the orchestra, which celebrated its 50th anniversary in 1997, has achieved world-class renown. It performs fall–spring in Symphony Hall at Woodruff Arts Center; in summer, the orchestra occasionally accompanies big-name artists in Chastain Park's outdoor amphitheater. ⊠ *1280 Peachtree St., Woodruff Arts Center,* ☎ *404/733–5000.*

Theater

Unlike cities with a distinct theater district or row, Atlanta has companies spread throughout the metropolitan area

Although these groups and some of the names on the marquee are not world renowned, you'll enjoy good, innovative theater.

Downtown

Academy Theatre. Founded in 1956, Atlanta's oldest theater company performs new works, some of them by area playwrights. ⊠ *501 Means St.,* ☎ *404/525–4111.*

Actor's Express. Near the CNN Center, cutting-edge productions of works by local and nationally renowned playwrights are presented in an intimate, 150-seat theater in the stylish King Plow Arts Center, which also houses artists' studios and galleries and a fine restaurant, The Food Studio (☞ Chapter 3). ⊠ *887 W. Marietta St.,* ☎ *404/607–7469.*

Onstage Atlanta. Onstage performs consistently interesting dramatic presentations, comedies, and musicals in its 130-seat theater. **ABRACADABRA! Children's Theatre** performs at Onstage Atlanta, each year producing five works that adapt children's literature for the stage. ⊠ *280 Elizabeth St., Inman Park,* ☎ *404/897–1802.*

Little Five Points

Horizon Theatre Company. Productions from Horizon include new works, including comedies, by contemporary playwrights. ⊠ *1083 Austin Ave.,* ☎ *404/584–7450.*

Seven Stages. Thought-provoking plays about contemporary social issues often feature foreign performers. ⊠ *1105 Euclid Ave.,* ☎ *404/523–7647.*

Midtown

Alliance Theatre. One of the South's best, the Alliance mounts everything from Shakespeare to the latest Broadway and Off-Broadway shows on its large primary stage in the Woodruff Arts Center. Gutsy alternative productions are produced in the smaller Studio Theatre downstairs. The **Alliance Children's Theatre** performs children's classics. ⊠ *1280 Peachtree St., Woodruff Arts Center,* ☎ *404/733–5000.*

Atlanta Shakespeare Tavern. In addition to works by William Shakespeare, this company performs classics of European theater, from Molière to Shaw. ⊠ *499 Peachtree St.,* ☎ *404/874–5299.*

Center for Puppetry Arts. A museum as well as a theater, the center presents new and classic works for puppet theater for both children and adults. ✉ *1404 Spring St.,* ☎ *404/873–3391.*

The 14th Street Playhouse. This state-of-the-art theater facility is used by a variety of companies including the **Theatrical Outfit** (☎ 404/872–0665), which makes classic plays new and new plays classic; **Jomandi Productions** (☎ 404/870–0629), the city's best African-American company, specializing in works by contemporary black playwrights; **Theatre Gael** (☎ 404/876–1138), which stages plays by Celtic and Celtic-American writers; **Jewish Theatre of the South** (☎ 770/368–7469), which performs new works with Jewish content; and **Barking Dog Theater** (☎ 404/885–1621), which produces modern American classics in a fast-paced, edgy style. ✉ *173 14th St.,* ☎ *404/733–4750.*

Whole World Theater. In a relaxed setting in a tiny warehouse black-box theater, this company presents modern improvisational theatrical shows combining traditional theater with comedy. It also stages full-length productions of works from the classics to modern theater, always with an off-beat slant. ✉ *1214 Spring St.,* ☎ *404/252–5233.*

Suburbs

Neighborhood Playhouse. Mainstream dramas, comedies, and musicals are performed in a 170-seat main theater in a former elementary school. In **Discovery Arena,** a separate black-box theater, original (sometimes bizarre) works by local playwrights are performed; **Explorer Kidz Theatre** stages original works for children. Both are units of **Neighborhood Playhouse.** ✉ *430 W. Trinity Pl., Decatur,* ☎ *404/373–5311.*

Stage Door Players. A nonprofit theater, Stage Door performs musicals and contemporary plays. Each year the company does six plays, a summer new-play festival, and children's theater. ✉ *5339 Chamblee-Dunwoody Rd., North DeKalb Cultural Center, Womack Rd., Dunwoody,* ☎ *770/396–1726.*

Theater in the Square. This award-winning company has become popular with audiences from all over metro Atlanta for its fine productions of modern classics and its numerous world premieres. ✉ *11 Whitlock Ave., Marietta,* ☎ *770/422–8369.*

Village Center Playhouse. This 300-seat theater-in-the-round, a former twin-screen cinema, houses on one side a community company that specializes in romantic pieces, musicals, uplifting dramas, and family oriented comedy. On the other side, the **Storybook Theater** is a year-round children's theater performing seven shows per season. ✉ *617 Holcomb Bridge Rd., at Alpharetta Hwy., Roswell Village Shopping Center, Roswell,* ☎ *770/998–3526.*

NIGHTLIFE

Since its beginnings as a bawdy railroad town, Atlanta has been known for having more bars than churches; in the South, that's an oddity. The city's vibrant nightlife scene, supported by a large under-40 population, includes everything from quiet coffeehouses to raucous sports bars, country line dancing to high-energy techno dance clubs, acoustic to grunge music clubs. Bars and nightspots are spread throughout the city and into the suburbs, but if there is a party central, it's in Buckhead.

Most bars and clubs are open every night until 2 AM–4 AM. Those with live entertainment usually have a cover charge between $3 and $10. For schedules of current and upcoming acts at clubs, consult *Creative Loafing* or the *Atlanta Journal-Constitution.* Always call ahead; clubs can have a short life span.

Bars

The Bar, Four Seasons Atlanta Hotel. Posh, elegant, and soothing, The Bar has the perfect corner for intimate conversation. ✉ *75 14th St., Midtown,* ☎ *404/881–9898.*

The Bar, Ritz-Carlton, Atlanta. The after-business crowd gathers at this elegant upstairs bar and lounge, where the martini types are numerous (32!), the bar nibbles elegant, and the music (every night save Sunday) is sophisticated. ✉ *181 Peachtree St., at Ellis St., Downtown,* ☎ *404/659–0400.*

Fadó. The liveliest Irish pub this side of Galway serves up fine food from the auld sod (salmon, Irish stew), the right atmosphere (lots of dark woods, intimate nooks and crannies, outdoor seating), and plenty of brews. ✉ *3035 Peachtree Rd., Buckhead,* ☎ *404/841–0066.*

Jocks N Jills Sports Bar. Atlanta's most successful chain of sports bars has decent food and drink and lots of wide-screen TVs. The CNN location is a popular gathering place after games at the nearby Georgia Dome and after meetings at the adjacent Georgia World Congress Center. ⊠ *1 CNN Center,* ☎ *404/688–4225; 4 other locations.*

Manuel's Tavern. Between Little Five Points and Virginia-Highland lies a 35-year-old neighborhood bar where patrons from all walks of life gather for drinks, bar food, and conversation. The 11 TVs (including two wide screens) attract a crowd when sports events matter to Atlanta. ⊠ *602 N. Highland Ave.,* ☎ *404/525–3447.*

Prince of Wales. This cozy English pub with good fish 'n' chips and superior brews on tap makes a comfy spot for homesick Brits. ⊠ *1144 Piedmont Ave., across from Piedmont Park,* ☎ *404/876–0227.*

The Star Community Bar. This bar is a popular gathering place for drinks and live music from swing to rockabilly and rock to alternative country. Don't miss "Gracevault," its memorial to Elvis Presley. The "Little Vinyl Lounge" downstairs is for cigars and martinis. ⊠ *437 Moreland Ave., Little Five Points,* ☎ *404/681–9018.*

The Vortex. Great burgers, a friendly atmosphere, and a long beer list keep both locations packed. The original, on West Peachtree, is hung high with outrageous paraphernalia; the second location has a Munch-inspired munchkin screaming at its entrance. ⊠ *1041 W. Peachtree St., Midtown,* ☎ *404/875–1667;* ⊠ *438 Moreland Ave., Little Five Points,* ☎ *404/688–1828.*

Coffeehouses

Cafe Diem. Lying between Virginia-Highland and Little Five Points, this longstanding neighborhood spot recalls classic Left Bank cafés, with outdoor dining and a hip, bohemian clientele. ⊠ *640 N. Highland Ave., south of Ponce de Leon Ave.,* ☎ *404/607–7008.*

Java Blues. This spot serves excellent coffee and a full menu. In the afternoons youngsters gather for chess; in the evenings young adults come for the blues (Thursday–Sunday) and the conviviality. Wednesday is open-mike night.

Wine is also served. ✉ *10 Whitlock Ave., Marietta,* ☎ *770/419–0095.*

Urban Coffee Bungalow. This stylish coffee bar serves great coffee, sandwiches, and homemade desserts. ✉ *1425-B Piedmont Ave., near Monroe Dr. and Piedmont Park,* ☎ *404/892–8212.*

Comedy Clubs

Punchline. Punchline, the best place to catch national performers, showcases three comedians every night. Some shows are nonsmoking. Reservations are required; it's worth the $1.50 extra to snag a priority seat. Light fare is available. ✉ *280 Hilderbrand Dr., Balconies Shopping Center, Sandy Springs,* ☎ *404/252–5233.*

Uptown Comedy Corner. This upscale club showcases national stars and local amateur talent, with an emphasis on black comedians. ✉ *2140 Peachtree Rd., Brookwood Sq. Shopping Center,* ☎ *404/350–6990.*

Dance Clubs

Club Anytime. A disc jockey spins popular music for rock-around-the-clock dancing. ✉ *1055 Peachtree St.,* ☎ *404/607–8050.*

Johnny's Hideaway. Frequented by the over-50 set, this longtime favorite has ballroom dancing to the big-band sounds of the 1940s and 1950s, Elvis ballads, and golden oldies rock. ✉ *3771 Roswell Rd.,* ☎ *404/233–8026.*

Kaya. A diverse club serving up bistro food and a mix of music (both live and DJ) for dancing, Kaya has a different theme—pop, disco, jazz—every night. There's cabaret on Monday. ✉ *1068 Peachtree St.,* ☎ *404/874–4460.*

Otto's. A sophisticated small club, Otto's has live music—usually jazz or blues—Wednesday–Saturday downstairs; a DJ plays high-energy music upstairs, beginning Tuesdays at 5 PM. ✉ *265 E. Paces Ferry Rd., Buckhead,* ☎ *404/233–1133.*

Oxygen. Dance music runs from techno to disco, beginning at 9 PM nightly except Sundays. ✉ *3065 Peachtree St., Buckhead,* ☎ *404/816–6522.*

Music Clubs

Acoustic

Eddie's Attic. Seating 225 people, this is the best venue for local and national acoustic acts. The now-famous Indigo Girls, natives of Decatur, had some of their first gigs here. ✉ *515-B N. McDonough St., Decatur,* ☎ *404/377–4976.*

The Freight Room. In the former train depot of a nearby suburb, this venue books top-notch local folk, bluegrass, and country artists, and it has a broad menu. ✉ *301 E. Howard St., Decatur,* ☎ *404/378–5365.*

Blues

Blind Willie's. One of the 20 best blues clubs in the country, Blind Willie's is definitely the best blues parlor in town for both music and atmosphere. The bands—local, rising stars, and legendary greats—play Mississippi Delta–, Chicago–, and New Orleans–style blues in a smoky, always-crowded setting. Covers can be hefty, starting at $10. Get here early as seats are in high demand; music starts at 10 PM. ✉ *828 N. Highland Ave., Virginia-Highland,* ☎ *404/873–2583.*

Daddy D'z. Near the capitol, this place cooks every night—serving both the blues (Fridays and Saturdays) and an excellent, inexpensive rib plate. No cover. ✉ *265 Memorial Dr., Downtown,* ☎ *404/222–0206.*

Fat Matt's Rib Shack. On the north fringe of Midtown, the shack resembles a small Texas roadhouse; it's a great place to eat barbecued pork ribs and, after 8:30 every night, to hear live blues bands. No cover. ✉ *1811 Piedmont Ave.,* ☎ *404/607–1622.*

Fuzzy's Place. This small, smoke-filled performance space is a neighborhood hangout that serves excellent Cajun food into the wee hours. TVs draw sports enthusiasts while music fans come for the blues and rock by local artists, including The Cold Chills, Francine Reed, and Barry Richman. No cover. ✉ *2015 N. Druid Hills Rd.,* ☎ *404/321–6166.*

Lou's Blues Review. Handy to Downtown, this dark and urbane blues room attracts musicians from around the South, but the house band, Lou's Blues Review, delivers extraordinary performances. Food is available, but it's not interesting. Cover charges run up to $10. ✉ *736 Ponce de Leon Ave.,* ☎ *404/249–7311.*

Smith's Olde Bar. A wide variety of talent, both local and regional, appears in this acoustically fine performance space. Undistinguished food is available at the restaurant downstairs. Covers vary widely, depending on the act, but are usually in the $5–$10 range. ✉ *1578 Piedmont Ave.,* ☎ *404/875–1522.*

Whiskers. A neighborhood tavern featuring blues and rock groups, Whiskers hosts some of the area's best local talent, such as Eric Quincy Tate. Bar food is freshly made. No cover. ✉ *8371 Roswell Rd., in shopping center at Roswell and Northridge Rds.,* ☎ *770/992–7445.*

Country

Buckboard Country Music Showcase. The area's biggest country music club has a house band (the Buckboard Bandits) and lots of good-time dancing. Celebrities like Billy Ray Cyrus occasionally pop in for its Thursday night showcase of musicians. A bar menu is available. ✉ *2080 Cobb Pkwy., in Windy Hill Plaza Shopping Center, Smyrna,* ☎ *770/955–7340.*

Cowboys. With 4,000 square ft of dance floor, Cowboys is *the* happening place for country music fans. Live music fills the air every night, and Wednesday–Friday and Sunday, its friendly staff gives dance lessons. ✉ *1750 N. Roberts Rd., Kennesaw,* ☎ *770/426–5006.*

Mama's Country Showcase. A club that looks straight out of Texas, Mama's has a mechanical bull to ride and a packed dance floor stompin' to the latest country rhythms. Live music is performed periodically. ✉ *3952 Covington Hwy., Decatur,* ☎ *404/288–6262.*

Jazz

Cafe 290. This showcase for talented local jazz bands and singers also is a casual neighborhood restaurant and bar. ✉ *290 Hilderbrand Dr., Balconies Shopping Center, Sandy Springs,* ☎ *404/256–3942.*

Dante's Down the Hatch. With two locations, this jazz music club and fondue restaurant has been a favorite for more than 20 years. Both locations are set up as sailing ships and come complete with crocodiles in moats. Downtown, jazz entertainers perform nightly. In Buckhead, the Paul

Mitchell Trio conjures silky smooth jazz nightly except Monday. ⊠ *60 Upper Alabama St., Kenny's Alley, in Underground Atlanta,* ☎ *404/577–1800;* ⊠ *3380 Peachtree Rd.,* ☎ *404/266–1600.*

Yin Yang Cafe. This trendy spot near Georgia Tech serves up mainly local jazz groups as well as tapas. ⊠ *64 3rd St., Midtown,* ☎ *404/607–0682.*

Rock

Chameleon Club. The under-30 crowd comes here for progressive rock bands such as Day Room. ⊠ *3179 Peachtree Rd., Buckhead,* ☎ *404/261–8004.*

Masquerade. A tri-level grunge hangout in a former factory, this club spins just about everything in popular music, from disco to techno to industrial rock. The interesting mix of revelers reflects the club's three spaces, dubbed Heaven, Hell, and Purgatory. ⊠ *695 North Ave.,* ☎ *404/577–8178.*

The Outer Edge. This warehouse setting can pack in up to 1,000 people to listen to local and regional alternative music bands. ⊠ *585 Franklin Rd., Marietta,* ☎ *770/428–1393.*

The Point. Little Five Points' denizens come here to enjoy up-and-coming rock and progressive music groups in a small club setting. ⊠ *420 Moreland Ave.,* ☎ *404/659–3522.*

Smith's Olde Bar. This acoustically fine performance space packs 'em in to enjoy some of the city's best rock groups. The restaurant downstairs serves undistinguished food. Cover is normally $5–$10. ⊠ *1578 Piedmont Ave.,* ☎ *404/875–1522.*

Gay and Lesbian Bars

A number of establishments are concentrated around Peachtree Street in Midtown. The publications *Etcetera* (☎ 404/525–3821) and *Southern Voice* (☎ 404/876–1819), available free in bookstores and at other locations, have further entertainment information.

Backstreet. Midtown's mainstay gay club, with a good mix of men and women, has been a mecca for leisure-seekers for nearly two decades. Dancing begins at 10, and there's a female impersonator show every Friday and Saturday at midnight. ⊠ *845 Peachtree St.,* ☎ *404/873–1986.*

Blake's on the Park. This video bar near Piedmont Park draws a fairly young crowd of male professionals. No dance floor, but there's a DJ and there's never a cover charge. ⊠ *227 10th St., Midtown,* ☎ *404/892–5786.*

Hoedowns. This is country-and-western dance bar for men and women that lets you try line dancing and the two-step. Special features include free dance lessons Sunday through Thursday, and no cover is charged. ⊠ *931 Monroe Dr., Midtown Promenade,* ☎ *404/876–0001.*

6 Outdoor Activities and Sports

N A CITY WHERE OUTDOOR RECREATION is possible almost year-round, sports play a major role. You'll find Atlantans pursuing everything from baseball to rollerblading in parks, clubs, and neighborhoods all over town. On hot, humid summer days, it's a good idea to exercise early and drink plenty of fluids. *Atlanta Sports & Fitness Magazine* (☎ 404/842–0359), available for free at many grocery stores, health clubs, and bookstores, provides information on current events.

Participant Sports

Bicycling

Expect to see bicyclists all year, huffing up Atlanta's treacherous hills or flying down them. Since the city has few designated bike lanes, your best (and safest) bet is to venture to **Piedmont Park** (⊠ Piedmont Ave. between 10th and 14th Sts.), which is closed to automobile traffic. The **Southern Bicycle League** (⊠ 1285 Willeo Creek Dr., Roswell, ☎ 770/594–8350) and **Cycle South** (⊠ 7210 Rte. 85, Riverdale, ☎ 770/991–6642) lead regular rides throughout the year for all skill levels. Bikes can be rented from **Skate Escape** (⊠ 1086 Piedmont Ave., across from Piedmont Park, ☎ 404/892–1292) and **Intown Bicycles** (⊠ 1035 Monroe Dr., ☎ 404/872–1736). You can also rent wheels and ride at **Stone Mountain Park** (☞ Greater Atlanta *in* Chapter 2).

Boating and Water Sports

At the state-operated resort **Lake Lanier Islands** (⊠ 6950 Holiday Rd., Buford, ☎ 770/932–7255), 45 minutes north of Atlanta, sailboats, houseboats, fishing boats, speedboats, and a variety of pontoon boats can be rented from March through mid-November. Similar boats, as well as rowboats and pedal boats, are available for use on Stone Mountain Lake at **Stone Mountain Park** (☞ Greater Atlanta *in* Chapter 2).

Canoeing and Rafting

The **Chattahoochee River National Recreation Area** (☞ Greater Atlanta *in* Chapter 2) protects a large portion of the Chattahoochee River as it slices through northern and western Atlanta. Rafting (Class I and II rapids), canoeing, and other water sports are popular. The **Chattahoochee Outdoor Center** (⊠ 1990 Island Ford Pkwy., Dunwoody, ☎ 770/395–6851) rents canoes, kayaks, and rafts for "shooting the 'Hooch." The **Atlanta Rowing Club** (⊠ Boathouse at 500 Azalea Dr., Roswell, ☎ 770/993–1879) provides opportunities to scull on the river. **REI** (⊠ 1800 N.E. Expressway Access Rd., ☎ 404/633–6508; ⊠ 1165 Perimeter Center West, Dunwoody, ☎ 770/901–9200) rents canoes of various sizes for $24–$37 a day.

Fishing

The cold mountain streams of north Georgia are excellent sources of trout; the closer Chattahoochee River, Stone Mountain Lake, and lakes Allatoona (40 mi northwest of Downtown) and Lanier have bass, bream, catfish, crappie, perch, sunfish, and other freshwater fish. Fishing licenses and equipment can be purchased from any Kmart or sporting-goods store, including **Fish Hawk** in Buckhead (⊠ 283 Buckhead Ave., ☎ 404/237–3473), which is an excellent source of information and supplies as well. **Orvis** (⊠ 3255 Peachtree Rd., Buckhead, ☎ 404/841–0093) is the source for Orvis fly fishing gear. **Bill Vanderford's Guide Service** (⊠ 2224 Pine Point Dr., Lawrenceville, ☎ 770/962–1241) will take you to the best fishing holes in Georgia. For state regulations and information, contact the **Georgia Game and Fish Division** (☎ 770/414–3333).

Golf

The many courses here attest to golf's popularity. Greens fees range from $20 to $30 for 18 holes played on public courses; carts are $3–$15 extra. Always call in advance to reserve a tee time.

The only public course within sight of Downtown is the **Bobby Jones Golf Course** (⊠ 384 Woodward Way, ☎ 404/355–1009), named after the famed Atlantan golfer. The immensely popular 18-hole, par-71 course is on a portion of the Battle of Peachtree Creek site. Another course on a Civil War site is the **Alfred Tup Holmes Club** (⊠ 2300 Wilson Dr., East Point, ☎ 404/753–6158). Built on a former Confederate breastwork; it's known for numerous doglegs and blind shots. Also within I–285 are the 18-hole, 72-par

Browns Mill Golf Course (⊠ 480 Cleveland Ave., ☎ 404/366–3573), the best operated by the city, and the **North Fulton Golf Course** (⊠ 216 W. Wieuca Rd., Chastain Park, ☎ 404/255–0723), an 18-hole, 72-par course with a superior layout but also some of the smallest greens and a bunch of streams and water hazards. With 18 holes, the 72-par **Sugar Creek Golf Course** (⊠ 2706 Bouldercrest Rd., ☎ 404/241–7671) straddles I–285 (11 holes on one side, 7 on the other) in southeast Atlanta and provides tree-lined fairways, several long holes, and good Crenshaw Bentgrass greens.

Outside I–285, the best public course is the **Southerness Golf Club** (⊠ 4871 Flat Bridge Rd., Stockbridge, ☎ 770/808–6000), with tough holes ranging from long par-4s to shots over water that require pinpoint accuracy. Of Stone Mountain Park's (☞ Greater Atlanta *in* Chapter 2) two 18-hole courses, **Stonemont** has several challenging, scenic holes; the original 18-hole course was voted one of the top 75 public courses by *Golf Digest*. **Lakeside Golf Club** (⊠ 3600 Old Fairburn Rd., ☎ 404/344–3620), just outside I–285 in southwest Atlanta, has a dogleg on nearly every hole. **Eagle Watch Golf Club** (⊠ 3055 Eagle Watch Dr., Woodstock, ☎ 770/591–1000), designed by Arnold Palmer, is a huge course that will please long-distance hitters.

Health Clubs

If your hotel doesn't have an in-house exercise facility, several clubs are open to the public for a small fee, including **Australian Body Works** (⊠ 3872 Roswell Rd., ☎ 404/365–9696; 13 other locations); **The Sporting Club** (⊠ 135 Interstate North Pkwy., ☎ 404/953–1100); **SportsLife** (⊠ 3340 Peachtree Rd., ☎ 404/262–2120; 5 other locations); and the **YMCA** (⊠ check local listings), which has 56 metro locations.

Hiking

On the outskirts of Atlanta are several small mountains with scenic trails. The **Chattahoochee River National Recreation Area** (☞ Greater Atlanta *in* Chapter 2) has 70 mi of trails of all levels of difficulty. **Kennesaw Mountain National Battlefield Park** (☞ Greater Atlanta *in* Chapter 2) has 16 mi of hiking trails. Three loop circuits of 5, 10, and

16 mi encompass every skill level. **Panola Mountain Park** (✉ 2600 GA Hwy. 155, ☎ 770/389–7801), 25 minutes south of Downtown, has 6 mi of trails, half of which require a guide. A regular pilgrimage by Atlanta hikers is the 1.3-mi trek to the top of **Stone Mountain;** the state park has numerous other trails if you don't mind the crowds. For loftier heights and overnight backpacking trips, the **Appalachian Trail** and several national wilderness areas are only 60–90 minutes away in north Georgia. Serious hikers will want to visit **REI** (☞ *above*), a good resource for equipment (including rentals) and trail information. Another good source for information and equipment rental is **High Country Outfitters** (✉ 3906 Roswell Rd., ☎ 404/814–0999; ✉ 4400 Ashford-Dunwoody Rd., Perimeter Mall, ☎ 770/391–9657).

Horseback Riding

For riding lessons and trail rides, call **Sweet Sunshine** (✉ 14295 Birmingham Hwy., Alpharetta, ☎ 770/343–9807). Near Decatur, **Vogt Riding Academy** (✉ 1084 Houston Mill Rd., ☎ 404/321–9506) gives lessons in a location more convenient to the city.

Ice-Skating

Parkaire Ice (✉ 4880 Lower Roswell Rd., Parkaire Shopping Center, Marietta, ☎ 770/973–0753), open year-round, is the only ice-skating rink in metro Atlanta.

Jogging

This is one of the city's favorite sports; the hilly terrain provides challenges even for professional runners. The top event is the annual **Peachtree Road Race** (Atlanta Track Club, ✉ 3097 E. Shadowlawn Ave., ☎ 404/231–9064) on July 4: up to 45,000 participants run a 10-km (6.2-mi) course down Peachtree Road from Lenox Square Mall to Piedmont Park. All slots for this race fill rapidly. Good for jogging are traffic-free **Piedmont Park** (☞ *above*) and a 3.1-mi loop in the **Chattahoochee River National Recreation Area** (☞ Greater Atlanta *in* Chapter 2). Contact the **Atlanta Track Club** (✉ 3097 Shadowlawn Ave., 30305, ☎ 404/231–9064), which organizes the Peachtree Road Race, or **Chattahoochee Road Runners** (✉ Box 724745, 31139, ☎ 404/916–2820) for information and other suggestions.

Rollerblading and Roller Skating

Piedmont Park (☞ *above*) is popular for roller sports, partly because the nearby **Skate Escape** (☞ *above*) rents Rollerblades and skates.

Swimming

White Water (☞ Greater Atlanta *in* Chapter 2) has a huge wave pool, several water slides, lockers, and showers. The beach at **Lake Lanier Islands** (☞ *above*) is open to swimmers in summer. Fifteen minutes northeast of Downtown, the **Dynamo Community Swim Center** (⊠ 3119 Shallowford Rd., Chamblee, ☎ 770/451–3272) has two 25-yard indoor pools and a 50-meter, eight-lane outdoor pool.

Tennis

There's at least one court in every city park for this favorite pastime. Organized tennis centers run by the city charge court fees from $1.50 to $2 per person per hour for hard courts and $2.25 to $2.75 for soft courts (Altantans pay the lower prices). The best public facility is the **Bitsy Grant Tennis Center** (⊠ 2125 Northside Dr., ☎ 404/609–7193), which has 13 clay courts and 10 hard courts and is open weekdays 8:30–7, weekends 8:30–6. **Piedmont Park** (⊠ Piedmont Ave. between 10th and 14th Sts., ☎ 404/853–3237) has 12 hard courts with night lights and is open weekdays 9:30–9, weekends 9:30–6. The facility has lockers, but bring your own lock. On the north side of town, try the **North Fulton Tennis Center** (⊠ 500 Abernathy Rd., at Roswell Rd., ☎ 404/303–6182), which has 20 hard-surface and 4 clay courts with lights and is open daily 8:30 AM–9 PM. The facility has lockers, but supply your own locks. Fees are $2–$3 per hour per person.

Spectator Sports

Atlanta has six professional teams, a major university, and an abundance of events. Tickets can be obtained from the individual teams; **Ticketmaster** (☎ 404/249–6400 or 800/326–4000), which charges a $2.75–$5 fee per ticket, also handles most professional and some collegiate events.

Auto and Motorcycle Racing

The **Atlanta International Raceway** (⊠ 1500 U.S. 41, Hampton, ☎ 770/946–4211), 20 mi south of Atlanta, is the site of several NASCAR race events, including the Coca-Cola 500 in March and the *Atlanta Journal-Constitution 500* in November. When attending events here, make careful note of where you've parked your car, as the lot is not well marked, and finding cars after dark is nearly impossible. **Road Atlanta** (⌧ 5300 Winder Hwy., Braselton, ☎ 706/967–6143), 30 mi north of Atlanta, is the home of the International Motor Sports Association (IMSA) and American Motorcycle Association (AMA) circuit road-racing events—stock cars, Grand Prix, and motorcycles.

Baseball

The **Atlanta Braves,** the 1991 and 1992 National League champions and the 1995 World Champions, play home games from April to October at Turner Field (⌧ 755 Hank Aaron Dr., at Capitol Ave., ☎ 404/522–7630), a short distance south of Downtown.

Basketball

The National Basketball Association's **Atlanta Hawks** is one of several teams that have used the Omni Coliseum, which is scheduled to be torn down. Until a new facility is constructed (1999), the team will play at the **Georgia Dome** (⌧ 1 Georgia Dome Dr., ☎ 404/223–8000) and at Georgia Tech's **Alexander Memorial Coliseum.** The regular season runs from October to April.

Bicycle Racing

Amateur and professional bikers race at the **Dick Lane Velodrome** (⌧ 1889 Lexington Ave., East Point, ☎ 404/765–1085), a short distance from Hartsfield Atlanta International Airport. Cycling classes are held Tuesdays and Thursdays in the evenings.

Collegiate Sports

The **Georgia Tech Yellow Jackets,** participating in the NCAA's Atlantic Coast Conference, play Division I-A football, basketball, baseball, tennis, wrestling, and other sports on the Georgia Tech campus (⌧ between North Ave. and 10th St., ☎ 404/894–5400). **Kennesaw State University** fields Division 2 teams in eight sports, seven of which received NCAA tournament bids in 1996–97; the baseball and softball teams were defending national champions in 1996 (⌧ 1000 Chastain Rd., Kennesaw, ☎ 770/423–

6284). **Morehouse College** (⊠ 830 Westview Dr., ☎ 404/215–2751) was defending national champion in cross country and won the 1997 Southern Intercollegiate Athletic Conference indoor and outdoor track and field championship. The college also has a successful tennis team, which has also won S.I.A.C. championships.

Football

From October to January, the National Football League's **Atlanta Falcons** kick off at the Georgia Dome (⊠ 1 Georgia Dome Dr., ☎ 404/223–8000).

Golf

The four-day PGA **Bell South Classic,** held at the Tournament Players Club at Sugarloaf (⊠ 2595 Sugarloaf Club Dr., Duluth, ☎ 770/951–8777), attracts the nation's best golfers. **Nationwide Championship,** a Senior PGA tour event, is hosted at the **Golf Club of Georgia** (⊠ 1 Golf Club Dr., Alpharetta, ☎ 404/303–0993).

Hockey

The International Hockey League (IHL) Atlanta Knights won their league championship in 1994, but the team has moved to Montreal. At press time Atlanta was in the running for an NHL team under the guidance of media and sports mogul Ted Turner; it was unclear where the new hockey and basketball sports arena would be located.

Horse Racing

The annual **Atlanta Steeplechase** (☎ 404/237–7436 for directions), held in the countryside north of Atlanta near Cartersville the first weekend in April (unless that's Easter weekend, then it's held the second weekend), features several races, a virtual parade of women's hats, and the chance to see Atlanta's elite, who arrive in their Rolls-Royces and Bugattis.

Polo

Between 2 PM and 4 PM every Sunday from June through October, the **Atlanta Polo Club** (⊠ Majors Rd. at Post Rd., Cumming, ☎ 770/316–9109 for Polo hot line) holds matches and tournaments. Admission ($15) is charged by the carload; picnic parties are the norm.

7 Shopping

ATLANTA IS AS CLOSE TO HEAVEN as it gets for shoppers in the Southeast, many of whom make annual buying pilgrimages here. Second only to Chicago in space devoted to shopping areas, the city has major department stores, haute-couture specialty shops, antiques markets, and an array of malls with nearly every possible chain business. Intriguing stores throughout Atlanta are in neighborhoods off the tourist track, providing a fuller picture of the city's diversity. Most stores are open Monday–Saturday 10–9:30, Sunday noon–6; downtown stores close on Sunday. Sales tax is 6% in the city of Atlanta and Fulton County, 4%–5% in the suburbs.

Shopping Districts

Buckhead

The heart of Buckhead is Atlanta's premier shopping district. Within a six-block area bounded by Peachtree, West Paces Ferry, and Pharr roads and East Shadowlawn Avenue, art galleries and more than 40 specialty shops sell everything from designer clothes to bass fishing lures. Lining Roswell and West Paces Ferry roads, and on the side streets leading off them, are exclusive shops. South of here, down Peachtree Road to I–85, small shopping centers and restaurants mix with residential areas. On the northeast edge of Buckhead, **Lenox Square Mall** and **Phipps Plaza** (☞ Shopping Malls, *below*) tempt shoppers with hundreds of stores.

Buford Highway

Buford Highway, in the northeast suburbs of Chamblee and Doraville from Carol Avenue to a mile beyond I–285, has stores that cater to metro Atlanta's enormous Asian population. The large **Asian Square Shopping Center** (✉ 5150 Buford Hwy., ☎ 770/458–8899) has an Asian grocery (☞ Specialty Stores, *below*) and many other shops. Nearby, **Chinatown Square** (✉ 5379 New Peachtree Rd., ☎ 770/458–4624) has a large Asian food market, restaurants, a bakery, and other retail operations. Discount clothes, furniture and herb shops, and ethnic eateries dominate the area.

Downtown

Although most Atlantans do not make a special trip Downtown to shop, the stores here—helped by conventions and trade shows—do a steady business. In between **The Mall** and **Underground Atlanta** (☞ Shopping Malls, *below*) is the venerable **Macy's** (✉ 180 Peachtree St., ☎ 404/221–7221), the last of the grand old department stores in Atlanta, with its high ceilings, crystal chandeliers, and marble floors. **The Limited** (✉ 209 Peachtree St., ☎ 404/523–1728), a favorite with downtown office workers, is near Macy's.

Little Five Points and Virginia-Highland

Within 2 mi of each other, the small neighborhood shopping districts of Little Five Points and Virginia-Highland are known for art galleries and funky specialty shops selling unusual antiques, books, clothes (new and vintage), gifts, jewelry, CDs, and more. Little Five Points attracts a younger clientele, while more affluent types gravitate to its neighbor.

Shopping Malls

City Malls

BUCKHEAD

On opposite corners, at Peachtree and Lenox roads in Buckhead, are two major shopping malls.

Lenox Square Mall. Atlanta's favorite, Lenox Square Mall has 268 retailers, making it the area's largest. The broad mix of stores includes Macy's, Rich's, Neiman Marcus, Banana Republic, the Disney Store, Louis Vuitton, Burberrys, J. Crew, F.A.O. Schwarz, and Geode (☞ Specialty Stores, *below*). There's also a large food court, three fine restaurants, and a multiplex cinema. ✉ *3393 Peachtree Rd.,* ☎ *404/233–6767.*

Phipps Plaza. Phipps has traditionally courted well-to-do shoppers with such offerings as valet parking and concierge services. Its 200 stores include haute retailers like Saks Fifth Avenue, Lord & Taylor, Parisian (a somewhat upscale department-store chain based in Birmingham, Alabama), Gucci, Tiffany & Co., Gianni Versace, and Pierre Deux. There are fine arts and crafts galleries as well as such mainstream stores as Nike Town and Alex & Ivy. Shoppers can take a break at the small food court and or one of five restaurants or watch a movie at the multiple-screen cinema. ⊠ *3500 Peachtree Rd.,* ☎ *404/262–0992 or 800/810–7700.*

DOWNTOWN

The Mall. Peachtree Center's The Mall has 30 retailers including Brooks Brothers, in the Gaslight Tower (a skyscraper in Peachtree Center), and International Records & Tapes, which has a stellar inventory of hard-to-find music. The Mall's stores and restaurants are popular with area businesspeople; business is fairly slow on weekends. ⊠ *Peachtree Center, 231 Peachtree St.,* ☎ *404/524–3787.*

Underground Atlanta. There are 46 retailers in this mostly underground shopping and entertainment complex. Stores include the Gap, Sam Goody, Habersham Winery (an outlet for a north Georgia winery), Hats Under Atlanta, and the eclectic Art by God gallery, which exhibits everything from fossils to artistic creations by Native Americans. Pushcart vendors selling everything—including books, original art, and tourist trinkets—dot the passageways. ⊠ *Upper Alabama St. at Peachtree St.,* ☎ *404/523–2311.*

Suburban Malls

Cumberland Mall. Just inside the I–75/I–285 intersection, this mall has about 150 stores, including Rich's, Macy's, JC Penney's, and Sears. Touch of Georgia specializes in all-Georgia gourmet foods and gift items.⊠ *1000 Cumberland Mall,* ☎ *770/435–2206.*

Gwinnett Place Mall. There's excellent shopping here—10 mi north of the I–285/I–85 junction—at Rich's, Macy's, and nearly 200 other retailers; several large strip malls surround it. ⊠ *2100 Pleasant Hill Rd., Duluth,* ☎ *770/476–5160.*

Northlake Mall. Just east of the I–85/I–285 intersection, Northlake gleams with a Miami-deco look and a skylit garden and food court. Macy's and a Parisian department store are anchors. ⊠ *4800 Briarcliff Rd.,* ☎ *770/938–3564.*

Perimeter Mall. Anchored by Rich's and Macy's, Perimeter gets high marks for family shopping, with Gap Kids and The Nature Company. ⊠ *4400 Ashford-Dunwoody Rd., Dunwoody, outside the north Perimeter near I–285 and GA 400,* ☎ *770/394–4270.*

Specialty Stores

Antiques

BENNETT STREET

Bennett Street, a short side street near the 2100 block of Peachtree Street, is a mecca for art and antiques buyers; galleries and dealers fill its former warehouses. The two places listed below have cafés for when you're ready for a break.

Interiors Market. This plain-Jane sister to The Stalls (☞ *below*) displays treasures from 45 antiques merchants in an old warehouse. Offerings include antique lamps and chandeliers, picture frames and paintings, ceramics, and 19th- to early 20th-century furniture. The narrow aisles and crowded, three-sided booths can feel claustrophobic. ⊠ *55 Bennett St.,* ☎ *404/352–0055.*

The Stalls. In a pleasant warehouse, The Stalls leases booths to 75 antiques dealers, mainly from the South. The eclectic antique or near-antique items on sale include ceramics and cut glass, lace and linens, folk art, and 19th- and early 20th-century furniture. ⊠ *116 Bennett St.,* ☎ *404/352–4430.*

CHAMBLEE

This working-class, ethnically diverse town is riddled with interesting shops and flea markets. Browse and cruise if you have time; if not, head directly to the locations listed below.

Atlanta Antique Center and Flea Market. This 80,000-square-ft warehouse offers good values on collectibles (including baseball cards and Elvis memorabilia), brass, furniture, and glassware from 150 dealers. ⊠ *5360 Peachtree Industrial Blvd., Chamblee,* ☎ *770/458–0456.*

Chamblee's Antique Row. A dozen antiques shops, some in former homes, and two antiques malls with another 40 dealers showcase European and American furniture, wooden and ceramic decorative objects, and jewelry. One store not to be missed is Moose Breath Trading Company (⊠ *5461 Peachtree Rd.,* ☎ *770/458–7210*), which sells 1940s neon signs, soda-fountain bars from the 1950s, mounted animal heads, kitschy plastic creations, and other oddities. It's a favorite with film directors and restaurants seeking nostalgia. ⊠ *3519 Broad St.,* ☎ *770/455–0751.*

Miami Circle. An enclave with more than 20 antiques and decorative-art dealers, Miami Circle specializes in furniture, a large portion of it imported from Europe. Prices are on the high side, but so is the quality. ⊠ *Miami Circle off Piedmont Rd., about 2 mi north of I–85.*

2300 Peachtree Road. Here is where Atlanta's elite shops. More than 25 stores—with expensive art, antiques, and decorative-art items—cluster around a cobblestone courtyard.

Beverly Bremer Silver Shop. Antique and secondhand silver flatware (more than 1,000 patterns), tea sets, and accessories fill this small shop. ⊠ *3164 Peachtree Rd., Peachtree Plaza,* ☎ *404/261–4009.*

Arts and Crafts Galleries

Abstein Gallery. This Midtown gem is one of the largest galleries in Atlanta. It shows established local and regional artists working in all media. ⊠ *558 14th St., 1 mi west of I–75,* ☎ *404/872–8020.*

Aliya—Ardavin. This gallery represents 30 of the South's hottest artists. Painting, sculpture, glass, and mixed media are represented. ⊠ *1402 N. Highland Ave., No. 6,* ☎ *404/892–2835.*

Berman Gallery. Specializing in ceramics, paintings, and other primitive-art creations by southern artisans, this was the first Atlanta gallery to show the folk art of Howard Finster. ⊠ *3261 Roswell Rd.,* ☎ *404/261–3858.*

Bobo's Monkey. Bobo's, an established Little Five Points gallery, sells cutting-edge designs by artists working in many media. ⊠ *441 Seminole Ave.,* ☎ *404/522–4123.*

By Hand South. Handmade crafts from southern sources, including pottery, glass, wood, and jewelry, are the focus. ⊠ *112 E. Ponce de Leon Ave., Decatur,* ☎ *404/378–0118.*

Camille Love Gallery. Camille is the source for fine contemporary work by African-American artists. ⊠ *309 E. Paces Ferry Rd., Suite 120,* ☎ *404/841–0446.*

Fay Gold Gallery. This avant-garde Buckhead gallery has won recognition throughout the South for trend-setting, sometimes controversial, shows by renowned contemporary artists, photographers, and sculptors. ⊠ *247 Buckhead Ave., East Village Square,* ☎ *404/233–3843.*

Fräbel. The award-winning glass sculptures of Hans Frabel have been Atlanta favorites for more than 20 years. ⊠ *695 Antone St.,* ☎ *404/351–9794.*

Jackson Fine Art Gallery. Jackson is the city's best place to buy the work of well-known photographers. ⊠ *3115 E. Shadowlawn Ave.,* ☎ *404/233–3739.*

Modern Primitive Gallery. Work by southern self-taught artists, many of them represented in the Smithsonian Institution and other fine museums, is this Virginia-Highland gallery's focus. Represented is Howard Finster, a former Georgia preacher and now an internationally recognized artist who has created album covers for the rock bands REM and Talking Heads. ⊠ *1393 N. Highland Ave.,* ☎ *404/892–0556.*

Out of the Woods. A standout in the Buckhead scene, Out of the Woods has an extensive inventory of work, much of it in wood, from contemporary and ancient civilizations. ⊠ *22-B Bennett St.,* ☎ *404/351–0446.*

Ray's Indian Originals. Ray Belcher, who is part Cherokee, and his wife Peggy own a TV repair shop; its top floor is a treasure trove of fine Native American jewelry and art. ⊠ *90 N. Avondale Rd., Avondale Estates,* ☎ *404/292–4999.*

Sidewalk Studio. This Virginia-Highland gallery shows the pottery, sculpture, paintings, and jewelry of more than 180 artists. ⊠ *1050 N. Highland Ave.,* ☎ *404/872–1047.*

The Signature Shop and Gallery. Items in all price ranges from nationally recognized artisans include baskets, pottery, and vases. ⊠ *3267 Roswell Rd.,* ☎ *404/237–4426.*

TULA Art Center. This former warehouse has 23 galleries and artists' studios selling photography, sculpture, paintings, textiles, and crafts at a variety of prices. ⊠ *75 Bennett St.,* ☎ *404/351–3551.*

Vesperman Gallery. Artsy and functional glass creations include sculptures, creative paperweights, vases, and perfume bottles. ⊠ *2140 Peachtree Rd.,* ☎ *404/350–9698.*

Booksellers

The Architectural Bookstore. Run by the American Institute of Architects (AIA), this store focuses on local and international architecture and design and also sells interesting cards and gifts. ⊠ *The Mall, Peachtree Center, 231 Peachtree St.,* ☎ *404/222–9920.*

Charis Books. Feminist books and cards, cassettes, T-shirts, and other sidelines draw an intellectual crowd; call for information about Thursday-night speakers. ⊠ *1189 Euclid Ave.,* ☎ *404/524–0304.*

Oxford Comics. A huge collection of antique and specialty comics, toys, and games (not computer, though) draws a diverse patronage. Late hours keep 'em coming. ⊠ *2855 Piedmont Rd.,* ☎ *404/233–8682.*

Science Fiction & Mystery Bookshop. This is the best place to find new non-bestseller titles in these genres, as well as hard-to-find backlist titles. ⊠ *2000-F Cheshire Bridge Rd., Cheshire Pointe Shopping Center,* ☎ *404/634–3226.*

Tall Tales. This small shop with a knowledgeable staff excels in regional fiction and travel books. There's also a coffee bar. ⊠ *1099 N. Druid Hills Rd., at LaVista Rd., Toco Hills Shopping Center,* ☎ *404/636–2498.*

Yesteryear. A mecca for antiquarians, Yesteryear deals in fine old volumes covering a wide variety of topics, but it's especially good for Georgiana. ⊠ *3201 Maple Dr.,* ☎ *404/237–0163.*

Cameras and Video Equipment

Wolf Camera. With its main showroom in Midtown, Wolf is the South's largest camera and video-equipment dealer, a one-stop shop for major camera brands, film, supplies, books, and 24-hour (often less) film processing. ⊠ *150 14th St.,* ☎ *404/892–1707; more than 70 other metro Atlanta locations.*

Clothing

CHILDREN'S

Caroline's Children's Boutique. Here you can find the highest-end garments for children from newborn through preteen. ⊠ *99 W. Paces Ferry Rd.,* ☎ *404/364–0233.*

Chocolate Soup. Practical quality casual wear for newborns through middle-elementary-school ages is almost always on sale here. ⊠ *6681-C Roswell Rd., Abernathy Square Shopping Center, Sandy Springs,* ☎ *404/303–9047.*

MEN'S

Bennie's Shoes. Men's fine dress and casual shoes, some discounted up to 70%, are sold here. ⊠ *2581 Piedmont Rd.,* ☎ *404/262–1966; 2 other locations.*

International Man. This upscale men's boutique sells sophisticated and fashionable clothes from such Italian designers as Moschino, Gianfranco Ferre, and Versace (the V-2 line). ✉ *3500 Peachtree Rd., Phipps Plaza,* ☎ *404/841–0770.*

Sebastian's Closet. In Buckhead, Sebastian's sells men's fashions by Hugo Boss, Jhane Barnes, and Donna Karan. ✉ *3222 Peachtree Rd.,* ☎ *404/365–9033.*

MEN'S AND WOMEN'S

Friedman's Shoes. Quality dress, casual, and athletic footwear from size 7 to 22, narrow, medium, and wide for men, attract professional athletes. Ladies' shoes sizes 4–13 are also available. ✉ *209 (men's store), 223 (women's store) Mitchell St.,* ☎ *404/524–1311 (men's); 404/523–1134 (women's);* ✉ *4340 Roswell Rd.,* ☎ *404/843–2414 (men's and women's).*

H. Stockton. This longtime Atlanta men's clothier has conservative business clothing, sportswear, and good service. Two of the stores (this one and Park Place) also sell women's clothing. ✉ *210 Peachtree St.,* ☎ *404/523–7741; 3 other locations.*

RESALE

Backstreet Boutique. Buckhead's upscale women's consignment shop sells such names as Adolfo, Chanel, and Donna Karan for a fraction of the retail price. ✉ *3655 Roswell Rd.,* ☎ *404/262–7783.*

Gently Owned. Bargains on lightly worn designer menswear include such regular brand names as Polo, Valentino, Giorgio Armani, Gianni Versace, Jhane Barnes, and Hugo Boss. ✉ *56 E. Andrews Dr., East Andrews Square,* ☎ *404/869–1881.*

WOMEN'S

The department stores in Lenox Square and Phipps Plaza offer chic designer names and great variety. Parisian sells the best-quality clothes at suburban malls, followed by Macy's and Rich's (☞ Shopping Malls, *above*). The following add another dimension.

Anthony Liggins. Liggins designs stylish wear for women, such as actresses Halle Berry and Jada Pinkett. Visit his Buckhead studio by appointment. His ready-to-wear work is available at Peoples, Mint of Beverly Hills, and Sandpiper (☞

below). ⊠ *254 E. Paces Ferry Rd., Suite 203,* ☎ *404/842–0621.*

Bill Hallman. This talented Atlanta designer specializes in comfortably priced "fashion forward" casual wear for both men and women; his Virginia-Highland store also carries designs from other sources. ⊠ *792 N. Highland Ave.,* ☎ *404/876–6055.*

Mint Beverly Hills. Women's clothing—ethnic print dresses, funky pants suits, designer dresses—fill this midtown boutique. ⊠ *595 Piedmont Ave., at North Ave., Rio Shopping Center,* ☎ *404/874–4656.*

Mitzi & Romano. This intriguing Virginia-Highland shop sells cutting-edge American and European clothes (Betsey Johnson, French Connection), jewelry, and accessories. ⊠ *1038 N. Highland Ave.,* ☎ *404/876–7228.*

René René. Local designer René Sanning is known for avant-garde clothes with a 1940s-retro look. All Sanning's designs shown at his Little Five Points shop are manufactured in Georgia. ⊠ *1142 Euclid Ave.,* ☎ *404/522–7363.*

Rexer-Parkes. Contemporary, elegant clothes from the likes of Nicole Miller, Tahari, Emanuel, and Calvin Klein are sold here. ⊠ *2140 Peachtree Rd., Brookwood Square,* ☎ *404/351–3080.*

Sandpiper. The focus is better contemporary casual and evening wear for sizes 2–12, some of it by local designers like Anthony Liggins (☞ *above*). ⊠ *4200 Paces Ferry Rd., Vinings Jubilee Shopping Center,* ☎ *770/433–2989.*

Wayne Van Nguyen. A young designer, Wayne concentrates on fun, contemporary men's and women's clothing for both business and leisure. One-of-a-kind design work for celebrity clients in the sports and entertainment industries gets publicity. ⊠ *342 Marietta St., Suite 1, near CNN Center,* ☎ *404/522–7555.*

Food

99 Ranch Market. A diverse group of customers is drawn to this large market with aisle after aisle of Asian grocery items, unusual fish, exquisite pork, poultry, and fresh produce. ⊠ *5150 Buford Hwy., Asian Square, Doraville,* ☎ *770/458–8899.*

DeKalb Farmers Market. Imagine 140,000 square ft of exotic fruits, cheeses, seafood, sausages, breads, and delicacies from around the world. ⊠ *3000 E. Ponce de Leon Ave., Decatur,* ☏ *404/377–6400.*

Harry's in a Hurry. A favorite of gourmets, Harry Blazer's markets present a dazzling array of prepared foods as well as produce, meats, seafood, wines, and breads, all in a pristine environment. ⊠ *1875 Peachtree Rd.,* ☏ *404/352–7800;* ⊠ *3804 Roswell Rd., Powers Ferry Square Shopping Center,* ☏ *404/266–0800.*

International Farmers Market. Fresh produce, a strong wine department, and fresh deli and seafood draw people of diverse ethnicities. ⊠ *5193 Peachtree Industrial Blvd., Chamblee,* ☏ *770/455–1777.*

Leon International Foods. Turkish coffee, dried figs, Tunisian oil, and other North African/Middle Eastern foods are the specialty. ⊠ *4000-A Pleasantdale Rd., Doraville,* ☏ *404/416–6620.*

Quality Kosher Emporium. Strictly kosher from the deli to the wine department, this store closes at 3 PM on Friday afternoons. Deli food (including unique, superior potato salad), meats, and bakery items draw a diverse clientele. ⊠ *2161 Briarcliff Rd., at LaVista Rd.,* ☏ *404/636–1114.*

Sweet Auburn Curb Market. A historic Atlanta landmark, this is a true farmers' market in an urban setting. Stalls are individually owned. Fresh produce, whole pigs and parts thereof, fresh flowers, and a unique atmosphere are the draws. ⊠ *209 Edgewood Ave.,* ☏ *404/659–1665.*

Jewelry

Geode. Local and national jewelry designers peddle their unique pieces here. ⊠ *3393 Peachtree Rd., Lenox Square Mall,* ☏ *404/261–9346.*

Illumina. The focus here is on fine handcrafted jewelry from local and national artisans. ⊠ *3500 Peachtree Rd., Phipps Plaza,* ☏ *404/233–3010.*

Mon Petit Chou. A vast assortment of costume jewelry from New York and Europe in addition to evening bags, belts, and hair accessories, fills this chic shop. ⊠ *3205 Paces Ferry Pl.,* ☏ *404/816–7891.*

Raiford Gallery. A massive timber frame building is filled with Judie Raiford's jewelry, furniture, ceramics, glass, wood, metal, and mixed media pieces. ⊠ *1169 Canton St., Roswell,* ☏ *770/645–2050.*

Luggage and Leather

Mori Luggage & Gifts. A good source of high-end luggage and leather briefcases, Atlanta souvenirs, and unique gifts and accessories for the home or office, Mori's is an Atlanta-founded and -based operation. ⊠ *3393 Peachtree Rd., Lenox Square Mall,* ☎ *404/231–2146; 8 other locations.*

Outlets

AJS Shoe Warehouse. In the city's warehouse district, AJS is the best source for discounted women's shoes (Joan and David, Unisa, Van Eli); they're open Friday through Sunday only. ⊠ *1788 Ellsworth Industrial Blvd.,* ☎ *404/355–1760.*

Ballard's Backroom Catalog Clearance Center. In the Chattahoochee warehouse/outlet district, Ballard's carries the uniquely designed rugs, lamps, tables, and pillows usually available only through its catalogs; it's open Monday through Saturday. Discounts can be as deep as 80% off retail. ⊠ *1670 Defoor Ave.,* ☎ *404/352–2776.*

K&G Men's Center. If you're patient and don't mind unsufferably rude service, you'll find values on designer apparel for men. Open only Friday through Sunday. ⊠ *1750 Ellsworth Industrial Blvd.,* ☎ *404/352–3471; 2 other locations.*

Men's Wearhouse Warehouse. One of three nationwide clearance stores for this chain, this outlet discounts thousands of designer suits, shirts, ties, and accessories; imagine getting an Yves St. Laurent suit for less than $200. ⊠ *1218 Old Chattahoochee Ave.,* ☎ *404/351–1060.*

North Georgia Premium Outlets. A total of 74 stylish stores sell discounted merchandise, including Barney's New York, Donna Karan Company Store, Timberland, The Gap Outlet, Stone Mountain Handbags, Bose (electronics), Music for a Song (discounted CDs and tapes), Anne Klein, and Calvin Klein. ⊠ *GA 400 at Dawson Forest Rd.,* ☎ *706/216–3609.*

Rich's Finale. Worthwhile discounts on the chain's merchandise can be had here. ⊠ *2841 Greenbriar Pkwy. SW, Greenbriar Mall* ☎ *404/346–2600.*

Stone Mountain Handbag Factory Store. Known throughout the Southeast, this outlet sells this brand's high-quality leather handbags at 20%–50% off the retail price. ⊠ *963 Main St., Stone Mountain,* ☎ *770/498–1316.*

Toys and Games

F.A.O. Schwarz. This purveyor of high-quality toys has a delightful stuffed-animal section and outstanding educational games, collectibles (dolls, cars, and action figures), and toys. ⊠ *3393 Peachtree Rd., Lenox Square Mall,* ☎ *404/814–1675.*

Learningsmith. A wide variety of games, videos, and puzzles for both children and adults fills this store. ⊠ *3500 Peachtree Rd., Phipps Plaza,* ☎ *404/364–0084;* ⊠ *4400 Ashford-Dunwoody Rd., Perimeter Mall, Dunwoody,* ☎ *770/730–8181.*

Store of Knowledge. Operated in association with Georgia Public Television (GPTV), this jam-packed store has loads of educational and action toys, books, puzzles and games. ⊠ *3393 Peachtree Rd., Lenox Square Mall,* ☎ *404/467–0021.*

INDEX

✕ = restaurant, 🏨 = hotel

NOTES

NOTES

NOTES

Fodor's Travel Publications

Available at bookstores everywhere, or call 1–800–533–6478, 24 hours a day.

Gold Guides

U.S.

Alaska

Arizona

Boston

California

Cape Cod, Martha's
Vineyard, Nantucket

The Carolinas &
Georgia

Chicago

Colorado

Florida

Hawai'i

Las Vegas,
Reno, Tahoe

Los Angeles

Maine, Vermont,
New Hampshire

Maui & Lāna'i

Miami & the Keys

New England

New Orleans

New York City

Pacific North Coast

Philadelphia &
the Pennsylvania
Dutch Country

The Rockies

San Diego

San Francisco

Santa Fe, Taos,
Albuquerque

Seattle & Vancouver

The South

U.S. & British
Virgin Islands

USA

Virginia & Maryland

Walt Disney World,
Universal Studios
and Orlando

Washington, D.C.

Foreign

Australia

Austria

The Bahamas

Belize & Guatemala

Bermuda

Canada

Cancún, Cozumel,
Yucatán Peninsula

Caribbean

China

Costa Rica

Cuba

The Czech Republic &
Slovakia

Eastern &
Central Europe

Europe

Florence, Tuscany
& Umbria

France

Germany

Great Britain

Greece

Hong Kong

India

Ireland

Israel

Italy

Japan

London

Madrid & Barcelona

Mexico

Montréal &
Québec City

Moscow, St.
Petersburg, Kiev

The Netherlands,
Belgium &
Luxembourg

New Zealand

Norway

Nova Scotia,
New Brunswick,
Prince Edward Island

Paris

Portugal

Provence &
the Riviera

Scandinavia

Scotland

Singapore

South Africa

South America

Southeast Asia

Spain

Sweden

Switzerland

Thailand

Toronto

Turkey

Vienna & the Danube
Valley

Special-Interest Guides

Adventures to Imagine

Alaska Ports of Call

Ballpark Vacations

Caribbean Ports
of Call

The Complete Guide
to America's
National Parks

Disney Like a Pro

Europe Ports of Call

Family Adventures

Fodor's Gay Guide
to the USA

Fodor's How to Pack

Great American
Learning Vacations

Great American
Sports & Adventure
Vacations

Great American
Vacations

Great American
Vacations for
Travelers with
Disabilities

Halliday's New
Orleans Food
Explorer

Healthy Escapes

Kodak Guide to
Shooting Great
Travel Pictures

National Parks and
Seashores of the East

National Parks of
the West

Nights to Imagine

Rock & Roll Traveler
Great Britain
and Ireland

Rock & Roll Traveler
USA

Sunday in
San Francisco

Walt Disney World
for Adults

Weekends in
New York

Wendy Perrin's
Secrets Every Smart
Traveler Should Know

Where Should We
Take the Kids?
California

Where Should We
Take the Kids?
Northeast

Worldwide Cruises
and Ports of Call

Fodor's Special Series

Fodor's Best Bed & Breakfasts

America
California
The Mid-Atlantic
New England
The Pacific Northwest
The South
The Southwest
The Upper Great Lakes

Compass American Guides

Alaska
Arizona
Boston
Chicago
Colorado
Hawai'i
Hollywood
Idaho
Las Vegas
Maine
Manhattan
Minnesota
Montana
New Mexico
New Orleans
Oregon
Pacific Northwest
San Francisco
Santa Fe
South Carolina
South Dakota
Southwest
Texas
Utah
Virginia
Wine Country
Wisconsin
Wyoming

Citypacks

Amsterdam
Atlanta
Berlin
Chicago
Florence
Hong Kong
London
Los Angeles
Montréal
New York City
Paris
Prague
Rome
San Francisco
Tokyo
Venice
Washington, D.C.

Exploring Guides

Australia
Boston & New England
Britain
California
Canada
Caribbean
China
Costa Rica
Egypt
Florence & Tuscany
Florida
France
Germany
Greek Islands
Hawaii
Ireland
Israel
Italy
Japan
London
Mexico
Moscow & St. Petersburg
New York City
Paris

Prague
Provence
Rome
San Francisco
Scotland
Singapore & Malaysia
South Africa
Spain
Thailand
Turkey
Venice

Flashmaps

Boston
New York
San Francisco
Washington, D.C.

Fodor's Gay Guides

Los Angeles & Southern California
New York City
Pacific Northwest
San Francisco and the Bay Area
South Florida
USA

Pocket Guides

Acapulco
Aruba
Atlanta
Barbados
Budapest
Jamaica
London
New York City
Paris
Prague
Puerto Rico
Rome
San Francisco
Washington, D.C.

Languages for Travelers (Cassette & Phrasebook)

French
German

Italian
Spanish

Mobil Travel Guides

America's Best Hotels & Restaurants
California and the West
Great Lakes
Major Cities
Mid-Atlantic
Northeast
Northwest and Great Plains
Southeast
Southwest and South Central

Rivages Guides

Bed and Breakfasts of Character and Charm in France
Hotels and Country Inns of Character and Charm in France
Hotels and Country Inns of Character and Charm in Italy
Hotels and Country Inns of Character and Charm in Paris
Hotels and Country Inns of Character and Charm in Portugal
Hotels and Country Inns of Character and Charm in Spain

Short Escapes

Britain
France
Near New York City
New England

Fodor's Sports

Golf Digest's Places to Play
Skiing USA
USA Today The Complete Four Sport Stadium Guide

WHEREVER YOU TRAVEL, *H*ELP IS NEVER FAR AWAY.

From planning your trip to providing travel assistance along the way, American Express® Travel Service Offices are always there to help you do more.

Atlanta

American Express
Travel Service
3384 Peachtree Road, N.E.
404/262-7561

American Express
Travel Service
4400 Ashford-Dunwoody Road
770/395-1305

American Express
Travel Service
2140 Peachtree Road, N.W.
Suite 245
404/355-2696

American Express
Travel Service
2184 Henderson Mill Road
Suite 12A
770/723-9488

do more AMERICAN EXPRESS

Travel

http://www.americanexpress.com/travel

American Express Travel Service Offices are located throughout Georgia. For the office nearest you, call 1-800-AXP-3429.